THESE
WILDS
BEYOND
OUR
FENCES

THESE WILDS BEYOND OUR FENCES

LETTERS TO MY DAUGHTER
ON HUMANITY'S SEARCH FOR HOME

BAYO AKOMOLAFE

North Atlantic Books
Berkeley, California

Published by   Cover art and design by Nathaniel Russell
North Atlantic Books   Interior design by Happenstance Type-O-Rama
Berkeley, California   Printed in the United States of America

These Wilds Beyond Our Fences: Letters to My Daughter on Humanity's Search for Home is sponsored and published by North Atlantic Books, an educational nonprofit based in Berkeley, California, that collaborates with partners to develop cross-cultural perspectives, nurture holistic views of art, science, the humanities, and healing, and seed personal and global transformation by publishing work on the relationship of body, spirit, and nature.

North Atlantic Books' publications are distributed to the US trade and internationally by Penguin Random House Publishers Services. For further information, visit our website at www.northatlanticbooks.com.

Library of Congress Cataloging-in-Publication Data

Names: Akomolafe, Bayo, author.
Title: These wilds beyond our fences : letters to my daughter on humanity's
  search for home / Bayo Akomolafe.
Description: Berkeley, California : North Atlantic Books, 2017.
Identifiers: LCCN 2017024072 (print) | LCCN 2017031790 (ebook) | ISBN
  9781623171650 | ISBN 9781623171667 (paperback) | ISBN 9781623171650
  (e-book)
Subjects: LCSH: Akomolafe, Bayo—Family. | Authors, Nigerian—Correspondence.
  | Fatherhood. | BISAC: BODY, MIND & SPIRIT / Inspiration & Personal
  Growth. | BIOGRAPHY & AUTOBIOGRAPHY / Personal Memoirs.
Classification: LCC PR9387.9.A39277 (ebook) | LCC PR9387.9.A39277 Z48 2017
  (print) | DDC 828/.9209 [B] —dc23
LC record available at https://lccn.loc.gov/2017024072

4 5 6 7 8 9 KPC 25 24 23 22 21

When you get to the edge, open the letters.
Read them, Alethea. We'll meet you there—
at the place the sun touches the horizon.

Contents

Foreword

Dear Alethea,

I met your father when he was a young man still searching for a proper channel for his ambition. This, more than our intellectual resonance, is what called us into friendship. You see, our generation faced a quandary. Full of youthful ambition, we had awakened to the wrongness of every ready-made goal that society offered as a way to express that ambition. First, we rejected the most obvious conventional goals of money and power, seeking outlet instead in academia, NGOs, science, or any other realm we imagined to be untainted. But as our understanding grew, we realized that every institution was part of the same world-dominating, world-destroying complex. There was nowhere for us to go.

With nowhere to go, perhaps we could find our own way. Perhaps we could channel our ambition into revolution, or into "building the alternatives." Yet when we tried that, we discovered the same familiar ways of thinking scaffolding our dissident organizations and our alternative programs. It wasn't just that society offered us the wrong map; it was the whole formula for making and following a map that was wrong. We saw that the revolutionary elite behaved not much differently from the financial elite, that countercultural idea celebrities embodied the same basic archetype as conventional experts. The very recipe for change-making was part of what needed to change: the smart guys in a room coming up with a brilliant idea, a plan, a blueprint, and then convincing the public and especially the elites to enact a change. And so, even the ambition to bring an important new idea into the world was lost to us.

Some of us, your father included, dabbled in the idea of an ambitionless life, an understandable refuge given that those who have tried to save the world have done it the most damage. We thought, perhaps, that ambition was a bad thing. But to suppress it was as impossible as confining steam in a boiling pot. No matter how hard one presses on the lid, it finds another vent.

That is what this book is: the eruption of a long-simmering ambition that has not yet quite found its object. What does ambition do, when it lacks a destination, an aspiration? It turns toward adventure, a foray into the unknown. The title of this book is apt then, not only in reference to its content but also in reference to its animating impulse.

It would be inaccurate to say, though, that this book of letters has no destination, just as it would be to say that an adventure has no purpose or a wandering no outcome. It is just that the purpose is never, in the end, what we thought it was. On the contrary, it is something that was unknowable, residing as it did in the wilds beyond our fences.

These letters are among other things a chronicle of a search for home; they are also steps on that search. Fittingly, your father eschews at the outset the possibility of success: "There are no beginnings that appear unperturbed, pristine and without hauntings. And there are no endings that are devoid of traces of the new, spontaneous departures from disclosure, and simmering events that are yet to happen. The middle isn't the space between things; it is the world in its ongoing practices of worlding itself." We are always in the middle, he says. The home he seeks never did or could exist.

Yet I have to say, it is not a delusion that draws him on this search.

It isn't that the bull's-eye, the destination, heaven, home, doesn't exist. It is only that it doesn't exist in linear time. It is like a crystal hanging above our entire timeline, refracting partial images of itself onto our world that we recognize as home. That is why the mystics tell us it is always there, closer than close. Nonetheless, our journeys away from home have their purpose. A will stronger than our own sends us on these journeys. If we do not someday leave home, then home will leave us.

Maybe, thought your father as he embarked on these writings, home will come through their completion. Maybe, he thought, I will have arrived somewhere. I certainly thought such a thing when I first became an author, loathe though I would have been to admit it. Can he say, "Now I've made it?" "I'm home now?" Perhaps not. Yet something has changed. I just talked to him on Skype today and got the sense that here is a man more at home with himself, more at home in the world, and more at home with his lingering homelessness than ever before.

I wonder if that is more because of you, Alethea, than anything else. It might be trite to observe that family grounds a man in reality and arrests his flights into unwholesome over-abstraction. It is relevant to mention it here though, since this is after all a book of letters to you. I remember you well, you know, your clarity of will and the aliveness of your eyes. We joked about betrothing you to my son Cary, also two at the time, whose will and eyes resemble yours. But I digress. All I mean to say is that it is quite natural that a book that is a journey to and from home, would take the form of letters from a father to his daughter.

I won't venture to name what I think the destination of this book may be, but I am certain these letters will take you somewhere, Alethea. The same goes for anyone who reads them. While it may be true that there are no real endings, no final homecomings, no place untainted with what your father calls the dust, the messy incompleteness of the world, it is equally true that there are endings, homecomings, and destinations everywhere. I do not think this book will take you to a middle and dump you there. I think it will make the middle feel more like home.

Love,
Charles

—Charles Eisenstein

Prologue

B/reach

Mama, I don't want to be alone again!

It's turning out to be a horrible Wednesday evening in Chennai. I pull myself up the old limbs of the ladder and look into the room through its lattice window. You are at the door on the other side of the room—your tiny fingers surveying the annoying contraption of steel and wood before you. The latch is, however, resolute. Firmly shut. Just before I surface, Mama has been speaking to you from behind the door. I can't see her but she has been trying to pass instructions to you on how to open the latch. She wants to sound reassuring and calm. Anything to put you at ease. Only those who listen closely enough, or those who know her as well as I do, can discern the desperation in her voice—the submerged strain of dread that threatens to surface.

"Alethea? Alethea! Alee! Listen to my voice," she bellows. Pleads. But you do not ... cannot listen. *I'm sorry, mama!* You already know how to say sorry. You are not even two years old, but the words you've been crying out arrive with the gut-wrenching urgency of an elder breathing for the last time.

Beneath me, the rung I stand on creaks uneasily, its protest followed by echoes of "Bayo, be careful ... take it easy" from those below who are trying hard to steady the feet of the ladder. Down the narrow and broken walkway that borders the building, and on the tiny street it creeps into, there are enquiring men with their *lungis* tied about their waists and some children peeping through whatever space the men's potbellies haven't taken. Two women clad in various stages of their *dupattas* point at me, moving their heads this way and that in animated conversation. I balance myself precariously on the old ladder, acutely aware of how far away the ground is. Up where I am, the air is stiff with the whiff of cow dung—an all too familiar motif of the city of Chennai. Inside the room where you had wandered while playing and somehow locked yourself up, the ceiling fan whirs on cavalierly, as if nothing is at stake.

Behind the door, Mama begins to sing *the wheels on the bus go round and round*, sobbing softly as her words flail at the wooden obstacle separating her from her only child. At this time, this is your favorite rhyme. I have coaxed you to sleep many nights singing this song, and you would sing with me, giggling happily when we get to the part where *the horn on the bus goes beep-beep-beep ... all day long*. Do you remember this? On this night, however, you bravely manage to stutter a few lines, choking back the sudden and very jarring distance of things, but only for a little while: your young resolve gives way—and the floodgates of tears are open again. It seems that the singing has only made it more apparent how dire your situation is. You are not comforted.

"Alee mama! It's Dada," I call out to you from the window. You turn around to find me. I will never forget your face: a ghastly portrait of fear, an existential query struck at the heart of my fatherhood. How could I have allowed this happen to you? Your face is covered everywhere with streaks of wet and dried phlegm, and your tongue is trembling with every passing wave of grief. "It's Dada, dear! Come to Dada!" I squeeze my arm through the rusty railing, adjusting my feet to enhance my reach. A flicker of hope shoots through your eyes, and you run across to me, trying to climb up the window, as if that would do any good. If I keep you close to me at the window, the concerned men who ran up to the apartment to offer their aid can break down the door with you out of its way.

I hold on to you for dear life, my hand close enough to wipe your tears as your eyes tell me that you are wondering why I am so close and yet so far away, why my attempts to fill the distance between us only concretizes it. I watch you turning pale, the familiar constellations of joy fading from your eyes. Outside the room, I shout out a signal into the room, and the men begin kicking at the door. It is a very strong door, made from proud wood. It would take more than a few kicks to bring the whole thing crashing down. In the meantime, you are out of harm's way. There I stand, on a borrowed ladder still vehemently protesting its enlistment, my palm curled up under your chin as your silence metastasizes into soft frightful shivers. "I'm here, my dear," I whisper to you, as the pounding on the door starts to get louder. More worried.

I'm here.

Let me hold you ...

✦

> *Home, the spot of earth supremely blest,*
> *A dearer, sweeter spot than all the rest.*
> —ROBERT MONTGOMERY

My dear Alethea,

Of all the critters that crawl across the earth's meandering planes, and hide in the shadows of her belly folds, a hush is perhaps the most difficult to find. You don't bump into one of these every day. That's not because they are rare; as a matter of fact, they are actually quite common, even right here in this city. And yet, it's very easy to miss them ... to go about one's business without having to meet one. Coming across hushes (they mostly move in packs, stringed to each other with their "tails") mostly depends on where you are and what you do when one or several show up. In a way, they are like slugs, or better yet, cockroaches, who, in spite of all the hideousness associated with their always unsolicited appearing, are magnificent and resilient creatures. *Did you know those infamous bugs can live without their heads for weeks? It gives a whole new meaning to having one's head in the clouds, doesn't it, dear?* But I digress. Hushes too, like cockroaches, are *present,* hiding in cracks, staring back out of the dark holes they often inhabit with yellow unblinking eyes, and scurrying past our busy lives with their hairy-scaly-tentacular kin, nary a sound made in their ghostly trafficking. They thrive best in the corners of our eyes, stealthily making their way up the wall or floating free in midair without a care in the world. There one moment, gone in the slice of a sigh.

We are strangely drawn to hushes and yet simultaneously possessed by a crippling fear to actually meet them. I have seen a burly local rat-catcher, you know, one of those intrepid night-dwellers that prowl Chennai's moonlit alleys looking for rodents the size of little dogs—I have seen one shriek out a perfect falsetto as two hushes no bigger than *gulab jamuns* crawled up his thigh. There are no myths or portraits or stories told with these creatures. No blue gods are adorned with their image; no place where they are at home, and I have been to many places. One gets the sense that while we regard them with dread, they couldn't be bothered at all. They really couldn't care any less. They are quite indifferent to the prospect of making friends with humans. They seem unafraid for their survival, and live vanishingly brief lives, breeding rapidly and often shamelessly feasting on their own young. So, no, the fear isn't mutual.

But that's about all most of us know—or want to know—about these inscrutable fellows. Of course, there is also the matter of how they leave annoying slime trails wherever they go, and secrete a horrendous foul-smelling liquid whenever anyone attempts to hold them too tightly. It's all too much: the most common gesture is to look away, maintaining an unwritten rule to act as though hushes don't exist. One might thus say that the things are difficult to meet because we've taken such pains to avoid them, to pretend they aren't there and keep on doing what we were doing before—and also because we don't exactly know how to look for them, or what to do with them, or how to give them names, or tether them to our schedules, and domesticate them into pets. They don't act like they want to be loved or cuddled or storied. They are too spritely to stay put. Indeed, to speak about them is enough to violate something quite fundamental to them.

So why do I speak of them, then? Why are they of any importance to you? It's because these letters before you have more than a thing or two to do with hushes.

I met a wild man once. He lives at the edges, where the wild things press their faces against the borders and make funny noises. This man knows hushes. Sorry, I should say he knows *of* them: I do not think anyone can claim to have befriended them entirely. Well, this wild man knows the thick silence that comes with waiting, the forlorn itch of unrequited wanting. He is *re*acquainted with death, with not knowing what to say or what comes next, with things gone awry. With yearning for sense or meaning where there is none available yet. He is a bank of many sorrows. Many griefs. He knows how to wheedle a hush with rapidly spoken more-than-words, thrusting his fist in the sixteen directions of noble things, rolling his eyes this way and that way, every gesture a feint. He speaks his incantations with tongue in cheek, with a gentle cadence in his full-mouthed enquiries. He says a hush is not a trifling matter, that a hush has a message to share, and that to truly meet a hush, one must approach it with hesitation. One must be prepared to be marked, broken, mocked, and dismembered. To sit with a hush is to meet oneself as if for the first time. It is to come *home*. And *this*, coming home, is why I write you.

✦

I remember the journey to this man.

The Wednesday sun shimmers in a cloudless sky. Not even an orphaned bird crosses the bright blue, save the stubborn contrails of airplanes long vanished from view. The metallic green motorcycle or *okada* we're on has seen better days, but it bleats and splutters in defiance, often snapping and coughing out its own white smoke like a flatulent old-timer doing his utmost to convince onlookers of his vivacity. The road we travel is unforgiving, threatening to derail our rude pilgrimage through Adó-Odò, this tiny western Nigerian town.

Mr. Gbóyèga, my rider and gatekeeper into the communities I hope to access, doesn't seem to mind this at all. For someone who arrived an hour and a half late at our agreed rendezvous point, and explained his lateness by saying "the time wasn't right yet," he appears to be in a real hurry. He doesn't mind the mechanical choking, the potholes, and the dust particles flying into our eyes—the same canopy of dust that has already colonized the inconsequential blur of tin roofs, market kiosks, angry mongrels, and broken-down cars on our sides. In fact, his head leans forward more perilously, and the onrushing wind steals into his *bùbá*, making him swell. From my vantage point, his knees jutting out the sides of the speeding bike seem like ossified wings. He looks like a huge toad riding a dragonfly.

We stop at a T-junction to ask for directions. A woman approaches us from her kiosk to answer Mr. Gbóyèga's questions about how to find "Bàbá." An older woman lingers near, as if to ensure the younger woman is giving these men the right directions to the wild man. She stretches her hand down the road, speaking Yoruba with Mr. Gbóyèga, resting her other hand on her hip, nodding her head slightly as he interjects, seeking clarity about whether a street she refers to is in fact the same one he has in mind. Her mannerisms. The local portrait of self-assurance. *Like many others, she must know him so well, or must have consulted him for her own troubles.* We ride past a gaggle of screaming half-naked boys jumping into what looks to be an oversize puddle or a stagnant creek. A line of hushes is scuttling up a nearby tree, winding round its eminent bark. I whip out my Nokia phone to take a picture of the boys for my memos—unsuccessfully: the tiny screen of my phone reveals an incoherent swoosh of pixels.

I delete the picture as the rushing wind distils Mr. Gbóyèga's voice into flapping noises, half-enunciated pidgin, and occasional droplets of spit: "Oga Bayo, we go soon *reash* Bàbá." My eyes are still squeezed to twin slits to keep out the dust as we enter a clearing of well spaced-out farmlands and unpainted bungalows, through which a single asphalted road runs in the middle. A thickset, bald, middle-aged man in a white bootleg "Reebokk" T-shirt and faded jeans stands at the jagged edges of the road, a few feet from the entrance of what appears to be his home. *"Bàbá nì ye,"* my gatekeeper-rider tells me, slipping back into his dialectal comfort zone. I can't blame him. The usual thing to do when a Yoruba person meets another is to speak the language—and as you might already know, dear, I am the birth child of an uneasy tryst between colonial nobility, the captive life-worlds of an indigenous people, and the shibboleth of an elite future for those who know the *one-tongue* well. I know enough of my own language to know Mr. Gbóyèga is saying that this man who stands before us, unassuming and quite unremarkable, is in fact the one who can answer my questions. *Bàbá nì ye.* This is Bàbá.

Moments later, Mr. Gbóyèga and I sit on small wooden stools just outside Bàbá's hut. He is inside, gathering a few things I suppose are fitting for the occasion of a guest. Mr. Gbóyèga's eyes are blood-red. I am concerned. I ask him if he is all right, and he responds with a coy smile assuring me that all is well. I can see into the wild man's shed. It is everything I had imagined it to be—perhaps just one ontological decibel away from the fictionalized accounts of Yoruba traditional healers in local films. In those videos, the ones we had to watch because our parents had had enough of Chuck Norris and his swashbuckling American beard, the healers are folk superheroes. They strut underneath cloud-pleated skies, through forbidden forests, flanked by black mountains and the moaning accompaniment of song, drum, and yearning. Their arms are usually tattooed with unsayable secrets, their dresses ordained like Christmas trees with tiny gourds and little pouches hanging everywhere on them. The more memorable filmic depictions of these men paint them as wide-eyed, cocky, and histrionic performers of the sacred.

The sparks really fly when two equally powerful *babalawos* meet: it's nothing like a Mexican standoff and its strategic tensions, where everyone involved is immobile and catatonic, like excitatory and inhibitory motor neurons firing at the same time, paralyzing the limb. Here, with Yoruba *babalawos*, or medicine men, there is mystery and movement and poetry and flair. Like a street rap battle. One wild man belches out an explosive tirade of poetic incantations, jabbing his forefinger toward the earth, stomping his unshod feet affectedly, smiling and frowning and spitting, shaking his head as if trying to expel an insect that crawled into his ear, and arguing his cause like a cosmic lawyer before a jury of half-impressed gods. The other leans in and listens; his jaw hangs open, frozen dramatically, and his eyes dart here and there—his hands delicately resting on his chest, feigning shock. He may even fall back two paces or three when the first man is done talking, spinning in a dizzy fit, doubled over in exhaustion, and then ... slowly and whisper-ingly ... he chuckles. He starts laughing, a very sinister foreboding kind of laughing, his hidden mastery becoming apparent as thunderous clouds (aug-mented by cheesy sound effects) gather behind them. The first medicine man is dismayed, or appears to be. He looks at the camera, at us, wondering why his spells aren't as efficacious as he had expected them to be, and scrambles for a pouch of herbs—just as his assailant returns lyrical fire.

This wild man is nothing like the overdramatized ones I used to watch on television—the ones about whom I would ask your Nigerian grandma:[1] "What are they actually saying?" to which she would reply, "I don't know myself. Their Yoruba is the *ko-ko* kind." By *ko-ko*, she would mean "deep" or "beyond ordinary," playing with the tonality of the Yoruba tongue. Bàbá is genteel, soft-spoken, and—do I detect a hint of bashfulness here? Sigh. Am I disappointed a wee little bit? Maybe. Sure, his shed checks all the boxes in my head. Over its entrance, a bulbous object soaked in thick black oil and spattered with feathers of an unknown bird hangs by a red thread. Behind it, a parliament of webs, thick with age, rich with the devoured carcasses of unwitting houseflies and ants. In a dark corner of his room, I notice four cow horns, brown at the tips and striated with aging fracture marks. A clay pot and a charcoal-black cauldron, several bags of unknown substances, a single-page calendar on the cement wall, and a thin rectangular sheet of asbestos roofing tile, darkened by smoke and peculiar use, are some of the items I list. Outside, on the shed's thatch roof, a red-headed agama lizard nods uneventfully.

"This is where I dey do my work," Bàbá says to me, in passable one-tongue-ian, as he nestles himself into a plastic chair overlooking our occupied stools. The expected introductions begin, and Mr. Gbóyèga greets him and thanks him for granting us audience. Bàbá nods his head slowly in response. Mr. Gbóyèga then tells him that I am here to ask some questions, that I am from the university down the road, that I do not speak Yoruba at all even though my name is as Yoruba as they come. He says "yes, sah" or just "sah" at the end of almost every sentence. There is a palpable quality of eager deference to Mr. Gbóyèga's speech and posture. It is as if he wants to squeeze himself into a disappearing speck of air. The way his palms hover around his face, as if he were a scrawny boxer pitted against a silverback gorilla. This isn't a joke: I may have wandered into the den of a wizard, who might very well turn me into a tuber of yam, or—if I'm lucky enough—send noisome spirits to haunt my dreams. I am thinking of your mother at home and her worries that I am going in too deep, and might fall off an experiential cliff if care isn't taken. Perhaps the veneer of bashfulness that I detect is the perfect camouflage for a sophisticated predator, and I may have just strolled past the wide-open fangs of a Cthulhu-like beast my curiosity cannot encompass. Almost imperceptibly, with infinitesimal—and intensifying—drops of wordless apprehension, my posture starts to look like Mr. Gbóyèga's.

Bàbá turns to me and smiles, as if he heard my thoughts and wants to assure me he won't kill me just yet. He tells me he will consult Ifá first to find out if my intentions are good or if he should discontinue the consultation. I think I know what follows, and I lean forward to see what he does.

In the "home videos"—as they are called locally—the priest usually carries around his bag of cowrie shells, the vacated abodes of aquatic elders that simultaneously resemble the non-eroticized vagina and the eye of the gods. Venus's vaunted birthplace. The cowrie is a symbol of overflowing fertility and life's remarkable ability to regenerate itself.

Once used in precolonial Yoruba lands as a unit of currency when perforated and strung together by a single thread, cowries swept to the shores of West Africa from the Maldives via North Africa to the Middle Niger in the eleventh century, and later, with the arrival of European traders at the Bight of Benin in the sixteenth century. They are arguably more popular with contemporary Yoruba people as divinatory agents than as mediums of exchange or fossils of a bygone geo-politico-economic era.[2]

In one method of accessing the mind of the gods, Ifá priests would bring out sixteen cowries … sixteen, or *eerindínlógún* … from a white container, lay them in no particular order on a mat or on the bare floor, and ask the one who seeks answers to pick one. The one cowrie picked, the fellow is then encouraged to speak to the shell, to whisper to the gods her questions, her prayers, and her fondest wishes. Her reasons for coming. This is called *onda aniyan*, literally "the fellow wants to know the minds of the gods."[3] The one cowrie, now threaded through and layered with a new discursive web of human longing, now bathed in tears, is returned to the hands of the priest—with some money.

The priest then picks two out of the sixteen, holds them in his fist, embroiders them with speech and incantations just like the seeker does with the one cowrie, and casts them to the ground. As the priest leans in, gazing at the configuration of little olive-white bodies before him, one of three interpretive possibilities is disclosed, depending on how the shells fall. The shell is closed if it lands revealing the swollen and smooth part, like the abdomen of a pregnant woman, and open if it shows its jagged crevice—the part symbolically linked to the female sexual organ.

If both shells are closed, then there is no hope, the divination is closed, and the reason for which the seeker has come to the priest cannot be helped. A responsible priest will relate to the seeker the outcome of his consultation. It is not his place to bend the answers to appease his "client," or tone down the precariousness of the situation by being overly generous with platitudes. He may refer the seeker to another priest, or promise to consult the gods privately in another divination. But the silent bellies of the cowrie shells, at that moment, are votes of no confidence from the thick flow and tide of the immanent sacred. If one shell lands on the belly, and the other shell is open, then the way is clear, but not completely so. There is hesitation in the air, marauders along the highway, poison in the last morsel of sweet pounded yam, madness in the family of one's beloved, or less-than-stellar success in a new business undertaking. If the shells, however, land open, the road is free of marauders, the feast is set for the eating, and the reason the seeker wants divinatory access to the more-than-human is blessed.

Bàbá reaches for something hidden behind the wall of his shed. I expect him to return with a container of cowries. He does, apparently. He comes back with an old paint container, the ones with plastic handles and steel lids. He places it on a third stool that had been leaning against a tropical almond tree near the shed. He starts to whistle and hum a playful tune, interspersed with murmurings I cannot make out. When he opens the container, instead of cowries, out spills disconcertingly black streams of little furry creatures. A menagerie of monsters. Hushes. The way they emerge from the old paint can reminds me of a dark demon coming out of a black hell, its thin fingers clawing for a hold of the surface. I am taken aback by the horror of it, but anchor myself in some cosmetic notion of masculinity—muffling the instinct to yelp. And the desire to look away.

It is the first time I am this close to the monsters. No one I know is so invested in them as to keep a seething horde of them locked away in a container. Some of the more insectoid hushes have made it to the ground and are stationary, beating their "wings" in place; others are snaking up Bàbá's arms, and the rest seem quite content to maintain the fetid status quo within the container. The curious miscellany of limbs, fur, probes, scales, sizes, and behaviors belies their categorization as a homogenous group. Perhaps the one thing that unites them—apart from their pitch black pigmentation—is the jarring silence that attends everything they do. Not a sound is heard in all the beating and flapping and crawling and jawing about.

"Yes-s-s," Bàbá says, letting the *s* linger longer than it should as he looks admirably at the festival of mute madness erupting all around him. Mr. Gbóyèga is nodding and smiling, wordless but obviously pleased with the proceedings. I cannot make any sense of this. What use have these creatures for Bàbá? As if to soothe my growing frustration, the wild man looks at me, and then turns to Mr. Gbóyèga. He speaks in Yoruba: "Tell him that they have approved of his quest. He is welcome here." I understand a bit of what he has just said, but listen to Mr. Gbóyèga elaborate on and on about the glowing hospitality I am receiving, reminding me of the time I worried about accessing persons like Bàbá, and why he never doubted that I am a good person.

"*Ó ti yá! Gb'eléyi!* Take this one, my brother!" Bàbá moves his chair toward me, grabs my hand and shoves a hush into it in one swift and seamless move—all before I can protest my strong aversion to creepy-crawly multi-legged things. But, with my face now contorted into a scowl of disgust, I leave it there where he places it, in my wide open palm, my hand frozen in panic, held as far away from the rest of my body as possible. There it is in my palm, nesting and writhing and turning this way and that, its matte black layers of shell covering contrasting with the innumerable glossy lenses that freckle its *one-two ... three ... seven, I count ... ten,* ten horns. Bàbá and Mr. Gbóyèga are laughing now, hitting their hands on their knees, and ragging at my expense. I have more than half a mind to throw the thing off, but for reasons beyond me—perhaps nothing more notable than replenishing my sense of depleted dignity—I hold on to it, hoping there is some grand indigenous gesture or something to be gained from my hard-won bravado.

Bàbá and the gatekeeper decide their making jest is quite enough, and the wild man looks up to me and says, "Whatever you came here for, tell *it,*" pointing at the hush that still rests barely mobile in my phantom hand.

I know why I have come here. I know what haunts.

A gentle, wistful wind blows through the almond tree near us, making trembling incoherent music with the green leaves on its mysterious way to wherever. A familiar ghost.

$$\cdot\!\!\bigstar\!\!\cdot$$

My father, *your grandfather,* is tall. His full head of hair rises more than six feet above the ground. He is handsome, with sideburns that have a precise way of telling you that he is a man's man—*and that he knows what it's all about.*

There isn't a strand of white hair that tarnishes his eternal youth. Perhaps that is because my mother always dyes it, sometimes twice a month, and always on Wednesday. We put a chair in the bathroom, and my sisters get clean white towels, all the while bristling with excitement. My mother, her own hair attachments folded into a homey chignon, wears the transparent nylon gloves that had come with the hair dye, takes a neat comb she had soaked in a bowl of hot water, dips it gently into the chemical mixture, and applies the stuff on his hair—always beginning from the front and then proceeding to the back. We all watch, Bimbo, Tito, *Wendy is too small to know what is happening,* and me, all four of us, our faces transfigured by the soft golden glow of the bathroom light, as the comb's teeth runs through the forest, ploughing the wild, leaving wavy subservient locks of hair in its resolute wake. It's appropriate, this golden hue in the bathroom. After all, he calls us "the golden family."

My father, his eyes are closed, his head tossed back and forth in the firm direction of Mum's busy hand. Suddenly he wiggles his nose, sending us cackling with glee—the kind of laughter an underling would give to patronize his boss's attempt at a joke, or the kind that happens because love does indeed make things lighter. Mum just sighs, shaking her head as she treats his triangle sideburns with the black stuff, careful not to let any of it fall anywhere on his face that there isn't hair, and then combing from front to back again. He likes it when his hair at the back extends a few inches away from the neckline, just like those high-heeled, bell-bottomed Afro crooners on his many vintage vinyl record covers. My father is cool like that.

When Mum is done, he kneels by the bathtub, and holds his head over its rim, as mum runs the water—*not too hot, now, darling*—and rinses away his age in a black whirl of youth. He towel-dries his head. He is reborn. From the Lazarus Pit like Ra's al Ghul in the *Batman* comics stuffed under my bed. When he steps out, when we all do, he lets us touch his hair and climb his back. He tickles us until we are at the edge of peeing on ourselves. Outside a moon massages the troubled shadows of the city of Kinshasa—the tensions that daylight, like a Band-Aid, cannot tolerate or appease.

My father will live forever because of nights like this. He will never grow old and leave us alone. Because he can't. He *just* can't. In the morning, he will be dressed in his immaculately pressed suit, holding a giant glass mug filled with milk, speaking gritty jaw-breaking French into his walkie-talkie, just before he kisses my head and swaggers into the embassy car that will drive him a few miles to work. It's the way the world spins: to finish the remaining morsels of pounded yam and okra soup he has left for me in his bowl; to watch him bounce into our home with a big bucket of ice cream; to know *that* inner gravity, that horrifying feeling of falling into a dark place, when he and mummy get into an argument—or when I can taste the acrid tensions in the air, and know (along with my sisters) that they are about to have a fight because dad has taken one too many Guinness Extra Stouts.

Yes, my father will live forever—and this is not merely a love-struck son's fantasy. He has met death before, but he always comes back. A young civil servant freshly returned with his family to Lagos, Nigeria, from his first deployment in Bonn, Germany, my father is driving home one day in his buttercream Volvo sedan. He reaches an intersection, and makes a turn to his right. A trailer driver approaching the intersection steps on his brakes and realizes to his horror that they aren't working. The trailer slams into the Volvo right in front of him, sending glass and metal and gasps spinning in a thousand directions. Young men drag the man out of the car, and rush him to the hospital. The policeman that stands at our door reassures my screaming mother that he is well. They don't say it till months after, but everyone who sees pictures of the totaled Volvo knows he shouldn't have survived the accident. But he does. My father is cool like that.

And when an entire platoon of rebel soldiers protesting the nonpayment of their salaries scale the fences of our mansion in Kinshasa, kidnap my entire family, and put a pistol to my father's head—threatening to dispatch with him as they have done the French ambassador hours earlier, my father escapes again, as we all do. In the morning, our dogs, Sasha and Beethoven, are gone. The aquarium in the wall is pierced through and bled out by bullets, some of which now litter the floor and the settees. We crawl out from the toilet where we have been held hostage by successive waves of insurgent troops, tiptoe past drops of blood on the floor left by wounded soldiers, and make our way—through gutters and swamps and hidden streets lined with silent hushes—to the Nigerian Embassy on 141 Boulevard du 30 Juin. My father carries my sister on his back, wearing no shoes, and with nothing but his pajamas on. A few weeks later, the Nigerian government puts us all— except my dad and his diplomatic colleagues—on a plane home. But even though I am just nine years old, I know with an adult confidence he will come back to us. He always does.

And come back, he does. But in a wooden box. We receive his body at the airport, *three days* after he feels a certain weight in his chest, decides to drive himself to the doctor, and then dies on his chair. He is forty-nine years old. The first time I see him after he returns is through the smoky window of a Volvo ambulance car, *through the shattered lenses of my own world*. I am flanked by my sisters and the dramatic tears and dress-tearing rituals of more than a few strangers. My mother, she has no more tears to shed. Her very soul bleeds.

There is a convoy of buses bearing dad's photograph on their wind-shields. We are preparing to undertake a long journey to his hometown in the middle belt of Nigeria to bury him. The wooden box sits still in the ambulance. Mute and ordinary, unlike the man it is pregnant with. I cannot see his face. I do not know if white hair has now sprouted on his temples, and sullies his eternal youth. I cannot know whether his mustachioed smile still haunts his full lips, whether he misses me, whether he can hear me claw away at the windshield as an uncle wraps his arms around me and carries me away. But I know my father will live forever—and this is not a love-struck son's fantasy. He will live in the father-shaped hole carved out of my body, with nothing but the remaining sinewy threads of hammered flesh left to my claims of embodiment.

He will haunt my dreams, my yearnings for arrival, and my visions of justice. My want of warmth. I will seek out his smile in a vast conspiracy of things ... in the warp, woof, swoop, and swirl of my days; in my teenage struggles for homecomings and transcendence; in my failed relationships and how I rationalize them away; in my longing to explain the world in one breath—a grand theory of everything, and in my hopes to always be held in place. He will stand with me—a gaping hole of abiding absence, a figure of things yet to be and things that might have been—as I stand in wait for my bride to join me under the decorated tree. And he will stir when I hold you in my arms the first time you insist on breathing. He will haunt us both.

My father is cool like that.

$$\cdot\,\text{✦}\,\cdot$$

That this ghastly creature of darkness is to be a receptacle for the arcana of my longings, a squirming shrine, my confession booth, unnerves me. I bring it close to my mouth—not too close. Bàbá watches. As if in response, it—the hush, *that is*—stirs. I cannot tell where its head or tail is, or if I should even be thinking about these things in these ways. But still it moves, as if it too wants to hear my prayer. I do not, however, know how to pray.

Though I know why I have come here, I do not have the words to dance out the wordless gyrations of memory and pain and hope, the undecipherable grumbling of a heartache so fragile, and the feeling that all is askew and that something needs be done about *that*. It is an itch somewhere down my back that my fingers cannot reach. There's so much to say. So much to feel. Feelings that are not *mine*, but emerge from the material grounds—the killing fields, the sites of charged yearnings and gravid voids—that make me possible.

I sing a mournful tune of the world that now is. Let me sing and rend my clothes.

I know a certain nasty feeling of loss. It comes and goes, of course. It comes in sudden glimpses of eternal afternoons, when the world seemed straightforward and the hallway of my many small hours had furniture that stayed put in the places you left them. Neat and tidy. Now that hallway is unfamiliar, and might (yet) have always been. Death inhabits the living. Peace is a Manchurian deal. Heaven needs its hell. Even diamonds aren't so polished as to remove the blood stains, and exorcise the ghosts, of families and communities thrown in burning heaps of casualties of modern luxury.

I am marked by an eager fury about occluded lives and italicized worlds—about the drums of war beating in rhythm with colonial exclusions, the imperatives of progress and late liberal power, ecological devastation and big oil—the same rhythms that are the soundtrack of our waking moments. The leitmotif of the normal.

I worry about what might become of sea turtles, water, mountains, and land—the intricate life-web of the more-than-human spun outside of story and intention, upon which we depend and by which we are *enfleshed*. I cannot solve the world's problems or even know how think of them—how to think of the rivers of petrol that drown the feet of yawning toddlers in the Niger Delta, where burst pipelines snake toward giant factories that promise development and progress. Or how to think of my skin and the infirmities that come with being a young black man in a world that prefers the pedigree of brighter colors. I wish I had answers. I wish I could be accepted without having to exert myself or stretch myself in acrobatic displays of cultural mobility.

With the loss of biodiversity, ocean acidification, air pollution, and ecosystem collapse, it seems we have come to the limits of the usefulness of technological "solutions," and manifestos of liberation. Will I leave you a world with no enchantment? No community? No surprise? A world that isn't constantly aghast with the many gestures, sensuous textures, and wide-eyed becomings of leaping whales, chirping swallows, scratching grasshoppers, and mingling love-stitched human bodies?

Will I be contained in a box like my father, or—like Achebe's Okonkwo in *Things Fall Apart*[4]—dangle from a tree, estranged from the very lands that bore me, a fugitive in my mother's womb?

Will your lot be an eroding island of warmth, surrounded—threatened—by pipelines, by cold cash, and by barbarous hordes of flesh-hungry beasts whose storied ties to humanity might be known if you listened to their own stories and found traces of yourself? Will you have enough money to get around? To live and breathe and dance?

What about the misery at our fences? What about Aleppo, Standing Rock, and the Gaza Strip? Am I paranoid about all of this, or is there really a rumor that mountains might one day be replaced with piles of obsolete television sets and smart phones?

I grieve my inability to grieve the losses that my people—the Yoruba people—suffered when ships pulled close, when schools stood tall, and steeples taller. When we learned slowly that the fullness of our lips, the color of our skins, the way we opened our mouths *yàkàtà* to enunciate words, and our imagined futures and notions of time were inferior and tacky, evidence of stunted development, needing the refinement of distant interference.

Do you understand what I speak about, babe? I know I have a reputation for speaking with more words than I need to. How best to say this?

Do you know how it feels to be possessed by agony, the one you try to repress with the unrelenting motions of the banal, but if it were left to its own devices, would scream out from your chest? You might know what I'm talking about if you know the city as your mum and I do: a sprawling edifice of anonymity and cultured indifference. A noman's land where stars are shushed by neon-lit nights, where new buildings, new roads, and new technologies do little to quiet the hollowness one might feel if one slowed down.

Maybe you know what it means to be without ground, to have one's feet planted in midair, to be dispossessed of one's own, to wander the face of the earth like a Cain—marked by a god—cursed to live a Sisyphean nightmare. To tug and stretch and thrash and flail about in one's skin, never knowing the stillness of mere nakedness. To know the burning sensation to stand up in response to a world so vast and incredible, and yet be beaten down by its suffering.

Do you know what it means to never be enough—not in an ideological way of not living up to lofty philosophies, but in the very ordinary sense of being framed out of the picture, or constantly looking over your shoulders, or being called a thing that feels foreign to you because you do not fit a particular regime of words?

I do not know how to meet this haunting, this feeling of alienation from community, from joy, from meaning, from my skin and from my "self"—so ably enacted by memories of his face, his brilliance, and his figure. I do not know how to appease this hole in my body, the shape of a ghostly presence, this series of cryptic questions tattooed on my palm, the meaning of which is not yet decided.

I do not know how to find home. And yet I am possessed by this longing, this embroidered absence that hisses within; I smell the evasive whiff of the Otherwise. A promise of reconciliation.

I am worried that I won't be there for you. That I won't last for long. That I won't be a good father. Won't rise tall enough. In fact, what can I give you, dear—that is not already haunted? That is not tainted and troubled with two shadows, instead of one? How can I hold you?

✦

The fluorescent tube flickers on, engorged with white humming light. Restless, electric humming light. Not the kind that soothes. It is the cold, clinical kind that keeps one on one's feet, that says "don't get too comfortable—keep moving." The chairs in the passageway are plastic and morose. There's nothing warm or homey about it. I think it's ironic that hospitals could be the least hospitable places. I can see down the lonely hallway, the perfect squares of milky tiles that cover its walls, the studious whirring of the mellow mocha fans above, the picture of an eminent looking Indian woman hanging near the reception, her forehead emblazoned with a *pottu,* her portrait garlanded with delicate arches of jasmine flowers. They say that during her time, she helped thousands of women carry their own children.

This is why we are here. This is why I walk five or more steps in one direction, and five or more steps in the opposite direction. Not that I am counting. I couldn't care less about numbers at this point, or being manly, or behaving appropriately. Yes, I am whispering "be a man" through my teeth, my taut lips lubricated by salty tears in free fall. *I can hear her muffled cries of pain through the door.* Oh, god. It must hurt. *It must hurt so bad.* Are they doing everything right? Is this how it's done? What if ... she'll be fine. She will be fine! I wish I were in the room. Why doesn't India allow husbands to stay in the same room with their wives giving birth? How would daddy behave now? Be a man. I'm a man. I'm a man. I can't breathe.

Lali's piercing yowl and stomach-curdling gasps of anguish reprimand me. Syreena briefly exits the hallway and retires to the hospital room we've been allocated. I know she cannot bear to hear her first daughter in so much discomfort. The minute hand on the clock on the wall moves backward. Or seems to. Is it broken? It's taking so long. I turn and face the door, hiding my tears from the uniformed sisters walking down the hallway. The door. Those maddening cries. She is a ghost, and her unfurling plagues me. I say a soft prayer to whomever. Then to the familiar god I was taught to think of as supreme. Then I pray to your mother's very femininity—to the cosmic circle of women who are invoked when a body stretches itself to make room for another body. Anyone's help is needed.

Please, don't take her away from me.

An eternity later, Lali's crying grows faint. And then an alto voice sprints through the air, mellow, delicate, quivering, but resolute and textured—like an aged flute. The tears flow even more freely now, and I stand still, my face contorted into a puddle of relief and—*ah-h-h* ... there's no need to put it to language! I stand there, looking at the frosted glass, *through the shattered lenses of my own world.* There are others! Where are they? I make to go bring the others that are with us, but they are already there. Syreena is still in the room, however. When I see her, she has no expression on her face. She asks if all is well, and I smile, exhausted. No, she has no expression on her face— none that is apparent to one who doesn't know how to look. None that can be felt by those who don't know what it means to suddenly, as it were, become a grandmother.

Dr. Vivek walks out through the door. His brow is wet and lined with threads of hair. He tells me, "So, congratulations, it is a girl," but says it with that Indian lilt so that it sounds as if he is asking me if it is so. I respond, "Yes, I know. Thank you, doctor." Through the door, I catch a glimpse of a nurse holding a clean white bundle in her arms as she walks swiftly to an adjoining room. There is no wah-wah filling the room, just—and this is amusing—something syllabic and frantic that everyone hears as "ee-lai," a phonetic match with the Tamil word for "no." "Your wife asks for you. Everything went very well. Don't worry," Dr. Vivek continues, and walks away. I run into the room. Lali is there, *your mother,* filleted into chunks of collapse and whispered acknowledgment. And yet she looks like an angel. I smile. She manages a smile, asks me to bring a few items in the box she had—as usual—made ready before we came to the hospital. She turns on her side, and closes her eyes. I lift her hand to my lips, and kiss it, and bless her. The music of your syllabic protests never dies out.

I am a father. *I am your father.*

It is Wednesday, the 10th day of July.

✦

I find words to say. Or maybe the words find me. I whisper them to the hush, and hand it back to Bàbá. He receives it gently, with both his hands. He now holds more than a hush. He holds the precious cargo of my prayers. He holds the very stuff of my fatherhood. He holds space-time. The space between us, you and me, is at stake. Everything turns on this.

I don't become your father the first time I hear you rip the air with your song, or when I later carry you close to my chest, shaky and afraid that I might do something silly and drop you. I tend to think it is the moment we bring you to your grandmother's home, the house your maternal grandfather—a Nigerian like me—bought for his Indian wife. I steal away from the festivity of laughter—often punctuated by *shh!-lower-your-voice-she's-still-sleeping* persuasions—and find a private spot. There, where no one else can hear, I say a short prayer to you. I make a promise to give you a home, to work for your future, to love you with my darkness, to be the ground upon which you stand to greet a whole new world. I promise to be your father.

This is why I am here, and why I sit with this wild man: because the only way I can meet that promise is to seek out the ghosts that haunt my fatherhood-in-the-making: the ones that linger at the edges of our collective imaginations of human agency, in the crevices of our protracted enactments of socio-politico-economic reality, in the blind spots of our scientific pronouncements about the nature of nature. How can I know what is at stake in such a promise unless I grope at and feel the strange shapes in the vast ecosystem of elided histories and stories that is our world? How can I make you a home unless I set out to encounter the universe halfway?

I take this seriously. This project to give you a "home" by striving to know the world in wholly new ways.

Bàbá places the hush in front of him on the floor. I realize he has now slipped from his chair and is sitting upright on the bare ground, his outstretched legs boundarying a small V-shaped space where the hush remains. He tells me my prayers have been heard, and then he falls silent. In the periphery of my vision, Mr. Gbóyèga shifts in his chair. He seems a lot more comfortable now, but his posture now conveys keen interest. Bàbá says something at length in Yoruba, holding his hand in the air, dropping it behind him as if pointing to something forgotten or lost or on the way. Mr. Gbóyèga stirs to life: "Bàbá is saying that we have chased away all the spirits into the forest. *Him say* if we want to do well for this world, we must to look for them. If we want to find our way, we must first come away from the road and become lost."

Bàbá is nodding his head all this while, watching Mr. Gbóyèga translate his words. As soon as this is done, he turns to me and continues speaking, Mr. Gbóyèga mediating: "My fathers who taught me this work—when they want to bless the people that come to them—they use ten cowries. The number ten is important for blessings to us." He pauses to take a breath, raises one knee and uses his hands to hold that leg in its folded position. "You must go and look for ten of these ones," he points at the hush in front of him, "if you want your prayers to be answered." He goes on to tell me that I am to go on many journeys to find answers to my questions, and that wherever I go, I must go to the edges ... *the edges in the middle* ... and that there are hushes—ten in total—that I must not only acquaint myself with, embrace and acknowledge, but pray to as well. He tells me I must learn how to create the right conditions for them to show up. I must learn to listen. "Only then will you find the answer to your prayer." I am told they will come in twos, or threes, or fours, or alone—no matter how I find them, I will somehow know which of them are the right ones to use for my ritual. What I am to do when I encounter the "right" hushes will feel improvised to me, but I do not need to worry—just because it feels useless doesn't mean it isn't important. Also, this might take years to complete and it could take a day. Who knows? I can begin anytime I want. It doesn't really matter when. Life will guide me.

Bàbá tells me a few more things before packing up and escorting us to the waiting motorcycle. The way home is silent. Even the old-man-motorcycle doesn't bleat and cough as much now. There is a calm wind blowing. Or maybe I am so preoccupied with Bàbá's words that I cannot hear the world seemingly outside of my head. *If you want to find your way, you must become lost.* And then the matter of befriending hushes. I do not understand why this is important. But the echoes of your heart-rending giggles stream through my other pair of ears. And eyes. Your dimpled smile. The day you start to crawl, dragging your feet behind you like two tails. The first set of rabbit teeth that burst through your pink gums. The time you utter your first word, *dada,* much to the playful chagrin of your sweet mother. The sound of blaring horns bring me back to life. Mr. Gbóyèga has been speaking. I ask him what he said. I am prepared to listen.

ALL THE COLORS WE CANNOT SEE

In My Father's house there are many mansions.
And if not so, would I have told you that I go to
prepare a place for you?[1]

Baby,

Here we are again, my dear. Right here, in the middle. In the riddling middle of things.

I am reminded of beginnings—when you first squeezed through the curtain, like a young performer before her first audience, eager to please. You came out—a masquerade in a village square of interested passers-by—*quite* intent on making your voice heard. No taller than a generous roll of ghee *dosa*, no larger than a loaf of bread, you fit neatly on my forearm, as if it were made for you.

On that first night, and the sleepless nights that followed, I whispered to you your secret name, your *Oríkì* or life-song—the one no one else (except your mum, I think … yes, definitely Lali, when she felt like it) was allowed to utter. The name *Maya*. For me, beyond its multicultural significance and spiritual connotations, *Maya* means you are vast; that the whole world, its many twinkle-twinkle-little-stars and the shadows between them, conspired in your emergence; and that—most importantly—I am indelibly marked by the small and seemingly insignificant promise I made you *to find you a home*. To topple regimes of knowing, petition water spirits, climb mountains, and be pierced by a thousand proboscises if only to inch closer to understanding what it would take to live peaceably in this world of dust, shadow, and burning sun. And, yes, huffing-puffing wolves.

But where to begin on this quest? What does a home mean in this world of shifting sands and eroding foundations? What good is home if it doesn't preserve you for a while longer than if you were without it? Hold on to these initial questions; I trust they, among others littered along the way, will later on become more meaningful to you as you read these letters.

Beginning with an account of my brief expedition to the frontier of an Indian city, a slum, where I visited in order to understand new ways of speaking about home, I would like to tell you a story of settlements we once occupied ... descriptions of the world and of home that were found wanting, leaving much to be desired. This story I tell is not *done,* in the past and therefore unreachable, or written in stone. It is just an iteration of the many stories I am sure you have by now heard about the world, our place in it, and what it means to be at home with it. The hushes Bàbá asked me to find are integral to the telling of this monumental story—and to my ultimate quest to find you a home.

This story—running through these letters—is the series of assumptions about being human and about the world that is often called "modernity." Modernity is home to us. Our flag is planted deep in this planet, this uncouth carnival of churning matter *we barely understand*. Not for a want of trying. We are doing our best to encounter the world and make sense of it by reducing it to utilitarian units for potential exploitation. We seek to meet the world by conquering it. We treat ourselves the same way—subjecting the "other" to the brute force of our colonial narratives (a legacy that runs in your veins).

But then this drive to mastery has spawned many dreadful things, and the focus of (Western) critical inquiry has shifted once more: rejecting the grounds upon which our cities and empires of selves are premised, we are moving our tents. Many have left their material belongings and the camp, and headed for the sea, roaming in desolate, postmodern waters—stricken with thirst but unable to drink the inhospitably salty water. Awash in a heady place. Lost with no possibility of redemption. There's a lot to say about these settlements, but what—for now—is important to note is that both of them, the modern and the postmodern, especially the former, are how we struggle against "nature" ... how it has become imperative to discipline it, to leave its logic behind, and float above its assumedly brute prolificacy. Spirit above matter.

So, here we are, our feet showered with gold dust and tattooed with paeans of mighty valor. Our cargo area filled with spoken secrets and many spoils from cultures plundered. And yet we are exiled from home. There is no arriving. We know no welcoming shores. We are like one abandoned ship I used to stare at when we went to the Bar Beach in Lagos. It was some meters from shore, neither tethered to safe land nor cast away in roving sea. Just hovering at the lip of a final resolution, stuck in the frustrating middle. Our days and nights are like that: filled with a certain feeling that something is missing, that there is something yet to be done, that the world could be more beautiful, more just, more inviting to leaf and limb. More like home. Perhaps a good deed here and there. Perhaps another hero who could swing his rope, anchor it to a stern, and pull us in. Perhaps another sacred book. The hypotheticals are endless.

So where do we go from here? Where do you go, my dear? This is the question that has brought these letters before you, right here, at this threshold. This is why we are here together.

Now, before the sun takes away her light, let us go on. It's an uncertain road ahead, dear. But let us not back away from taking it.

Do you remember what you and I learned in those nightly moments when I—with some exhaustion from repeating it so many times—told you your second-favorite bedtime story, of the three little pigs, with your tiny legs playfully thrashing in the air, and with *Mary* the red-haired rag doll clutched close to your chest? Yes? We agreed that a lesson to learn was that when you build a house made of straw or sticks the big bad wolf is sure to huff and puff and blow it away. The moral of the story seemed to be that what one needs is a house of bricks. And if one could afford it, steel comes quite recommended. And why not go even further? High walls, barbed wire, a moat, and closed-circuit television cameras thrown in for good measure—one cannot be too safe where wolves could willy-nilly blow one's abode away and eat you up!

Early in my own life, in my teenage quest for final settlements and homecomings, I hoped I could afford the luxury of a house made of bricks—a safe place, warm and friendly, where I belonged and was free from the wintry desolation of a material world I had come to despise. I was a young kid a few licks away from the terrible, terrible loss of a father and best friend—and I hated the world for my predicament. Something had to be wrong with this carnivalesque riot of things. Death was so unnatural. So wrong. Consequently, I dreamed of a home that would take me away from the pains of being enfleshed—away from this body of death, this deadening mangle of dust and grime. Away from the inanity of a world that, were it left to its devices, would rapidly descend into some kind of protozoan immobility.

I longed for a pristine beginning, a clean start. A time before corrupted time. A time of innocence. Do you understand? I write about pure beginnings, corrupted middles, and redeeming endings. Home evoked a notion of future reconciliation and of bravely slugging through the tangle of the ordinary in order to arrive intact at the unspoiled gates of the real. For me, life was an arrow—the entire world and its history a single shot fired from a benevolent archer. To live was to come awake mid-flight, never fully at home in the fugacious sceneries of our days. Home *wasn't* this annoying unsure spin of hellos and goodbyes, of dying fathers and interrupted joys. Home was the glowing red bull's-eye in the faithful distance. The *end* of the archer. The permanent. The point of the plot.

I wish I had *this* to give you now: *you know,* this bull's-eye I write about—for, whatever I might come to say about it, I must admit, there is more than a small measure of comfort and relief to be gained from thinking about home in this way. H. P. Lovecraft, what with his preoccupations with terrifying primal beings and monstrous entities, knew a thing or two about the comfort I speak of:

> *The most merciful thing in the world, I think, is the inability of the human mind to correlate all its contents. We live on a placid island of ignorance in the midst of black seas of infinity, and it was not meant that we should voyage far. The sciences, each straining in its own direction, have hitherto harmed us little; but some day the piecing together of dissociated knowledge will open up such terrifying vistas of reality, and of our frightful position therein, that we shall either go mad from the revelation or flee from the deadly light into the peace and safety of a new dark age.*[2]

This "safety" of the shore, this fear of voyaging too far and falling off the deep end of all things, of staying put, of maintaining originality and the seal of the pure, is a powerful thing indeed. The world is too complex, too tedious to be apprehended in one gaze—perhaps reason enough for Markus Gabriel to insist that the world does not exist and that "an overview of the whole is impossible."[3] Hence one can at the very least sympathize with the psychic need for an End, which guarantees that the Middle, the vast continent where we all must number our days and count our blessings-curses, will one day be blown away like a house of straw and sticks, giving way to a new heaven where many might arrive.

I wish I could offer you this story of arrival, a tale of a city in the horizons with which you could warm your weary bones made hard and brittle by cold, long pilgrimages. A map to teach you how to go, why to go, when to go, and what to look for when the place you seek stretches unforgivingly in the taunting distance. Firm ground. An origin myth—a story of when things were just fine and innocent. A portrait of paradise lost. A resolute forefinger trained in the firm direction of home.

But I can't. I will try to explain why in the course of these letters: the problem with *safe shores* is that they are never too safe from the ocean they pretend to protect us from. Indeed, the anxious work of keeping the ocean to its watery confinements, and of hoping it does not *arrive* too heavily on the shore, is futile. Not because rising tsunamis might someday tear apart our little islands, but because the ocean never *reaches* the shore. There is no simple arrival here; that's an inadequate portrayal of what is happening. Instead, the ocean *enacts* the shore (the stranger without is already within). It happens the other way around too—in one single move. The shore performs the ocean—a co-constitutive mutuality that makes doubtful the prospects of xenophobic havens, where the pure are inside and the Gentiles are out. *The inside and the outside are not easily divided.* By acting as cleaning agent for ocean debris, the shore characterizes the ocean; and by the mereness of its material complexity, the ocean creates shorelines. The heavens we seek are secreted by our own longings and performative quests for a final, static home. We want to get "there"—whether "there" is a beautiful techno-utopic world, or a more just arrangement that works for the many and not just the few. But there is no "there"; there is only a yearning, an aching, a struggle for "there"—and in the struggle, we change.

But let me not get ahead of myself.

There's a lot I'd like to tell you, and these letters are the only way I know how to.

Let me also say this, dear—just before the night comes and you no longer have any light to see my heart beating between these lines: I have written you these letters—though at times it might seem like these words are exercises in meeting my own self. And the resulting effect might be passages that feel too dense, too thick for your easy reading. I am not so sure, however, that this is without merit. In meeting myself, in working through the knotty issues that becloud my mind, I make myself more available to the nuances of our relationship. I become your father over and over again—in new unexplored ways. But most importantly, these letters urge you to slow down. If there are words you don't understand, check them up. Contemplate the knots and the entangling turns of phrase. The slowly eaten morsel rewards the patient mouth with juices that the rapid eater may never know.

Right.

Where were we? Middles. Origins. Arriving. *Maps.*

Maps are comforting, for reasons I have just highlighted. I spent my mid- to late teenage years tracing paths and seeking maps to lead me to fixed existential settlements—mostly to the exclusion of a functioning social life (I had often nursed fears that your early passion for writing and scrawling almost-alphabets on every surface you could find meant you would also live a very solitary, internal life—like mine—which is full of haunting ghosts and often unbearably lonely). As you grew to know, my life was irreparably changed when dad passed. It was difficult watching my mum become a shadow of her once full self. Oftentimes she would bow her head in soft, jerking sobs of sadness, doing her best to assure us—as she hastily (and futilely) wiped the tears away from her tired, ringed eyes—that everything was going to be fine. I was young, just coming away from fifteen, but I was old enough to know she had no clue what the next day might bring. In the place where there once was the soft golden glow of assurance crept shadows of foreboding, like distant rainclouds dispelling the naive blue of a sunny sky. We were a little tugboat of a family—and we had lost our sails and compass, adrift in the oblivious vastness of the sea.

Cast about so rudely, without land in view or the promise of being saved, I desperately needed some sort of stability. I needed this mad dance of the elements to cease their obstinacy. There had to be a place, a truth, behind this nihilistic spin of things. For my sake, I had to find it, this endorsement of a master seated in the midst of a disagreeable audience.

I didn't go anywhere "fun," and always had a book about me—a sticky habit that would later annoy your mum when we met, and sometimes made her erupt in passionate pleas to me to come out of my "shell." She used to say, "I married a mind with a body attached," which—her sarcasm notwithstanding—would have coincided seamlessly with the Christian view of the primacy of mind that we were both raised with.

Growing up, soon after your grandpa passed, and after I graduated from secondary school, I would wander about my neighborhood—actually from our home to my mother's shop down the street, where we sold delicious chicken barbeque under a canopy I often set up by myself—with a Walkman

firmly attached to my jeans pocket. A single black cord—a life vein, to me—
would snake up toward my ears from the clunky plastic thing, streaming
urgent dispatches from the frontiers I sought, the final settlement where only
the deserving arrived. The place I wanted so much to believe now held my
father in transfigured wait.

With my Walkman, I held open a breach in the deadness of the sky; I had
his final instructions not only for how to live *a good life* in the hostility of the
time being, but how to eventually find *him*—how to right the wrong that was
done to us, done to the very fabric of the world, when he closed his eyes on
that deathly surface, a man in his prime.

I lived in a bubble, pored over the Bible, and kept multiple journals. My
inoculated distance from the familiar, my cultivated indifference to the material middle, had the effect of making me feel I belonged to a better commonwealth, a vaster conspiracy of nobler selves who knew the hidden codes
behind the swirl and indiscipline of the everyday. The stable behind the
apparent.

Of course, it wasn't my father's actual voice that I heard when I pressed
"play" on my Walkman over and over again—blocking out the unadorned
sounds of the prosaic in my quest for the sacred. It was the voices of others
who knew the way to where his soul floated, waiting for me. And to hear
them was the closest thing to pacifying his ghost. What I heard every day—
as I drifted in the liminal space between being a teenager and becoming a
man—was soothing medicine for my existential exile. *My firm ground in lieu
of the firmest.* Sanctuary. It was the rushing of a waterfall splintering into a
million haloed paeans to a beautiful world; it was the song of a company of
holy people. And when they sang, I felt giddy with electric pulses shooting
out of my head: the foretaste of rapture. Their voices made my insides tingle,
made me want to squeeze myself into the warmest cradle the universe could
contrive, and giggle with endless excitement.

You see, I was raised in the Christian south of Nigeria, at a time when
there was a church on almost every street in Lagos, at every turn—each a
funny adjective different from the previous in their titling. I doubt much has

changed even now. Every day of worship, you could hear the shrill voices of pastors urging their flock to pray "in the spirit." To dance away their sorrows and troubles. There was drumming and preset electronic piano tunes accompanying even shriller voices in song. The biggest, richest pastors in the world were Nigerian; they knew their stuff. They wore fine suits and drove finer cars. They stood behind proud lecterns and told everyone that God wanted them to live the best life they could—and that, like them, we all could find the secrets behind a victorious earthly existence.

The thought that these men hadn't a clue about God or the home I sought never did completely untangle itself from me. But I knew no other way, no other bolder map or hope for restoration. So when I wasn't at church, I had my Walkman. I would listen only to "Christian music" (some of which I played repeatedly and eventually labeled "The Soundtrack of My Life") and, even more frequently, to my father's prized collection of audio cassette recordings of an old American preacher called Finis Jennings Dake—who in 1963 published an annotated reference Bible with an intriguing spin on the familiar Christian creation story. These were the same recordings I woke up to on most days we went to church when we lived in Kinshasa, filtered through one of those very expensive sound systems only a few of my father's peers were privileged to have.

With my Walkman, I was part of the resistance, tuned in to frequencies that skirted the expedient, just a beckoning inch away from the extraordinary. At night, away from television, I reached out and groped for those signals from home. Dake's Appalachian drawl would crackle, burp, and snap into place, against a constant hissing background noise of rolling tape. I didn't mind. He would reannounce God's eternal manifesto, the original innocence of Lucifer before Isaiah saw him fall … like lightning. There were hundreds of thousands of cross-references and annotations in my father's giant gold-rimmed Dake's Bible; I read every one of them, underlined most of those side notes, and even accidentally burned a few pages one night when I fell asleep by a glowing candle, while serving with the paramilitary youth corps for Nigerian graduates.

Many things Dake said were quite fringe, unknown to the larger population of churchgoing Nigerians that I belonged to, but this only endeared me even more to his message. His teachings had the right dose of controversy, eccentricity, eloquence, and rational unimpeachability I looked for. When I learned of the pre-Adamites who lived in the thin space between the very first verse of Genesis and its second, or about the Millennium, or about the Nephilim, giant offspring of a perverse time when angels left their first abode and lusted after the daughters of men, I felt I was being initiated into an elite group of apologists—those who had peered through the breach, and whose eyes were undone by the beauty on the other side. His conversational sermons and booming voice only added to the sense of authority I felt when he spoke about "God's eternal plan." Moreover, he was a white man. He had to know what he was talking about.

Listening to the cassette tapes, all forty of them, milky-brown and stoic, dwelling on different topics (from "The Simplicity of the Bible" to "New Heaven and New Earth"), made me feel closer to my father, who at one point in his final years nurtured some hope to be a preacher—you know, of the more intellectual sort. We both shared a repulsion for the "dancing, sweating, devil-chasing" clergyman, whose displays of fervency had a funny way of emptying surrounding wallets. Dad wanted to retire from the Ministry of Foreign Affairs and open up a church. I dreamed of him serenading his flock with cool, persuasive commentary, with dictionaries, and with a head full of hair and books—and no convulsing sips of Holy Ghost juice or its symptomatic glossolalia. If he lived long enough, he might have been like Dake.

It was simple, really: the songs and messages that flowed into the privacy of my hearing offered me a simple way to make sense of that which seemed to resist sense-making. I had always known the stories and doctrines of our family's faith, but for the first time, in the troubling years following my father's passing, I needed them. *I needed ground*—a point I have already stressed. And so the world was reduced into a thin timeline that proceeded from the initial, splendorous appearing of all things. In a burst of the divine inexplicable, God created the sun, moon, and stars. Crickets, cats, and cows. "He" made them all. The Bible didn't say he created dinosaurs, but I figured they were referred to in the old book of Job, where God urged his wavering disciple to "consider Leviathan." Everything was accounted for. Everything was "good." Until something went wrong along this appointed line of emergence.

Sin.

The Fall.

Eve listens to a snake, and indulges her desires to taste the succulent fruit of a tree—the very one God expressly forbade them to eat from. She later brings her "treachery" to Adam, the *first man*. Though all of creation becomes cursed, the first man is absolved of his complicity and is made to be the hesitant accomplice in this cosmic tale of degeneration. The blame for everything gone awry sits squarely at the feet of those with bodies like yours, my dear. Woman. *Eve.* Her punishment? She must ache and squirm and scream in the unutterable pain of giving birth to another human being.

I came to believe this, among other things—and, more importantly, to trust that a divine plan of complete restoration was afoot. That one day, I would have reasons to dismiss my abiding pain, and that because the Christ promised a home in the heavens, a place of many mansions and thrones, *dustless realms,* I would finally feel the mustachioed kiss of my father's lips on my cheek again.

In the same way they were part of dad's arsenal of sanity, those tapes became my refuge. My map. I listened to them, wore them out, and broke some of them from overuse. With each listening, the emptiness felt a little less empty. Home resumed its song, its dutiful and lofty soprano above the carnal tenor of the world. I listened. Hard. Biding my time like a soldier of a spectacular ending imprisoned by the meantime. Stuck in the edges in the middle. Awaiting rapture.

But it is here, right here in the contested middle that we often learn that our maps, however elaborate, are not the whole picture or the terrain they pretend to represent. And that home is not simply the fixed dot at the end of dashed lines, motionless and given, awaiting the ones who come marching in. Let me tell you the little things that I have come to learn while I still can, right here in these middling places, still trying to reach out to you: everything begins in the middle. There are no beginnings that appear unperturbed, pristine and without hauntings. And there are no endings that are devoid of traces of the new, spontaneous departures from disclosure, and simmering events that are yet to happen. The middle isn't the space between things; it is the world in its ongoing practices of worlding itself.

✦

Heaven was my first post-dad vision of home. Paradise. Eden updated. The "shiny city set upon a hill which cannot be hid."[4] The place the Christ offers his disciples, the ones washed of their sins. The place he is urged, by a dying criminal, to bring him into at his end. The itinerant evangelist, Paul, in one of his ecclesiastical letters, narrates a near-death experience in which he visits the "third heaven," where he hears things too sacred to be put into words, reinforcing the mysterious quality of this place beyond places. This bull's-eye.

In the Book of Revelations, exacting dimensions are given of an opulent city made of pure gold descending with "the glory of God," boundaried by twelve gates, founded upon twelve foundations, and inscribed with the names of the twelve tribes of Israel. The author of the text warns us that none whose name is missing from the Lamb's Book of Life shall be deemed worthy of entrance into this city of "clear glass," jasper, and one hundred and forty-four-cubit walls. Talk about immigration control raised to the power of infinity!

Such an indescribable abode, the prospect of a final destination, open only to the redeemed, and outside the degradation and ruin of the material world, inspired Saint Augustine of Hippo, a fourth-century theologian-philosopher who shaped Western Christianity, to write:

> *For we are but travelers on a journey without as yet a fixed abode; we are on our way, not yet in our native land; we are in a state of longing, not yet of enjoyment.*

But let us continue on our way, and continue without sloth or respite, so that we may ultimately arrive at our destination.[5]

Those words were once music to my ears. They gave me a sense of diplomatic immunity or "red passport" status—the kind my family enjoyed when we traveled the world together. I told myself home was far away. I was just passing through.

Augustine's longing for "native lands" made sense in the context of his struggles. In his incomplete autobiographical work, *Confessions,* he equated his body with sin itself, speaking of his battles with concupiscence and "adolescent stirrings," a godless lust, and how the carnal lump that was his body was his one source of inner turmoil—getting in the way of him and his devotion to God.[6] Perhaps more than any other theologian, Augustine was influential in shaping Western attitudes to sex. In trying to answer the question of how sin came into a perfect world, Augustine (along with Irenaeus and other early church writers) helped articulate the idea of "original sin"—the notion that the flesh is depraved, ridden with guilt, sewn through with corruption—an unfortunate yet prolific generativity of despair. Consequently, he longed for release. Escaping the entrapments of embodiment, and finding the unmediated joy of finality, figured prominently in his view of a surer home. The purpose of home was the soul's absolute reconciliation with the ground of being—a daunting task in a material world that is the very breeding ground of alienation. Thus, Augustine looked forward to the purging of the afterlife—the destination that coincided with ultimate arrivals and new beginnings.

In Augustine's meditations, I found an eloquent (though provisional) way to voice my longing for a heaven, and spent solitary moments imagining what living there might look like, perhaps much to the chagrin of the flamboyantly suited pastors I pestered with my unsettling questions. I had very practical questions. *Is heaven an exalted version of suburbia? How are those mansions allocated, and are there different residential standards—with the most sanctified immortals occupying, say, five-bedroom duplexes, as against the standard issue of three-bedroom apartments? Or is heaven one vast sprawl of identical homes?* Perhaps I was going about it the wrong way—maybe heaven was less a utopian arrangement and more of a state of deindividuation, a melting back into the celestial soil whence we came. A returning to soul dust, if you will. But then why take pains to build separate mansions, to fortify a city with multiple foundations and ordain it with exotic stones and physical dimensions if there's no one around, save an undifferentiated divine soup of cosmic goo?

The more I explored my emerging map of home, the outlay of my future abode, the more worried I became. The Judeo-Christian doctrine of an afterlife, even one that Paul suggested we must suppose is beyond our ability to fully describe or comprehend, presented itself with some troubling inconsistencies. For one, this idea of pristineness began to unnerve me. The more I leaned into heaven's flattering sprawl, the more its eternal foundations seemed to collapse under the weight of its own aspirations. I had questions about the nature of the "soul"; whether people were still enfleshed in bone and skin (and what that meant for Augustine's arguments against carnality); whether there was normal (or perhaps cyborgian) sex and reproduction and—consequently—an ever-expanding population of humans without the winnowing threshold of death; whether people felt pain, grief, and the bodily limitations that define our earthly lives; and, how long forever was.

Heaven-as-home started looking suspicious, evoking the same feelings I had watching a particular episode of the animated television series *The Simpsons*.

In that episode, called "Brick Like Me,"[7] Homer wakes up in an alternate universe and finds himself a subject of a utopian Lego-brick Springfield where "everything fits together and no one gets hurt." At first, he feels fully at home in this plastic-shiny town without real consequences, where a Lego helicopter could drop out of the sky, and heads could be severed from their bulbous torsos—only to be followed by a cavalier shrug of the shoulders of onlookers. Things fall apart, but they can easily be put together again. In this world, everyone has a place—every step is literally an interlocking of a Lego unit and a planned layout of plastic blocks. There is no room for errancy.

When Homer starts having disturbing visions of a fleshly world, where his skin is mushy and not smooth, where his hands branch out into squishy tentacular protrusions (or fingers) instead of mechanically efficient claws, and where a "flesh monster" shows up in the mirror in the place of the stenciled flatness that is his face, he panics and seeks help. He learns of an alternate world—actually, it seems to creep up on him, especially in dissociative flashbacks and socially embarrassing moments—where things do go wrong, very frequently.

Learning he can decide which world to make his ultimate reality, Homer considers the implications of choosing this squishy, messy, and monstrous realm over his safe plastic heaven. In the world of skin and blood and membrane, he'd have to grow old, might lose his job at the factory, and worse, risk losing the affection and attention of Lisa, his daughter. But when Homer realizes in a moment of triumph that "the fact that kids grow up is what makes our time with them special," and that the reward for a life well lived is the "gentle slumber of death," he leaves Lego heaven behind.

Like Homer's schizophrenic responses to Lego Springfield, you might feel there is something disturbing about a place where everyone belongs and no one gets hurt. I know I did. Could it be an engendered cynicism? A failure of imagination? Perhaps we have lived so long in a world where things go wrong that it is hard—maybe impossible—to imagine one where things go according to plan, without fail. Perhaps we should broach the subject of utopian longings with a good dose of intellectual modesty, and not try to get ahead of ourselves, then.

And yet even this sentiment of modesty and capitulations, a gesture parallel to Pascal's wager, proves equally unsatisfactory. Pascal's wager is an apologetic line of reasoning devised by Blaise Pascal, a seventeenth-century physicist and mathematician, who advises the seeker to trust that God exists, since doing so has more pragmatic benefits (among which is escaping eternal damnation) than disbelieving. It's the "What have you got to lose?" and "What if you are wrong?" argument. Apart from the fact that Pascal doesn't answer the culturally charged question of which god we ought to believe in, and proposes a simplistic account of belief that treats it as a simple matter of choosing between beliefs, the wager glosses over the remarkable eventfulness of wrongness. For Pascal, the choice is between zero and one. "Why choose nothing, when you can settle for something?" he asks. But the binary is misleading. The zero isn't an empty, dank, lifeless gray zone where nothing moves and stirs. There is spontaneity and color and comeuppances and surprise and politics. There is life here too. There is beauty in this meantime.

For me, the idea of heaven cut too cleanly, too firmly, between life and what purportedly comes after it. Cynicism and a critical lack of imagination might have played a role in how I gradually began to shrink away from the bull's-eye, but who was to say that these things—my cynicism and stupidity—didn't have genealogies of their own? Did they not come bearing gifts, substantiating the world in different ways, opening me up to other possibilities I hadn't considered? Is darkness merely an absence of light, and the middle merely the space between two points—or is darkness just as embodied, resilient, and voluptuous as proud light, and the middle just as much a destination as the "end"? It seems to me—even now—that brokenness is generative. Creative. The void speaks. A crack is a different phenomenon, not merely the empty jagged space that has been created by the fracturing of a surface.

The Japanese understood this as they evolved their ancient art of *kintsukuroi,* which involved the active smashing of ceramic objects, and then re/pairing the pieces with lacquer dusted with gold powder—producing pieces of ceramic delicateness.

You'd notice I did something queer to the word *repair* with the intrusive slash. I mean to point out that something more complex than a mere putting back together again is involved. There is no "return" to pristine conditions—there is only a *re/turn,* a coming back to the new—which is itself threaded through with the old. But more on this later.

The ancient practice of *kintsukuroi,* where a ceramic piece is even more beautiful for having been broken, speaks with the eloquence of the between, and entrusts us with a richer world where cynicism, despair, and failure are not orphaned apparitions of an immaculate world trying to expel its demons, but part of how the world substantiates itself. The practice disturbs the neat divide between wholeness and brokenness, instead making them contingent on each other and co-constitutive with each other.

What the vaunted city of gold and high walls excludes isn't all that's ugly, but other forms of beauty. Heaven is as such irredeemably incomplete—for this much we are told: in heaven, there is no sickness, no sorrow, no regret, no death, *no dust*. We are missing something in not being able to decay, fade away, or suffer—in not being able to err, fall off the highway, or beat out new paths through fields of barley.

I often like to think that *the Fall*—that great mythic rift in the scheme of things, the crack that tore everything apart—was more devastating than we might think. Not only did it occasion the cursing of mankind but perhaps also the death of God the Absolute—giving way to god experimenting with finitude, with decay, and the "gentle slumber of death." Maybe the Fall unraveled him so much that the all-knowing is depicted in unflattering circumstances shortly after the deed is done—walking in the garden *seeking* Adam.

> *Then the LORD God called to the man, and said to him, "Where are you?" He said, "I heard the sound of You in the garden, and I was afraid because I was naked; so I hid myself."*[8]

Could the Fall event have been so incomprehensibly potent that its effects leaked backward and forward into time, recreating all in its carnal memory, reconfiguring the godhead, and infecting the absolute with its contingency? Could the project of repair, of putting everything back together again, seeded in the redemptive work of Christ (according to Christian theologians), sweeping across thousands of biblical epochs—involving the parting of the sea, the carving of the tablets of stone, the seeking of Canaan, the period of kings and judges, the rise of the Roman empire, the time of prophets, the virgin birth, the incendiary ministry of a remarkable rabbi, the crucifixion of Jesus, the time of the apostles, the repeated failure of men to live holily, the promised purge of fire and brimstone, and the promise of a future heavenly home—could all of this be the masterpiece of a God tired of his eternity? A trickster's ruse behind which lies a shocking subplot, the details of which suggest that in spite of appearances to the contrary, God isn't really as interested in saving us from sin as he is in teaching us to immerse ourselves in its ongoing fullness? Could it be that when the forbidden fruit was tasted, the middle spilled through its hermetically sealed container, corroding the beginning and the end, so that it is not quite the case anymore that life flies toward a given destination or home? And, even more scandalously, could the idea be playfully mooted that Eve (and Lilith before her)—in an ironic twist of plot—was all the while God's partner in his self-redemption from the plastic and dustless Lego realms of the absolute? The thought of it! To think that the "chief cornerstone the builders rejected," the female, is the one that redeems. And that none less than God himself is the beneficiary of her mischief.

Maybe, then, there is no return to beginnings. No prelapsarian rendezvous. We must learn to live in the Fall, right here in the middle of things. Not "after" it, as if the Fall were done with, or "before" it, in the exhausting longing for Eden restored. If the Fall infected what was, what might have been, and what might yet be, then a gospel of the Fall is the thing to preach, not so? The absolute splinters into shards of the contingent—and here, this very middling ground—is the gold-powdered lacquer that embraces the fragments in a vast network of many becomings.

This middle—what with all its tensions and exclusions—is beautiful, dear. Do you already see that too? In the transgressions of the middle against its once noble walls, like an opening of Pandora's box, we are left with a reimagination of "the" afterlife, and thus a reconsideration of the home-as-fixed-destination thesis. The afterlife is not devoid of life or an immaterial place of postbecoming that is "unaffected by empirical accidents of the physical realm [and] immune to the fluxes of becoming and destruction."[9]. Neither is it a single place with boundaried walls, opulent pillars and beams. Like dust—as it *is* dust or a re/turning to dust—the afterlife is not invulnerable to the evanescence of the middle. It is not the apotheosis of the ordinary, and it is not a transfiguration into disembodiment. The afterlife is in the middle, substantiated by partial recuperations, and never not broken (such might become clear as we both sigh through these letters).

In a sense, we are already living with (and because of) the afterlife. As the world (itself partially made real by our performances) grates upon us, we shed our cutaneous cells and hair and pieces of ourselves, contributing these into a commonwealth of dust that includes other beings and their shedding. Edges bleed in traces of becoming, melding dying and living, beginning and ending, into an always pregnant middle. A thick middle. None can escape this "universal proliferation of dust"—this rebuke of Shiva the destroyer—whose medium is dust and whose art, Michael Marder reminds us, is to "pulverize composite beings, sparing neither you, nor me, nor anything around us."[10] He writes more:

> *Dust chronicles both the gradual break up of beings and how they get a second lease on life, the opportunity to lead a posthumous existence in a random combination of their remains. If there were a god of dust, the "god beyond God" Borges invokes, then it would most likely be Hindu Siva-the-Destroyer. Lest we be misled by his terrible attributes, Siva is not an external annihilating force; he is the temporal gist of finite beings, whose gradual or rapid manner of passing away is, at bottom, what they are. His actions uphold the living order, which needs change, dying away, and rejuvenation. And, last but not least, he destroys death or puts an end to the misconception that death is the end of existence, just as dust teaches us about the afterlife of its sources in the contingent communities they establish.*

We are a constant falling-apart, a becoming-dust—and this applies not merely to surfaces, as if the boundary between surface and content, outside and inside, were that clear. We fade away in eddies of dust, and heaven itself—with all its gold and jasper and angels—will not refute the arguments of dust's redemptive-destructive work. The rapture is taking place right this moment, as it always has—in the ongoing dis/appearing of the never-whole, in the purging of Eve's children: God, world, and all. In seeking home, we are coming down to earth, and we will not arrive intact.

You are probably asking about my dad: what becomes of him, if he is not to be located in an immaculate place—at secure finish lines, where the saints go marching in? I figured, not without some difficulty, that it appeared he had changed address. He didn't disappear into an existential black hole. No. I couldn't trust that. That's not the sense I got as each golden brick of heaven crumbled into dust, expelling its last occupants—and as I risked my first unsure steps into a cluttered world infused with the sacred. He was present in a way that queered presence itself, and—I realized—even closer than before: no longer awaiting his son at the end of time, arriving at my deathbed to whisk me into roiling prairies. He was right here in the middle, where I was—thus even closer. Maybe he was like that rusty and eminent ship I used to stop and stare at when we went to the Bar Beach in Lagos: neither tethered to safe havens nor cast away in roving emptiness. I knew this with every singeing memory of our time together. The effects of his haunting—experienced as a gnawing compulsion to make sense of the world—were no less loud than when heaven was supposedly the place I had to return to in order to find him. Perhaps his dust comingling with sky and soil flirted with the air around my ears, whispering my name. A mild haunting trace away.

✦

Shouldn't we then give dust her due? Pay more attention to it?

Look around you, love. Slowly. Do you notice this sunset? It's the only one you'll ever see. Tomorrow, you'll see another one when you come to this edge—but then it will be another sunset, incalculably different from the ones you've already seen. Such is the miracle and wonder of the world. Everything moves, nothing stays or congeals long enough to ever be fixed into being. Everything is caught in the trance of becoming.

Do you feel the gravity of things? The way the ground feels beneath you? The tension in your chest as you pull in oxygen and dust, thereby disturbing the boundaries between the inside and the outside? Life and death? Feel the gentle drumming of your heart within, its music rippling through your entire body so that you—in almost imperceptible moves—are never not dancing. Never not flowing. You are moving, even though you sit still, here at the precipice.

Do not close your eyes, if you can manage it. I'd rather you meet the inchoate festival of colors and contours, the seemingly random stance of objects around you—their gritty materiality a scolding of our very old exile. Take in the muck and grime and beige dust. Priests of the middle. They have escaped our reckoning because of beginnings and longed-for endings. Comprising roving communities of remnants of human and animal hair, grains, pollen, pulverized stars, fibers, minerals, pollen, and dust mites—and lacking an essential identity or core integrity—dust unsettles foundations and neat borders, and yet gives birth to the world. The trickster surrendering to her own trick.

In Yoruba folklore, the higher God lowers a chain to the nether region, where Oduduwa, ancestor of all people, descends into what would later become the city of Yoruba people, Ilé-Ifè. The first settlement for earth's citizens. Oduduwa comes down the chain hanging on the corner of the sky with a pouch around his neck, containing a rooster, some earth, and a palm kernel. He meets the tipsy waters, swaying this way and that. There is no place to rest his feet as he hangs by the chain from heaven. So he throws the earth into the water, and deploys the rooster, who scratches, flails and scatters the dust far and wide with its wings, making continents and huge land masses wherever the dust settles. Oduduwa plants the palm kernel, and makes his home on earth. But the dust never settles. It may be said that that ancient rooster, restless and eager, still disturbs the dust—and it is disturbed dust, always flowing, that makes us and makes the world over and over again.

We cannot account for ourselves, and the world by which our breathing is sustained, without paying homage to dust, to this graceful contingency that imbues all and resists wholeness and lastingness. This mysterious wafture without denouement. Perhaps a libation—the practice of ceremoniously pouring drink to the ground—is not so much about quenching the thirst of bloodthirsty gods or appeasing haunting ancestors, as it is about unsettling dust, summoning Shiva to intervene, if you will, and remembering that we all—hunter and hunted, sacred and mundane, master and slave, homeless and homed—are enchanted by our co–becoming-threadbare. In that ritual, we honor our fading, and yet pray for sustenance and well-being. Dust appeasing dust in preposterous palimpsests of becoming.

Dust gives us place, while reminding us that it isn't ours to own forever. We cannot toss our proprietary claims at an ideal, at thought, at place, or at bodies, since the generativity of dust resists permanence and undercuts lasting presence. In my revised reading of the biblical story of creation, which hopefully will not long abide the chastising gaze of time, God curses man— but only apparently. "Dust thou art, and unto dust thou shall return." It is at once an annulment of the project of eternity and wholeness—or a tongue-in-cheek invitation to us to learn alongside the many others how to live in the midst of the fade—as it is God's own declaration of freedom from his shiny lamp, where he had not known the merest joys of finitude. It is his convocation keynote address, spoken to himself and to us as we collectively graduate from the eternal to the finite. Once immortal, we all will now have to learn limits. We will have to make do with hints of ideals, the dust trail of essences we will never catch up with. But this is a difficult lesson to learn, because it comes with the message that we are not unilaterally in control of our circumstances. We are not sovereign. "Dust … gives lie to the human presumption of power and control."[11]

The real implication of all this talk about dust is that in consideration of the real, or of home, we can no longer march "straight to the things themselves, because that path would only bring us to the cul-de-sac of ideal and ideally dustless entities."[12] The world can only be spoken of incoherently, not because we don't have all the details but because the details themselves show up only in traces, in residues, in hints of what might yet be or what might yet have been. Burrowing deeper will not bring us closer to the essence of things, or home at last; it will only generate a lot more dust.

Is it any wonder that those of us in the mechanical heart of modernity cannot tolerate dust's presence? Does this tell us a bit why our cities— especially cities in the rapidly industrializing world—aspire to be dustless, shorn of any insurgent memories of our disappearing? Are Babel towers and phallic structures how we propose to escape the fact that we are dying (and being reborn in ongoing cycles of regeneration), *along* with everything else—and that no matter our ideological preferences, we all sympathize with this *becoming-dust* of things? Is there something here that coincides with our obsession with cleanliness?

These are the questions I learned to ask one hot Wednesday afternoon in Chennai.

In the room where, for most of the day, I am hunched behind a computer, in the unfortunate act of keeping myself relevant, I can still hear your cheerful voice in the hall, singing songs with no determinable lyrics. Lali is in the bathroom. I am busy, as I always seem to be, but I leave my chair and the seductive wink of the screen to see what you are up to. Through the crack of the room door now ajar, I watch you—as a sceptic taking a walk in the woods would watch a ring of elves dancing around a bonfire. As a prisoner might watch the moon gleaming through his bars. You are happily preparing a tea party for your *sisters*—"Mary," "Sister," "Fairygirl," "Sophia," "Ms. Miracle," "Bumblebee," "Fluffy," and the naked plastic doll with blue threads for hair and one leg. Your little feet move nimbly and tiptoe past your guests. That morning your mother had twisted your curly hair into dreadlocks so that as you danced, swaying your hands and weaving your way through the audience of dolls before you, you looked like a shaman catering to her white visitors. Eventually, you bring out your small kettle and pour out pretend-tea into many tiny white plastic cups. And then you are silent for a while, crouched next to a queer assembly of plastic and cotton "sisters," your attention stolen by Max and Ruby's opening theme song on television.

A familiar guilt washes over me.

You had come to me many times prior to that moment, inviting me to play with you. I didn't have the time or the patience. I had stuff to do. With a barely veiled frown, I succumbed to your demands on my time, and allowed you to pull me away from my chair, only to be stopped in my tracks when we got to the living room. The whole place was a filthy mess of spilled rice, littered alphabet bricks, and blotches of Plasticine stains on the floor—not to mention your tea set pieces flung across the room. The clutter was overwhelming. I'm easily triggered by clutter—especially the kind that defies easy interventions like the slide of a tall broomstick or the temporary inconvenience of squeezing oneself under the chair to pull out a stranded toy. Muttering under my breath, doing my best not to scream, I had reached for the broom and tidied the place up—firmly insisting that you put away your toys. You did so, crying that way you cry—talking at the same time, registering your protest with groanings that will not be uttered.

Now, standing at the door, watching you sit so still, nothing littering in sight … something feels a bit off. Dare I say it? Unnatural. Out of place. Isn't it funny that order could feel out of place? For me, at this point in time, the painful regret of my previous reaction to your wild play, coupled with the forced orderliness of the room, troubles me. Are my little devils getting in your way, preventing you from knowing the tactility and virtues of your felt surroundings? I suppose so. My obsessions with keeping our small apartment spick-and-span—even to the point of ridding the thin places between the floor tiles of its revenant communities of harmless specks of dust, and getting irritated when our appliances are enveloped by a thin film of dust—remind me of the old existential anxieties that prefigured my reach for a disembodied home. For the sky. Like Icarus of old, seeking to escape his material imprisonment in Crete, my unease with clutter is a psychic riddle that leaks into the sociopolitical, telling a story of dislocation and separation.

Dislocation is what "Euro-American modernity" produces in abundance. An ironic observation—since the stamp and force of modernity is an assertion of humanity's place in the world. The irony lies in the fact that in emphasizing permanence—*that is,* in striving to push back against the corroding and destabilizing effects of dust, and in striving to rise above the finiteness of matter, modernity escalates our being out-of-place.[13] Specifically, modernity is about matter … or unease with matter—"nature," so-called—and the consequent desire to tame *her,* rein *her* in, and put *her* in the family way.

In a sense, modernity offers the prospects of returning to heaven. The myth of modernity proposes a home ("a secularized eternity"[14] as Frédérique Apffel-Marglin would say) in a world that is progressively conquered by scientific and technological advances: the more we come to know about how the world works, the likelier our chances for successfully colonizing it. The many modern practices of world-making (home-making) compel us to see ourselves as alone and uniquely imbued with the powers of agency, cognition, and conation. We are a noble race in a desert, surrounded by a pagan orgy of forms and bodies we are pitted against in a game of survival. It is us against the world. Us against dust.

As our fences grew (pretending to enclose within them a circle of anthropocentric agency, and distancing the wilds beyond them, where dragons and beasts and mindless weeds sprout like an uncontrollable plague), the promise of arriving at a universal, totalizing, and complete knowledge of the world keeps a steady pace—disturbed now and then by the interrupting sounds of the wilds. With science and its supposed abilities to mirror unvarnished truth, the war is supposedly being won. We are getting "better." War and brute superstitions are being stamped out; we are gaining control over aspects of the world we would have thought beyond our control a few decades ago (there's talk of men visiting Mars soon, propelled by engines that can achieve unfathomable speeds). Soon, we say, monoculture would replace nature, or eventually rise so far above it as to be called its master.

Of course, this imperialistic thesis of modernity made colonialism possible. And science, purportedly apolitical and neutral, was in cahoots with the economic and cultural agendas that led to the exploitation of black, brown, and even white bodies. On account of our "primitive ways" (or lack of proximity to the ultimate truths modernity was intent on categorizing), we—your father, my mother and father, *their* mothers and fathers, and those before them—were given a dishonorable place in nature. The Negro was three-fifths of a proper person, a white man. The Negro woman was probably not even accounted for—or was many decimal places behind in the scheme of things that her value did not register in the equation. The home that modernity built was built on the bent backs of the inappropriate.

And yet, even with these painful histories, there is nothing inherently nefarious about modernity. Indeed, if we could give a fuller account of modernity (and no one can), and how it "came" to be, we might need to reawaken old anxieties produced by desires to preserve the ephemeral, to supplant the troubling contingency of things.[15] We might have to listen to the old pre-agrarian European wanderer whose battle against the elements, whose quest to save his family of wanderers in the face of swift and punishing climactic changes, taught him to see himself as apart from the weather and instructed him in the art of cultivation—anything to enhance predictability.

In the quest to stand resolute against the sandstorm, to affirm our place in a bold stance of anthropocentricity, and ensure a home for posterity, we only accelerated and enhanced the felt disconnect between us and the world around us.

·✦·

This concept of modernity will show up very often through these letters—not merely because your mother and I are embedded with others in this epoch, but because "it" is also a popular gathering place where stories about what we once had, homes we once built, futures we once thought given, cultures we once embraced, powers we once sustained, and liberties we once enjoyed are told and retold with nostalgic breaths.

In this loose assembly of bodies, manifested in the media, in the ways we govern ourselves, in the ways we name things and educate our children, we are desperately trying to investigate our circumstances, to ask what it takes to live well, to struggle with aging and dying, to know when to be wary of the other and when to be hospitable. To know what home means. We may not frame our everyday this way but we are constantly performing these investigations, driven by questions and stories our modern circumstances make possible: with films that explore extraterrestrial civilizations, we wonder about alien others and come to terms with the strangeness of our own forms and material circumstances. With fiat currencies, we are inquiring into our well-being and survivability on the earth; and with schooling, the questions about what it means to responsibly account for ourselves in a changing world come to bear.

Western science is often thought to be the oracle that grants us access to the deeper secrets of the world—the singular series of practices that offer us our best chances at resolving our most pressing dilemmas, a strategic stance to assume as the dust settles. To the question about our place in the universe, science[16] says we are unique, unrivaled for our evolutionary achievements. To the question, "Why do I feel so alone and feel like crying all the time?" or "Why do I feel tired even after I have had a good night's sleep?" science presents a conceptual framework that offers a way to think of your experience as the fallout of unhealthy life choices—with the potential for betterment. And to the question, "Where do we go when we die?" science thrusts out a chastising finger-wag, banishing such thoughts as nonsensical.

In short, Western science—and I say "Western" to acknowledge at least one layer of its particularity—teaches the modern world how to see, how to make meaning. Seeing clearly, getting it right, offering an answer, striving till we get there, reaching for the stars, finding the truth, never stopping, arriving intact, making it happen, being the first ... these impulses substantiate our modern lives.

Seeing clearly, especially, discloses a particular relationship with the world. The expectation is that the world around us is explainable, that we can arrive at answers to our most fascinating riddles. Never mind the dust! Just stand this way, push out your head that way, and squint a bit—and you should see the real masquerading behind the indiscipline of finitude. Modernity presupposes that the truth about ourselves can only be accessed indirectly, via representations of things themselves. The truth can be revealed if we harness ourselves and deploy our gifts to hold open the breach in the veil, where the real or "pure knowledge" spills into the ordinary.

The scientific method (about which I am very certain I will write in subsequent letters) is thus ennobled with the burden of sorting out what is true and what is false. And today, not just our technologies … not just our smart-phones and television screens and internet-y activities owe their being to this metaphysics of seeing, but the ways we navigate the world, the things we avoid, how we make love, how we think, and how we think about thinking are all partially produced by these particular ways of seeing that lie at the heart of the modern world.

The thing with seeing is that it comes with its own set of paradoxes—one of which is that greater clarity or higher definition is always a trade-off for panoramic depth. There's an Eastern saying for this dialectic: name the color, blind the eye. It means that "seeing clearly" is a practice of occlusion. It means that the premise of modernity—to arrive at the heart of things—is not an arriving at all. For every "resolution" offered to our pressing questions by our present circumstances, there is a possibility discredited or rendered invisible. The dust never settles.

No definition of modernity captures its essence, and that is because there is no essence, no ideal explanation to arrive at. We can only speak with a lisp about these matters, with a humbling stutter. Even the idea of modernity is a product of a Eurocentric analysis that looks "back" on "history" and arranges it in convenient thematic clusters amenable to contemporary discourse.

I think it is important to keep this in mind, and I have often had to remind myself—as a citizen gestating in this "age," sharing troubling questions with others—that modernity is not evil. Modernity is not a thing in itself, with its own walls and furniture, independent of other periods, sprouting unmediated. Neither does the term *modernity* aptly describe all the power relations, opinions, subjectivities, appetites, longings, or possibilities it supposedly "contains." Things aren't just that neat. Modernity might be an assemblage of practices of unease with the world, but its roots are the branches of the ongoing previous. As such, it is also part of the wafture of dust—no more cut off from the premodern (which we often tend to romanticize and talk about as if it were a time when things were all right) than the ocean is from the shore.

And yet there are some things that feel true and pressing about our world of clock time, long weeks, headline news, and occasional skirmishes with nature—things some metaphors might highlight: one might say that to be modern is to be in a constant state of ornamenting our exile, constantly changing the wallpaper to screen out the jarring effects of the world, a mass forgetting. Burrowing deeper to arrive at the ideal. Trusting that the dust will settle so we can see clearly.

There are many that trace modernity to those moments during the European industrial revolution of the late eighteenth century, when small-scale, agrarian, home-based production methods transitioned to mass production in large factories. These major changes in European culture came in on the back of the Renaissance, which declared man to be the practical measure of all things, and therefore instigated a return to Greek and Roman literature after the "Dark Ages."

The rapid industrialization of the landscape continued to reinforce the premise that man sits at the heart of the universe. The world was shaved of its sacredness, and the narrative of innovation became the central imperative of the new expansionist project. Today we are subjects of a neoliberal hypercapitalist system that seeks the rapid, largely unregulated, laissez-faire conversion of "nature" into resources and profit. It has changed the way we live, the way we educate ourselves, the way we understand knowledge and produce it, the way we eat and encounter food, the way we relate with the world *outside* and with the world *inside*.

But every world comes with its own shadows. The very logic of modernity and its quest for the universal, for expansion, for "naming the thing itself once and for all," inspired events that undercut its own foundations. Made possible by the technologies of travel that colonial impulses necessitated, many nonwestern cultures and worldviews became accessible. Meeting the strange "other" in colonial moments preceded institutionalized slavery and racism, but it also opened up channels of cross-cultural interactions that challenged the imperialist power of modernity. Soon, some began to react against modernity. There's no one name for this critical engagement, but we'll focus on "linguistic constructionism" as one aspect of these cultural conversations.

While the claim persisted that "pure knowledge" was possible, and that nature was perfectly disclosable to society, open to language, and separate from it, the linguistic constructionist's seditious dissatisfaction with, and opposition to, tenets of modernity began to air. Some would date this to the 1960s, when antiestablishment, antistructuralist views started to gain credence.

Considerable attention turned to the politics of representation—the social interactions, political contexts, situational dynamics, environmental variables, and gender biases that came into play when "pure" knowledge was produced. Postmodernists scoffed at the idea of the pure. Pure universal knowledge indeed! No such thing, they proclaimed. Representation (I'll write more about representation in the next letter) wasn't an act of mirroring the truth; it was the practice of creating one's own truth to the painful exclusion of other truths. There is no outside, no God's seeing eye; just the stories we tell. In a milieu that was largely predicated on the idea that truth was universal, the idea of difference and diversity mounted an insurgency.

The dust murmured in the air, and the most austere and most eloquent speakers coughed and choked on their claims to building a universal home. Being one given to the arts, to drawing and painting, one of my favorite ways of thinking about these monumental tensions within modernity—and postmodern critiques of modernity's regimes of visuality—was in learning how Picasso's cubism emerged from his interactions with African art.

Cubism emerged as a result of a growing weariness with the limitations of perspective drawing, a form of Renaissance response to the challenge of producing the illusion of depth on a two-dimensional surface. In most Renaissance art, the disseminating source of geometric lines could be discerned in the way the objects depicted adhered to it. Their contours and bodies aligned with a static unseen point in the distance. A type of disciplining, all-seeing God-eye. Space itself was empty of perspective, abstract, and unproblematic—serving only as a palette for the mathematical (and therefore immaterial and invisible) reproduction of reality. In African art, to-be cubists met a refreshing form of expressionism, free from the anxieties of exacting representations. These sculptures and paintings did not pretend to be photographic imitations of a world that was *outside;* they acknowledged subjectivity and played with emotions, and—in the case of paintings—honored the two-dimensionality of surface, instead of seeking to deny its characteristics. As such, the collage-like multimodality and polyvocality of cubist works radically reimagined space in Western art as populated, thick, and animated—instead of being empty and uninteresting.

Remember those crazy portraits you used to draw on your "Buddha Board"? The wet strokes of your tender brush that appeared as dark paint on the bright screen? Your mum and I, looking at the irregular lines, would ask you, "What is that? Is that a fish?" and you would say, "No, sillies! That's a dragon dancing on a tree." No matter how hard we squinted, we couldn't see what you saw—but we smiled all the same. It didn't have to look like a drunk dragon to be true to you that way.

When observing a cubist painting, one is usually struck with its queer deviations from "proper" form. Picasso's *Les Demoiselles d'Avignon* comes to mind with its depiction of five nude women (a truly scandalous piece for its time) with splintered faces and restless, anarchic lines. With a turn to language, to cultural diversity, postmodernity (or, specifically, linguistic constructionism) rejected the Euclidean imperatives of modernity and its quest for universal truth. Some critical of modernity came to doubt the given-ness of the idea that culture, language, words, concepts, and stories were separate from nature. In their opinion, the goal of "pure knowledge"—to describe (and ultimately control) nature in a painstakingly reductionistic manner—didn't stand up to rigorous scrutiny. Language and nature were, for those who proposed a paradigm of many truths and no grounds, related. Different cultures had different realities. Truth was annulled, and story was enthroned in its place.

And yet these reactions to modernity only added more inches to the walls we had already built. Dust swirled in the crazy distance—at least in the distance of our imaginations—like a madman peeping through the gaps in the fence, shouting loud obscenities at the passersby within the village.

The idea that the world is story was very fond to me. For a while. I learned to say with many others that there are no facts—that all the world is "energy" or consciousness or the reverberations of our own voices. I learned to think of everything in terms of stories told, stories that embraced, and stories that pushed away. A fair and just world was a mere syllable away, squarely in the orbit of our control.

But then, if reality were a story, then everything … every susurrous crevice, every untoward follicle, every amphibian burp, every unanticipated moment … would have to make sense. That may not count as a credible counterargument against linguistic constructionism, but it was my first baby-step into an aesthetic reconsideration of the story-is-all rejection of modernity. A world where everything is moored to logic, to power, to syntax and plot and scheme and expectation and meaning, leaves no place for magic, for the inextricability and beauty of a glimpsed sunset.

Something was missing in the linguistic constructionist's account of the world. The linguistic account was a shore without oceans—a neat and tidy island that refused to consider the grating bodies that rubbed against its squeaky-clean universe of words and names. In positing that language was critical in our account of the world, constructionists presented powerful insights that are very important to keep close in our search for new settlements. They rejected heaven, because it wouldn't have been able to contain everyone; too many people and possibilities were cut out. They won the battle over denaturalizing nature. But it was a pyrrhic victory: the new practices of focusing exclusively on language to understand what was happening in the world failed to bring in the contributions of the world in its own emergence. Just like paper currencies were once promissory notes backed up by stores of gold and other valuable artifacts, but were gradually exchanged as money itself, discourse came to be considered as the only thing that constitutes reality. *Facts* became arbitrary (as opposed to being pre-given), and it became fashionable to speak about your truths versus my truths in a new socio-political milieu that denied the existence of anything outside experience. The significance of the nonhuman world was overlooked, and the architecture of anthropocentrism, polished in modernity, was updated to cement our desired distance from the discipline of dust. In short, postmodernity failed to satisfactorily address the dichotomy of language versus nature upon which modernity, the other half of this moiety, based its problematic quest for home.

In "trying to evade [dust], we become dust all the more."[17] The banishment of matter from our descriptions of home has, in both instances of modernity and postmodernity, coincided with the globalizing threat of a neoliberal monoculture of war, blood, and suffering. We have lost, and are losing, species as our ecosystems undergo drastic changes. The loss of biodiversity, ocean acidification, desertification, and climate change are just a few of the challenges postponing our longed-for flight away from dust—a situation reminding us that we are of the soil—"dust thou art."

What is considered economic activity or productivity is limited to a set of practices that *men* engage in—that of repainting the world with the colors of their patriarchal angst for flight; what many female-identified bodies do when they are hunched over, breastfeeding their young, and mothering the soil, tends to be considered secondary to the real business of converting the commonwealth of forms and gifts into products and profit. What the material world does; how it miraculously regenerates itself; how it initiates, makes possible, destroys, enables, experiments with, and seeks to understand the genius of an anthill, the patience of a tapering stalactite in a limestone cave, the politics of wolves in a hunting pack, or the performances of bees in search of new locations for a hive—is hidden away. In the cracks on heaven's walls. The dust swept under its ornate rugs.

A home that proliferates refugees is no longer home. No longer at ease. A certain gravity pulls us "back" to the material—not the old atomic conception of material that was useful to old industrialists, but to a different one that gives it its due and acknowledges its contributions in worlding the world. What might "home" look like if we respected the world around us? If we came down to earth, and did not try to escape its sensuous rhythms in phallic perforations of the sky? It is not immediately clear. Perhaps you know.

Whatever the case, if we are to know how to even ask questions aright, it is to the cracks we must go. The dark alleys where the rejected and mad ones can no longer abide the excruciating sanity of the city. The shadowy places where Lilith, long rejected from heaven, and her children—those who speak with plants and know the mischief of the earth—still roam. We must go to the slums, where the poor make their home. We must listen for the ghosts that haunt our performances of escape, and investigate the contours of our vision. Will we find new homemaking possibilities along the spectrum of how we can make do with our planet? Will we find alternatives to the modern project of escape, and the linguistic denial of the material world? Will we happen upon colors that we might not yet see?

To begin Bàbá's ritual and my quest for hushes, I thought I'd begin in the dusty places—in the forgotten edges of my adopted city. It was there in a slum—in the pursuit of my hushes and of new ways of thinking about home—that I learned a valuable lesson about story and the elegance of being met by something deeper than words. It was there the wild hushes taught me that with regards to "home," I must speak with a lisp and write to you with a groan that will not be corrected or comforted.

✦

For the umpteenth time, my eyes fall open. Through the paper-thin aqua-green brick and cement wall, I can hear the sound of those growling dogs ... loud and menacingly close. I stir uneasily on the floor where I am stretched out. I want to sleep, but I can't. And barking dogs are the least of my worries. I am imagining cockroaches crawling out from behind the steel containers near my head, or worse, a cat-size rat squeezing itself through *that* big gaping crack in the wooden door, and nibbling on my feet while I sleep.

"I give tea, *tell me*" Kutti, my host, says, his voice keeping me awake. He is sitting on a wooden chair just next to my head, still chewing on *paan*, which he will later on spit out the door. His wife, Geetha, is folding some clothes, moving expertly between the sleeping bodies of her mother, her aunt, her aunt's husband, and her two children. Her daughter is coughing. "Thank you, Kutti. I'm very fine." Geetha says something to him in Tamil.

"Dosa, *tell me*," Kutti says, a few moments later. "Very full, very full!" I reply, gesturing with my hands on my belly to show how much I enjoyed dinner with his family an hour earlier.

"Light? Light, *tell me*."

I answer that I do not need the light, and that—yes—he can switch off the single bulb glowing in the corner of the room. The light bulb goes off, and darkness falls. A traveling troupe of singing mosquitoes descends on me, singing ominous tunes in my ears as I feel a tiny needle-pinch on my right foot. I rub the sore spot with my other foot, tuck both away under the blanket Geetha offered me, adjust the sack of clothes that is my pillow, and try to make myself as comfortable on this single wrapper as I possibly can. Kutti had told me earlier in the day that he wakes up at 6:30 a.m. every day to prepare his children for school, and that we'll need to get up early to have a bath. As I imagine what that might look like, the thought occurs to me: what am I doing here? Why am I sleeping on a cement floor, with seven other humans, in a hundred-square-foot, fifty-year-old shack—one of many homes in a cramped Indian slum? What am I looking for? Is this what Bàbá meant when he invited me to become lost in order to find my way? And will I find any hushes for the ritual?

Are Lali and Alethea safe?

Will something deadly come through that old rotten wooden door?

Before you were born, while you roiled the insides of my belly, your father and I decided we were not "bringing you into the world" … it just wasn't the right metaphor for how we wanted to hold you. That sounded like you were not of this earth, and that you were coming through parting clouds, descending from the naive into the real. You were more real to us than a hovering ghost or a visiting messiah. So we learned to say that you were coming out of the earth (not into it), that you were the domino effect of many parents—including animal and plant parents, and that you were a gift to us.

You are wise, not a tabula rasa. You have the royalty of mountains, the determination of swooping hawks, the experience of bursting pollen, and the joy of opening flowers written into your bones. This is the reason we said, once you were born, once your jelly father held you in his hands, and once I breathed in your face, that we would follow you just as much as we wanted to instruct you. That we would listen to your questions not merely as things you didn't know but as clues about what we also might need to unlearn. This has been our journey—to follow a child like the disciples of a rabbi follow hard behind the sandals of their master. And the questions you ask! Oh, how delightful! How surprising!

One day, we are preparing to take you out to see your Bama down the street, for fellowship. You are dressed just the way I like. Yes, I admit I often treat you like a doll I didn't have growing up—a point your father never fails to remind me of. The shiny black shoes. The little jeans. The bow on your cornrowed hair. The bangles on your hand. And the oversize plastic glasses on your face. With that dimpled smile your father bequeathed you. You are my angel.

We are leaving behind your father at work, writing his letters to you. I'm dressed and ready to go. I walk to the opened door, but you are not there. As I turn from the door to call you, I see you right by me: there you are, standing with a big smile, holding on to my leg. You say, "I want to make kaka!" "Kaka" is, of course, how we have learned to say that you want to shit. "Susu" is how we say you want to piss. We walk over into the toilet and I put you up to sit. I leave to the kitchen to sort out something and let you do your business—you like to be left alone until you need me again. I return moments later to clean you and pick you up. As I wash you up, you ask a question: "Where does all the kaka and susu go after I use the toilet and flush it?"

I call on your father, and he rushes out to hear me relate everything that has just happened. When I'm done, he takes a pen and writes the question on a yellow piece of paper stuck to the toilet door. We have many papers stuck on many things in our little house. He writes your question and today's date. And then we both turn to you, staring at you, you—blushing like you've just broken one of the seals in the Book of Revelation. "How about we find out together, love?" your father asks, smiling. You nod an adorable yes. A new adventure opens up to us—to follow the enchanted trail of shit and piss. To know a world that is more magical than we, educated and princely, ever knew was possible. To listen to one who came out of the earth, who still remembers faintly her melodious tunes.

CONSIDER LEVIATHAN

We live in the orbit ... of things that exceed us.

Alethea,

I wave my sister-in-law, your aunt Ifeoma, good-bye. She reciprocates by chuckling, shaking her head as she rides away on her Honda scooter. She must think I'm mad.

Ifeoma's laughter is taunting and, at some unexplored depth, troubling to me. At this point, left alone at the gateless entrance to an expansive slum of more than a hundred families, with women bearing colorful plastic jugs of water on their hips *casting eyes* on the dark-skinned stranger in their midst, I feel a bit abandoned. Marooned on an island, albeit one of my own making.

On the way here, Ifeoma had asked me a question I had asked myself over and over again in the weeks preceding my journey.

"So ... why are you going to this slum?"

I still had no complete answer—just a rambling stretch of tangential remarks about fatherhood, about finding beauty in the most unexpected places, and thinking about home in new ways. I had assured her that all was well. That there were elements to this that I did not fully understand. I did not tell her about the hushes, or Bàbá's talk about getting lost in order to find one's way, or what I had—three years ago—whispered to the hush that sat motionless on my outstretched palm. I did not fully elaborate on the peculiar feeling I had that this was an adventure I needed to embark upon—a prayer quest. I did not tell her about your grandfather's lingering absence, the traces of a revenant whose footfalls are a strain in my life's leitmotif. Soon after my half-intelligible commentary had melted into the buzzing, beeping, and whooshing sounds of Chennai's hetero-vehicular road users, I thought of you, dear Alethea. It's how I ground myself in what needs to be done.

I thought of your dimpled smile.

Your impassioned arguments correlating the sincerity of our love for you and your access to chocolate.

The way your mouth gradually stretched open for you to cry a few seconds before any actual sound came out.

The way you screamed "I can do it myself" when I wanted to help you to the toilet to pee—a thunderbolt of self-assertion at such a precious age—only for you to come back seconds after, not a bit crestfallen or embarrassed, asking me to help you with unzipping your little skirt.

Your manner of chastising me—"Dada, you are being very rude!"—while your little head swiveled from side to side. And the way you apparently forgave me when I apologized for being naughty—with wordless silence, followed by a redeeming kiss planted on the side of my neck.

I thought of *mama*, her belly already bulging with your sister- or brother-to-come ("sister, brother, and puppy!" you always insisted, squeezing your face into a disapproving scowl). I thought of her angelic face, the pronounced curliness of her mixed-race hair, and how—even now—I still marvel that I had been so favored to be embraced by someone with her beauty.

You are now three years old—inching closer to your fourth year in a few months. You are looking more and more like your mother—your perfectly round head stretching out to accommodate the nuances of her chiseled facial features … a development I am more than grateful for.

I miss you. Already. I feel this weight of longing as I stand here at the threshold of madness. I want to hold you up in the air and watch you do the "super girl"—your eyes aglitter, your arms pulled out in front of you, and your excited voice screaming "Aga-a-ain!" after we both crash-land into your mildly irritated mother. This is why I am here, and why I leave your mama, *my Lali,* and your sister-brother-puppy with you for a while: so that even when my bones are too old to hold you up, we can both rest in the knowing that my arms would no longer be needed, neither would your mama's, because you'll be flying without them.

With eyes that do not blink, I see Bàbá—standing there, motionless—a phantom emissary of something-yet-to-be-done. He smiles. Ten hushes, he says. *Find them. They will teach you how to pray for your daughter. Then you will find your way.* Where do I begin? I am confused. Can they tell—these delighted kids laughing and staring at me? Can they see my nakedness and naïveté through the embroidery and ornateness of my invisible Researcher's Clothes?

Kutti is lying down on a spread of clothes when we step into his home. It is a sunny Wednesday afternoon. I say "we" because a friend of the family, Velu, has joined me. We had spoken earlier about my feckless attempts at understanding Tamil: I had confessed to him then that I didn't even speak my own language, Yoruba … a detail I had in times past—to my chagrin—brandished to others as one would flaunt a peculiar body quirk just to arouse sympathy or (in most cases) to cover for the fact that I was poor at making conversation. Velu offered then to help translate Kutti's words for me, an offer that came with the silent caveat of Velu's own poor command of the one-tongue.

Kutti scrambles to his feet, wipes his eyes, scrunches the wrappers that serve as his bed, and greets us. With a sleepy smile, he asks us to take our seats. The challenge is finding where to do it: there are two wooden chairs—occupied with wrappers—facing a mattress-less wooden bed that takes up a third of the entire living space. Velu, apparently quite familiar with these circumstances, sits on Kutti's bed like it's nothing. I remind myself that in India—at least these parts of South India where your mother comes from—the common courtesies I was raised to observe back in Nigeria are not recognized. You could walk into another's house for the first time and make your way to the bedroom, without so much as a hello thrown along your merry way. I have often wandered past our neighbor's apartment, her door flung open, with all the goings-on in full view of passers-by. Me? I grew up behind closed doors, and was trained in the high art of landing a good knock on the door. Where there's no bell to ring, three taps, four well-spaced sighs, and—if still no response—three taps. Or maybe two. *Just in case you are not wanted.* The point is that I grew up with a fairly rigid sense of privacy—a very Victorian sensibility about where my space begins and where yours ends—tempered only by some sentimental account of the goodness of African hospitality.

In Kutti's shack, I quickly learn, there is literally no time or space for such frivolities. Space is performed differently here, not as a limited resource or a private chamber for one's own air supply. Everything bleeds into everything else, and in this scandalous perversion of boundaries, politeness is often fatuous. Well, I won't be asked twice: I move the items on the chairs to a side, and make myself as comfortable as I can.

Though this is my third time visiting Kutti and his wife, Geetha, I will be staying here for the first time tonight. I had asked him if I could stay over a week ago, and though I couldn't make out what he had said prior to a friend translating his response, the way he threw his hands and smiled felt like he was saying "Please come! Why even bother asking?"

So I look around, taking it all in. Looking for insight. Looking to be spoken to. Trying to force a question or two from the way the objects are arranged, the way dust lingers beneath my now unshod feet. I notice that the rough and uneven walls are constructed with red bricks, their earthen hues seeping through the aqua-green emulsion that pretends to cover them away. I run my fingers lightly across the gritty surface of the wall behind me, as if to entice it out of its stony silence. As if to reduce its empirical vagaries into the reliability of words, sentences, and story. As if to tickle out an epiphany.

Farther into the room, on an asymmetric shelf designed with painted stone slabs—embedded into the largest wall—an incredible diversity of items sits frozen in dust behind thick sinewy spider webs. A small television set in the far corner of one of the cluttered compartments of the shelf harks back to the questionable policies of a previous Tamil Nadu government, which had—in its efforts to alleviate extreme poverty—embarked on a scheme to distribute free fourteen-inch television sets across the state. *What do you think, dear?* Does this not create nail-biting window-shoppers out of these people, who must now treat every flashy ad that blazes across their screens as a capitalist indictment of their precarity? It is unclear to me how the television helps Geetha sweep the floors, bathe her children, or tend to Kutti's mother, who lives in an even smaller box a few feet away. And yet, am I too quick to reduce these people to victims? To strip them down to some kind of basic (and necessary) subsistence, and thus denying them the frivolity and complexity I allow myself?

Five feet above, a tiny fan with short thumb-like blades spins rapidly, every hectic revolution jolting the rod that connects it to a bamboo stick, which in turn acts as a support beam for the asbestos sheets that are both roof and ceiling. Broomsticks and wooden canes stick out from the dips of the undulating sheets. In a corner of the room, a dirty worn-out cricket bat rests against the wall.

My gaze slides to a framed painting of young deity Krishna with an older woman. Nesting close to their blue-skinned nobility is a framed picture of Kutti and Geetha, which opens into the tiny space that is the kitchen. There's an oxblood fridge in there, a gas cooker connected to an orange gas cylinder, a stone slab upon which rest endless stacks of steel pots, tiny plastic containers, a bunch of bright yellow bananas, and rusty cooking utensils of every tribe and shape mounted on a wall holder. The kitchen ceiling hangs so low that I hit my head on its fan when Geetha invites me to survey the place. As I retake my seat next to Kutti and Velu, she generously offers me drinking water in a dented steel cup. I thank her and take a sip. The water *tastes* like something. Water shouldn't do that.

I am taunting myself, querying my motives, second-guessing the appropriateness of my very presence, even as the scribe within scours every material surface, every turn of texture, every whiff of feeling for story. For meaning. For a hush. I feel like an extraterrestrial prospector, looking for a new home, inspecting the ruins of a forsaken planet, probing it for life—for signs that it can support my narrative.

And yet—as elitist as that sounds—I question if I am even doing it "properly." If I were employing traditional qualitative research modalities—especially of the phenomenological kind—I might have articulated guiding interview questions to orient myself in the "field," to help me know what to look for, and when to know I am saturated with enough responses and insights that it feels safe to leave. I'd have come up with a list of things to explore, and taken recorded audio memo notes of my observations—just as I did when I visited Bàbá. But this isn't "research" in that sense; this is a coddiwompling, stumbling into things. Into the throbbing heart of a stranger's world.

I keep trying to recall why I am here, as if to find myself again and again in my mirror: to learn how Kutti, his wife, Geetha, and their two children are making a home between the cavities of the normative; to find wholly new ways of thinking about home by seeking out what troubles our present visions and practices of home-making; to find the beauty in Kutti's life where it might be easier to merely conclude that he and his family are the poorest of the poor—and the only proper response is therefore charity; and to pray for the world you will live in when I am no longer there to care for and protect you. But my clarity of purpose also accentuates my feelings of helplessness—I do not know how to make any of these happen, and I wonder if I am not *using* this family, exploiting my status as a foreigner, and interrupting their everyday practices of getting by with my project of promise-keeping.

Reassuring myself that I had previously asked that none of my academic credentials be shared, and that they know that I am more than willing and happy to do household chores or help in any way—if only to be briefly woven into the embroidery of their life—I "return," as it were, to the quiet shuffling of feet, the irritating persistence of a scourge of dangling mosquitoes, the clanging of pots and steel containers just a few feet away, the rapid-fire Tamil conversation that is already underway between Velu and Kutti … and now, the smiling faces of children and their mothers peeking through the door to catch a glimpse of the black foreigner that is visiting.

I catch Velu's attention and indicate that I'd like to say something to Kutti, who is now sitting on the wooden bed next to Velu, smiling and nodding his head excitedly. "Teach me how you live. Tell me how you spend your day," I ask Velu's Kutti—acutely aware that reporting one's life as if it were a simple narrative stream flowing from one end to another is a tall order. And yet we dive—into welcoming waters.

An auto-rickshaw driver for most of the night, Kutti is a handsome little man with ear studs, a thick mustache and a generous mouche under his lip, so that if you squinted his mouth would look like a parenthetical remark. And true to form, he offers more smiles than words, partly due to the fact that his mouth always seems to be busy, his teeth reddened and words muffled by his fondness for *paan*—a mixture of heart-shaped betel leaves, tobacco, areca nuts, coconut shavings, and other ingredients. I have only known him a short while, but this much I know: Kutti loves chewing *paan*—a vocation shared by the boisterous population of Chennai, if the red splatter marks strewn across the city's streets are anything to go by. At the entrance of his home the spat-out mucousy residue of his chomping and chewing glistens in the glare of the sun ... close to my flip-flops.

Kutti offers a few words in response to my questions. He tells me about his love for his children and his wife, how old his home is, and how he wants for nothing more than what he earns every week—no more than three hundred rupees, with a third of that more than enough to put *dosa*, *idly* (rice cakes), and some Samba rice on the floor. I am finding this hard to believe, but Kutti smiles, insisting that it's enough—and when he can't eat, when death seems close because of some sickness, he is ready to walk into a mist too thick for an accompanying other. He doesn't seek a "better" home, and even when he agrees with the general consensus that he is "poor," he doesn't consider himself a victim of giant monolithic power structures.

A story is emerging, I tell myself—*maybe not a neat one* ... at least not the usual fare of those that paint the world as an obvious war between the powers-that-be and the little people. I am reminded of Avery Gordon's chastising remark, reminding me that "even those who live in the most dire circumstances possess a complex and oftentimes contradictory humanity and subjectivity that is never adequately glimpsed by viewing them as victims or, on the other hand, as superagents."[1] Could I discover deeper nuance as I listen for story? Perhaps as I gain insight after insight, a hush would stroll into my field of vision—and I can do the prayer rites.

Let's get back to Kutti.

Though considered the lowest of the low, his work keeps Chennai running like a more laid-back Swiss clock: setting out around 6 p.m. every evening, Kutti rides his three-wheeler vehicle through slender streets, picking up passengers and dropping them off, navigating tricky terrain and reaching places inaccessible to cars—even to the popular small cars motor factories have flooded the streets with. He will often work on the streets till the wee hours of the morning, getting home exhausted to his wife, his young children, his in-laws, and those who come in to spend the night in his shack—a trend that may explain his fondness for chewing the stimulating ingredients of a *paan* mixture.

In light of the rapid urbanization of Chennai (as is the case with other metropolitan cities in India) and an uptick in rural-urban migration—due perhaps to modern schooling, the loosening of cultural ties and imperatives, and the increasingly tenuous promise of jobs in the city for those who can make it there—there is hardly room anymore for people like Kutti. The bumps and grooves of the lands his grandparents might have learned to communicate with as home have now been flattened and filled up by mega-ambitious residential projects designed for the rich. Land spaces that have belonged to families for generations, and which many families often refuse to sell away, are very often appropriated by wealthy corporations with additional support from banks and bribed court officials. Kutti and his kin must survive along with the many others that India's envious rush to heaven cannot account for and has no space for. They must live in these borderlands in the middle of the city, as refugees of a protracted war against things. Against dust.

And yet Kutti is not a "victim" or subject of modernity's eliding power in the totalizing sense of the word; there is a complexity to this "slum," to him (as Gordon considers in her remarks above), which is borne out in the ways these practices of huddling together undercut the capitalist extractivist rationality of "scarcity" and "never enough." Because the self—that rusty screw that holds the chug-chug-chugging machine of modernity and its manifesto of estrangement together—is so closed up, so ontologically distanced from everything else, modernity produces an exhausting verticality, forcing upward movement or transcendence by denying the significance of our connections with others. Over here, something more than mere proximity is at work. There is an abundance here, in this mishmash reliquary of humans and nonhumans, in the modesty of this crevice. I have heard the rumors—a whisper here and a whisper there in the shadows of the fat pillars that uphold the regimes of the familiar—reports of other worlds pressingly close to ours where the usual laws of social mobility and ascension are suspended, as it were. What does Kutti know of these realms?

Later, we take a walk through the slum. I had expected the place to be a broken china plate in a sink filled with grime and spit. I am mistaken. Even though the slum shares a fence with a large sewage dump—an unmoving cesspool of fecal matter, plastic bottles, boots, cans, nylon bags, carcasses of unknown animals, and unfathomably large rats hovering over the deep like holy ghosts, all melted into a viscous semisolid chemical river of shadow, gloom, and black poison—there is an attention to hygiene and a keen desire to take care of those that visit. This is evidenced by the rows of water jugs outside the homes, which Velu tells me are used to clean one's hands and feet before entering. A few women are sweeping their surroundings as I squeeze my way through the housing rows. A very narrow passageway, no wider than two feet across, snakes through the entire area. The rows of homes are all capped by overlapping asbestos sheets, sloping down on either side into the passageway, so that at one point there is hardly room enough for a decently sized neck to glide through. On the roofs, there are cats licking their paws, abandoned clothes, browning sacks of whatever, a Sky satellite dish, potted plants and flowers, bamboo mats, and the outdoor units of split air conditioners. No hushes, no epiphanies—just this gravity of objects in this remarkable species of home in the between-places.

Kutti prances on, introducing me as his friend to everyone we meet—women washing their cement floors, washing their dishes, tracing out the geometric patterns of *kolams* with chalk, men sitting with their grown children indoors watching television, and a chained albino dog barking its protest when I get too close.

Kutti wants me to take pictures; I had felt using my phone's camera might be rude, inappropriate, and objectifying, but he insists—at times worrying that I am not capturing as much as I could. No one seems to care that I lift my device to take photos of them in front of their homes. A woman holds her little child, probably two or three years old, and urges her to give me a high-five. Some do not feel welcoming or responsive when I say hello, while others suppose that some kind of procession is ongoing, and want to tag along—just to know why I am here. An eighty-four-year-old man, missing many teeth, and carrying planks on his head, comes close to me and starts to tell me something. Velu and Kutti wave him off, and speak with him—and then ask me to "come, come."

The camera, an extension of colonial visuality in the way it freezes movement into an officialized snapshot and initiates photographic archiving, becomes my digital hand of friendship. Or, in ways I cannot yet access, my distancing rod, affirming my place of power over these people. I "capture" everything I can—sometimes meeting the pixelated versions of those human bodies before we find each other in voice, skin, toothed smile, and the customary steel cup of water—or tea. When we get back from our tour, Kutti's aged mother is sitting on the stone steps of a neighboring shack, with younger women surrounding her. I had met her during previous visits, and learned that she was married off to a man when she was seventeen years old, and had seven children for him. Her hands had served many homes, scrubbed many floors, fed many babies, and taken care of her children. Her hair is a shimmering white. Her smile, a cunning and yet affectionately cordial invitation to come closer. Kutti curls up to her, like a cat to her amused owner, hugging her, holding her fingers that are bent from too much handling, and drawing her attention to my lens. I am content just to watch mother and son, but Kutti, again, insists I record the moment. So I do, as the other women look on. I am struck with how intricately dense, connected, and abiding the relationships in the slum are. How anonymous the city feels in contrast.

Density. Enfoldments and entanglements of thick lives in thick lives. A democracy of objects. A wild place of skin, white hair, stacked pots, calloused knuckles, and knowing glances. For those recovering from the fantasies and insanities of flight. This Indian slum, hidden behind a phallic Samsung glass building, cordoned off by asphalt, shushed by the traffic of cyborg saints seeking glittery heavens to go marching into, and forgotten in the headlines that tout India as a fast-developing nation with abilities to launch satellites into space, tells a revisionist story about the dark places modernity supposedly saves us from—a story that presses the modesty of our occupations to live on earth. This place seems like the wild lands where the eloquence of the modern breaks down and splinters into the cacophony of many gasps—where humans and nonhumans, in chaotic and oftentimes risky configurations, are learning to press closer and closer to each other and live with each other.

At the risk of romanticizing Kutti's conditions—and I hope I do not—this place feels to me to be a sanctuary of sorts.

✦

As the dusking sky turns a shade darker, Kutti and I walk through a park not too far away from the slum, both of us mostly silent. I do not know what to say to him, or how to say it if I did know. Velu is now gone, after receiving a call from his office. It is just me and this familiar stranger who has opened his home to me. A few inches shorter than me, Kutti walks some paces ahead, his dirty beige uniform—traditionally worn by rickshaw drivers—engulfing his small frame. We walk past a large public compound where several water tankers underneath overhead pipes are lined up, and some men—assumedly the tanker drivers and other operators—are pulling on fat hoses, fetching pails of water and washing big tires. There is a blue notice board painted with contrasting white Tamil fonts alongside the English words Metro

Water. "Metro water," Kutti says to me, pointing at the busy compound. "Have bath, water," he adds, confirming my suspicions that this is where he gets water for his family to have baths, among other things (but where is the bathroom? He hasn't shown me that yet). He meets a few people coming out the compound—big, husky men with their sweaty protruding bellies— shakes their hands, and points at me. I can only make out "friend-eh" from what he says to them—the rest of what he says is as undiscernible to me as the rest of this remarkable day away from you and mama.

We arrive at a small kiosk where he insists I must have a cup of tea or a cigarette if I'd prefer the latter. I decline both, but—after wondering if I am hurting my host's cultural sensibilities in rejecting his offer—request the small paper cup of tea. The cigarette is not even an option.

Meanwhile, the mosquitoes are relentless in their thirst for blood—and Kutti notices I am quite preoccupied with slapping and kicking them away from me. So, we walk the short distance to his home, where he picks up the keys to his auto-rickshaw, calls upon his son and daughter—Vicki and Nandini—and then takes us to where his vehicle is parked, just across the street. The first thing I notice is how much care and attention Kutti has put into keeping his *auto* in pristine condition. Unlike the others I have been in, Kutti's auto has padded leather seats, under-car LED lights and neon-lit tires, colorful graphic inscriptions on the yellow chassis, and insufferably loud sound speakers. Soon, Vicki, Nandini, and I are zipping through the streets with Kutti at the handle—a steady pulsating stream of local music blaring from the bug-like vehicle. I know a good many countries I have been to where we would have been locked up and reprimanded with sunken brows and an outrageous fine. Not in India. Not here. This place, these people are a fierce river—and though that river is now bordered by reinforced concrete riverbanks, so that the once joyful splash of flowing water is now the bovine mumbling of a gutter, Shiva—that subversive god that mocks all gestures of arrival—still roams these parts.

Vicki grabs my camera-phone from my pocket, focuses it on his little sister, takes a picture, and edits it—draining it of its color and settling for an aesthetically mature grayscale result. I commend him for his keen eye and photographic sensibilities. When we come to a stop, we meet other auto drivers, strategically parked outside a wedding ceremony to whisk guests to their homes when their partying is done. They shake my hand, and tell me their stories—they tell me about paying their electricity bills, taking care of their families, and ask what kinds of South Indian dishes I enjoy eating. After an hour or so, Kutti receives a call from Geetha, and we ride back home, where Kutti's mother is seated in her little space, coughing and bent over in pain. As I wait outside her room to help her into the vehicle, a big rat gambols past me, oblivious to the frightened human standing just a few feet away. Kutti and I help his mother (and little Nandini, who has a cold or some other ailment that is making her cough) into the *auto,* and drive to a nearby hospital. Many doctors in Chennai situate their practices in their residences, allocating lower floors in their duplexes for consultations. Kutti tells me—in the best way he possibly could … with chunks of almost-one-tongue words held together by a flurry of gestures, sighs, and head-tossing laughter—that taking care of his family's health care needs is easy for him to do: drugs are cheap, and there are shared homemade remedies among people living in the slum.

When we get home, there are others in the house. Many others. I find out that we all are going to spend the night in this tiny room—seven adults and two children in a space that is the size of a kitchen storage room in some of the new homes and apartments offered in the market. I am not alarmed by this—perhaps because Geetha has already whipped together a promising mixture of rice flour. She pours the fermented mix in her medium-size *tava* on her cooker, lightly greases the flat frying pan with generous drops of ghee oil, and then pours the mix in the sizzling pan, flattening the batter in spiraling hand movements. She offers me two golden pieces on a steel plate—and would offer me a dozen if I didn't gently say no.

It is night outside, and a mob of stray dogs are arguing with each other under the rising moon—their throaty growls and treacherous motives as mysterious to us as Kutti's attempts at conversation are to me. From what he says, I can make out "6:30," and suppose he is saying we have to be up early. I am in agreement. I lie down in the "kitchen" on the spread of wrappers, which Kutti and Geetha have laid on the floor for me. Tucking myself into the thin layers of clothes, my every shrug attended to by a murmuration of mosquitoes, I try to shut my eyes—not before thinking of you and wondering if I would eventually meet any hushes.

I spring up from the ground when I hear faint voices at the edges of my fuzzy awareness. Kutti is folding his wrappers away, and—out of view— Geetha's aunt is saying something inaudible. I check my phone: 6:23. Outside, there is no canine altercation, just that peculiarly soft warm shade of blue sky that recommends that you do not take things so seriously—the one before the stoic whiteness of daylight impervious to nuance or negotiation. I am not sure how to think of my short experience here, but I do feel at home in a strange sort of way. Of course, I have only come one day, and have the luxury of returning to more familiar (and comfortable) circumstances—but, at this moment, I say good morning to Kutti. He smiles, asks me if I slept well (to which I give an enthusiastically positive response) and says "Have bath, water," performing that endearing head wobble as he does. As I search my backpack for my bath kit and towel, neatly arranged by *Mama*, I imagine there is a public bathroom somewhere provided for the slum-dwellers—perhaps a little hut where one can have a little privacy. At least I am hoping this is the case.

Kutti leads me out of the shack and onto the street. We pass the motorcycle workshop in front of the slum, cross the street, and walk into Metro Water's graveled compound. No one's there—just the yellow tankers set against the light blue of morning's slow yawn. We stop behind one of the tankers, and Kutti says here.

Here. Here in the open is where I have a bath.

As if to demonstrate the viability of his baffling proposal, he gets behind the tanker, grabs a heavy red lever attached to a greasy ball valve, and cranks it open. A pipe shudders and spits, then pours out a single thick column of cold angry water. He shuts it off. "Soap?" he asks. "I have it ... here," I say, as I bend over to search my bath kit, looking for something more obvious than soap and less alarming than the next few minutes I am to live through.

When I eventually get in the crosshairs of that hollow pipe (while Kutti stands in the corner watching), and just after I squeeze the lever a full ninety degrees to the right—suddenly overcome in a rhapsody of splash, morning blue, and mechanical coherence—I feel something ungraspable I cannot fully account for. Something profound. I gasp as the water deals a blow to my body, making me buckle under its hydraulic wildness. A homecoming of a very fleeting sort.

Mind you, dear, I am not speaking about some kind of ecstatic state or moment of "self-actualization." I do not suddenly feel "at one with the universe," nor am I granted a revelation of the pureness of things or greater clarity about why I am with Kutti at this point. This is not a piercing light blinding that angry traveler on the road to Damascus. I am not levitating a few feet off the ground in weightless glory. My head is not orbited by a halo of hushes. This is not an epiphany. And yet, there's not much more to turn on; it seems the more I struggle to grasp it, the more it withdraws from being fully held—so that I am almost limited to writing to you about it solely in terms of what it is not.

Are you wondering what I'm prattling about, dear? I'm sorry. Words fail. It's so difficult to characterize. It is like describing the color red to one who is blind. How do you do that? What particular configuration of words is enough to grant one direct empirical access to the distinctness of red? I am momentarily lost, with no cardinal direction, with every orifice on my body trembling with animal alertness. Perhaps it might suffice to say—to speak about this in positive or productive terms—that this feeling, which I do not suppose is new or extraordinary, is a chimeric thing. It is one part an intoxicating expansiveness achieved by touching the virgin newness of a moment; another part a desire to kneel before the ferocity of that which has been encountered, and must be approached with hesitation.

My chest expands, my breathing intensifies, my pupils dilate. My body becomes a trembling antenna, the excited needle of a compass, or—better yet, a vibrating tuning fork in resonance with another body. The wild rush of water on my bare skin rekindles memories I did not myself create. It feels like an exhilarating adventure. And yet it feels like meeting a bellowing monster. It feels like being stopped in one's tracks. As if behind this tanker, in the direct line of this pipe's intervention, I have met the universe halfway. Or I have been met halfway.

As we cross the street, heading back home, I recognize that I have lost my voice. It's as plain as that. I'm shivering from the cold, but my warmth is not the only thing displaced. The whole experience is breathtaking, in the literal sense of taking my breath away—and my "soul," like Peter Pan's shadow, has been exorcised and now roams free in the littered wilds. The narrative I had anticipated I would write you—this story about my journey to Kutti's home, about his beautiful children, about the close others that press in and are entangled in his performance of selfhood, about the giant social project of modernity that rendered him a refugee even in his mother's womb, about the complexities of the conditions in the slum about modern power, about complex identity, and building a home in small places—has been intercepted by the intelligence of veteran gravel and rushing water and hulking tanker and suede-blue morning. The unstoppable force of story has met the immovable object of vital matter. And my words must now nod toward the unspeakable that stands in the way of my becoming lost. A full account is no longer possible. I have met an obstacle in the force of that burst of truck water and the breakdown of my inner playwright—and a different sort of eloquence is now needed: the eloquence of a gasp.

✦

When we were little, my sisters and I—especially me—thought it a thing of pride that we didn't speak Yoruba, the language my mother and father spoke fluently. During birthday celebrations or some other excuse to get together, my father often shared folk proverbs with his friends; in the jocundity of their renewed kinship, they would throw in their wise sayings like playing cards on a table, clapping their hands as the more impressive sayings with the more mysterious sentiments piled to the top of the heap. If I were within hearing range, I would block my ears with my hands in mock nonchalance. My dear father, noticing, would often approve—with haughty laughter. Being a diplomat, he preferred that we spoke good one-tongue. I suppose he was of the classical school of thought that believed in the nobility of his own traditions and dialect, but also trusted in schooling, the Bible, and the Western values in his catholic upbringing. When he left us, I put away the childishness of closing my ears, and listened to proverbs wherever they were uttered.

One which I learned recently says:

À ńpòyì ká apá, apá ò ká apá; à ńpòyì ká oṣè, apá ò ká oṣè; à ńpòyì ká kànga, kò ṣé bínú kó sí.

What that translates into is:

We make circles round the mahogany bean tree, but it is too much to handle; we make circles around the baobab tree, but it is too much to handle; we makes circles around the well, but it is nothing to jump into in anger.

I find that truly compelling, don't you? That the world cannot be embraced or encircled or paraphrased inspires a sense of awe in me—a feeling that the home I sought for you and now tell you about through these letters is a big place.

This is what Tortoise found out the hard way—as the Yoruba story goes—when, one day, he sets out to gather all knowledge to himself. To become the wisest of all. He takes a hollowed-out gourd—the one with the big pregnant belly and the narrow neck hung out thirstily to the world—attaches a string to it, places it on his neck, and goes on his way. When he meets eagle, he takes eagle's wisdom of flight and stuffs it into his gourd. From lion, the wisdom of strength and courage; snake, his notorious cunning; mountain, her proud silence and resoluteness; the sea, his radical hospitality; and human, how to make a fire. When Tortoise's project to encapsulate the world is done, the next thing to do is to secure his precious cargo. He chooses the Iroko tree, tall and durable, able to withstand the onslaught of untoward winds. He plans to take it up, tie the gourd at the topmost top of the tree, and camouflage it among Iroko's deciduous leaves. But no matter how hard he tries, Tortoise can't wrap his stunted limbs around the large hardwood tree's trunk: the gourd, heavy with the world's wisdoms, is between him and the tree, and weighs down heavily on his neck. As he battles with gourd and trunk and despair, a snail crawls by, observes Tortoise a while, and says, "You know you could simply put the gourd on your back and climb the tree. See if that doesn't help." It does. Tortoise swings the gourd to his back, climbs the tree, and reaches the top—only to be confronted by a paradox. Even though he has all the wisdom in the world, he is not the wisest. The poor snail, slow and pathetic, is the one that has given him a way to climb the tree. Tortoise removes the cloth he has tied around the gourd to secure its contents, and releases them into the air. The world will not be embraced, owned, or encircled. It is "too much to handle."

This indigenous notion of a thing being "too much to handle"—of the world retreating from our constant attempts to grasp it, to circumscribe it with words, with culture, with knowing, with definitions, or with discussions about identity and power—coincides with an emerging tradition that seeks to bring attention back to the material world. It is as if we, citizens of eternal flatlands, supposedly burdened with God's rare breath and the curse of sentience, now seek depth and shadow. We want to be met in this stretched-out and awkward muteness of daylight—but we are and have always been. Only now, we are slowly coming to terms with the significance of those encounters. The world, once laid bare before us—too docile to resist the advance of our attempts to understand it, too meek to rebuff our claims of inheritance—is mounting an insurgency, forcing us to reconsider our place in the cosmic scheme of things.

It turns out that there are things beyond story—beyond human subjectivity. Beyond experience. Like what, you ask? Well, the inner lives of bats, for one, the affective states of machines, the creativity of swerving atoms, and the romantic affair between churning ground and charged sky—an attraction so alive we often glimpse the severity of their lovemaking as lightning. Red is not just a word or an idea; there is "something outside" what we can say or think about it—"something" in its doing that slips away from the best descriptions, even those that come from verbose writings like mine.

I am not playfully employing figures of speech here—I do mean that there is a curious sense in which objects ... nature ... matter ... things are coming back into focus, and their reemergence is both a terrifying thing to consider and yet our most stunning source of hope for understanding home and homecomings.

You probably haven't forgotten my account of heaven in my previous letter (you always had this stunning ability to remember things your mum and I had long forgotten), but I think it serves to briefly survey the ground covered, why we are at this point, and why the spaces opening up before us are very important to my quest to fulfil my promise to you. I think it is important that I stress how I have come to see that the home I offered you— over and over again in silent whispers and with long-held gazes of disbelief mixed with gratitude—must take into consideration a world of nonhuman participants ... things that will not be paraphrased, encircled or reduced to the discussions we have about them.

Let's revisit that account by way of a different set of coordinates.

In the previous letter, we began with heaven—the home in the distance I desperately wanted. Modernity was a kind of heaven—a project of transcendence that probably had some of its lasting philosophical roots in the work of French philosopher René Descartes.

In the seventeenth century, Descartes took to himself the task of *ending* the world, erasing it in one swoosh of intellectual rigor. I'm serious; there was even *motive*. He had had a tumultuous childhood, which involved losing his mother a year after he was born, and bearing the pains of what some suppose was tuberculosis. I'm pretty sure that his eschatological background and faith were just as significant in shaping what he later on became quite famous for—insisting that the world was essentially made up of two kinds of stuff: mind stuff or thought and, well, stuff. Ideas and things.

To Descartes, the world didn't count for much—it was too unwieldy and unserious. In his time, Descartes believed philosophy needed new heights to scale, and had become so confused about its objectives that it felt true to say it exchanged its noble gowns for the torn and tattered rags of the marketplace servant. What was needed was certainty—the definite, exalted, rigorous and systematic empiricism of the sciences that arrived at unshakeable truth propositions about reality. In his *Meditations on First Philosophy*, Descartes announced a disciplined and methodical skepticism that pointed to that absolute metaphysical ground he sought: he would systematically doubt everything that existed, until he arrived at a place where denial was impossible. And so he did away with mountains, rivers, and estuaries, beavers, trees, burrowing worms, and the soils they aerate, glowing sun and pollinating quasars. He even doubted his own body's existence—considering it expendable on his quest to find the holy grail of absolute knowledge, which was to be the foundation of his philosophical system.

Descartes soon found out that the one thing he couldn't eliminate was his weapon of choice: he couldn't doubt that he was doubting. For him, the mind was the one stable thing in the universe, primary and foundational—everything else was ephemeral. *"Cogito ergo sum,"* he then declared—Latin for "I think, therefore I am." With that, Descartes ruled a thick, unbridgeable line between thought and mental stuff—composing the world into a prolific collection of binaries (mind versus matter, soul versus flesh, God versus human, man versus woman) and—some might argue—inaugurated new geometries of contact with the physical world.

If what Descartes claimed to be true doesn't sound new or out of order, then his Cartesian philosophies are just as pervasive and widespread as many agree they are—or it could be that he merely happened upon what should be obvious to any sane person. I mean, even *you* were once livid with my suggestion that cows could talk if you listened well enough! You were just two years old, but during our daily walks (which, I regret, started to become less frequent as I grew busier and busier), when we passed a certain decorated cow that lived, fed, and defecated freely on our street in India, I would ask you to say "hello." You would reply, gripping my hand as we came closer to it, that "cows don't talk, Dada"—which I would counter by asking you how you came to know this, and to which you would respond, matter-of-factly: "I know everything, dada. You don't know everything."

It does seem painfully obvious that cows don't talk, that we possess some internal quality of awareness that stones don't possess, that when you leave a box of toys under your bed they don't peep out after you are gone, and that the world truly would be mute, inert, and small if we—humans—were not around to grace its undulating surfaces. And while we might allow a slice of the divine in animals with big brains and bodies, we cannot bring ourselves to acknowledge that "dead" things—pebbles, tables, combs, and the toxifying carcasses of slain rats—are worthy of consideration—except as property or trash.

From the seventeenth century onward, the period historians of European timelines often mark as the beginnings of the Age of Enlightenment, Descartes's reductionistic doctrine helped consolidate the discursive practices of humanism (the system, their concerns, and human subjectivity as central to the world), the development of the scientific method, and the industrial revolution. Our world of towering steel and asphalt owes its unrelenting quest for growth and its desire to climb more and more into dizzying heights of disembodiment to that vision of the material world as a dead, dank, deaf, and dumb place.

Matter doesn't seem to matter. Yet, it is not so easy to dismiss it completely. In fact, it is possible to think of the history of *Western* philosophy and science as a history of its tense engagements with matter and form.

Are you following, dear? Stick with me. This matters.

Mind was thus the frontispiece of Cartesian thought. Great *mind*. Wonderful *mind*. The essence of the human being. The extended thread of stolen divinity in soil brought to life. Promethean fire. It was the one thing that stuck, and remained resolutely eminent the more you tried to get rid of it—for doubt only circled round and proved it. It was the one thing that separated us from the brute world around us.

Several philosophical traditions followed Descartes's map—hoping to pitch their tents in a way that honored and adhered to the formula given them by the French reality-cartographer. One of those traditions, representationalism, concluded that home was reachable (so good news, right?), but that it was only accessible via a specific set of coordinates.

Put differently, representationalism is the view that the mind never really perceives objects as they are; it merely perceives mental images, or representations, of those objects external to the mind. All we have are short-lived and naive interpretations of the world that are subject to the chaos of our lives. However, all these interpretations couldn't possibly be correct. Only one tells the real truth about the world out there—if the plastic "chair" I presently sit on is really a spirit, an ancestor come back, or senseless atoms cohering to form a structure. So, you see, we don't really interact with the world directly—our bodily knowledges cannot be trusted, except sanctioned by the final authority of science. All of our experiences, all our knowledges, all our wisdoms are incomplete and inferior—and, whether we like it or not, are already inside a funnel that progressively leads to the narrow end, where only the pure … the real … is produced.

Representationalism says the world outside our minds is objective, empirical, and ontologically motionless, external to and independent of our opinions or discussions about it. This idea is closely allied with positivism, which assumes a scientific unity at the heart of all reality—whether physical or social reality—and doubles down on the belief that the only way home is via the mediation of rationality and the logic of the scientific method. For representationalism to work, it needs its Cartesian heart—it must first assume the world is divided into two or made up of two basic properties: mind inside and matter outside. The twain never do meet, or they shuffle around each other—two irreparably estranged sides. At times, they do correspond with each other; the lines fall in pleasant places, and we get it right: mind syncs with matter, and *correct* theory is born. Pristine truth. Alchemical gold birthed through the filth of by-products.

Modernity is about investing energy in the politics of getting it right—in painstakingly numbering the table, naming things, creating hierarchies and categories and protocols for arriving again and again. It is about creating spatial-historical maps that contribute to "creating a world of things in themselves, where everything seems clear, objective, indisputable, in which the abstract is mistaken for entities and tangible links."[2] Other ways of knowing that were not founded in scientific rationalism led to dark, wild, and horrible places. One needed the cold, calculating tools of rationality to tell what the world is really, *really* like. Just the cold, hard facts—no colors and poetry allowed.

But then other critical traditions, later to be assembled under the banner of postmodernism (a word coined by French philosopher and literary theorist Jean-François Lyotard in the late twentieth century), observed with dismay the coalescing of power around a *"few men,"* whose procedures and practices the rest of us were to accept as likelier to grant us access to the real world. Postmodernism stepped up and named the game—saying it was not about truth or discovery, it was about the consolidation of power. Whether intended or accidental, science was a cultural project of denying the significance of other cultural modes of knowing. Postmodernists thus rejected these supposedly irreproachable institutions of rationality, deconstructing them as instruments of political control, not discovery. They rejected the structure of the funnel—or Tortoise's wisdom gourd.

Linguistic constructivism studies within the broad tradition of postmodernism sought to show that modernity was really a cultural pretension to superiority and supreme access, one which produced ethically challenged arenas that excluded the contributions of women and colored people. Science wasn't apolitical, innocent, or neutral; rationality wasn't cold and clinical. Science was just as compromised as those other forms of knowing it rejected as incomplete. Wasn't it more than a bit suspicious that science seemed predominantly occupied by white men?

To the question about what reality is, then, or how we were to come to understand ourselves in relation to this quest for home, they replied: *leave that alone.* Abandon it as a derelict project that leads nowhere, and toss it away in uncharitable depths and shadows. Our proper concern shouldn't be about what reality is, but how we speak about it, how people profit and gain from speaking about it one way instead of another, how white slave owners exploit black cotton-pickers by saying they are "naturally" inferior, three-fifths of proper men. Follow the smell of power, be suspicious of anyone claiming to know—once and for all—the truth about reality. There is no one home to arrive at; there are many realities, each arbitrary, not fixed and still like the modernists say. The laws of physics were not written by God—they were promulgated by a conspiracy.

Linguistic constructionism thus took on the postmodern mantle of turning attention to the complicated dynamics of discourse, of language, of words—or how we create meaning, the politics of sight (or how perception is already irretrievably burdened with human subjectivity ... so that our hopes of discovering the *real* world outside of our representations of it were largely hopeless), and how the material world therefore dwells at an inscrutable distance from our cultures and rituals of knowing. The energy moved from *what exists* (ontology) to *how we know* what exists (epistemology)—and new settlements sprouted in the now conquered fields. In time, these ideas percolated into mass culture and especially subcultures concerned with consciousness and social change, spawning memes of "change the story, change the world." We took it for granted that all that mattered were our stories, our language. We rescinded our commitments to an empirically verifiable world, because it reminded us too much about what we had vomited and left behind. *We gave language too much power.*

At some point in my search for settlements—for my place in the world and how to navigate its dumbfounding intricacy—I was of the opinion that linguistic constructionism provided a map and an ethics that spoke to my disaffections with heaven or with imperialistic arrival points that did not account for *diversity*. Your mother—her body a mulatto sermon rebuffing the neat notions of identity and belonging I grew up with—significantly influenced my appreciation and longing for a world of difference (I'll give you all the cringe-worthy details of how I fell in love with her, later!). A world that was better off because of the many perspectives, cultures, and ideas that populated it, and not in spite of them.

But constructionism was a halfway home: there was something missing in its explanation for reality—something I did not have a name for, but often imagined to be *really old* ... too old for the fashion of names. Too old to be bothered. So I lingered at the perimeters of my blind spots to catch a glimpse of this ancient one, this barnacled rock, this swerving giant mass of a monster that lived in the interstices between ideas and things, between story and objects, between epistemology and ontology.

Like Job of old, that biblical character whose unfortunate circumstances were prompted by disruptive immortals trying to prove a point about human frailty or loyalty, I was confronted with questions I had no answer to. Things that were too much to handle. Things that could not be encircled. In the Book of Job, when the eponymous protagonist angrily protests his treatment in the hands of a deity he had presumably been faithful to, God finally approaches him—after what seems like a period of silence—and provides puzzling non sequiturs that feel tone-deaf and irrelevant (at least to a large swath of modern readers) to the matters at hand. He asks the man with sore boils over his body if he was there when he laid the earth's foundations or when he shut up the seas behind doors. He boasts about the chains of Pleiades and Orion's belt, ostrich wings and ostrich eggs, the strength of horses, the obstinacy of an ox, the glory of a hawk in flight, mountain goats giving birth, and the spontaneity of rain. By the time he asks Job to "consider Leviathan," describing the oak-thick limbs and valley-rumbling movements of this unidentified monster that will not be culled or encircled or tamed, it is clear that God has no direct answer to the damning charges brought against him. He has something better.

The thing is, we live in a world that is largely populated by nonhumans, whose material effects are yet to be fully appreciated. That we understand the world through story, via discourse, does not foreclose the possibility of a material world that stretches *beyond it*—or, to put it in less tensile terms, a world that includes discourse as part of its material becoming. If we have no access to the so-called world-as-it-is, the colorless, silent realms outside the mediation of discourse (or if there isn't a world there, just an "in here" or "what we make of it"), and if we must continue to depend on these representations to mirror a mysterious nonworld hopelessly far away from us, then the Cartesian structure that social constructionism set out to dismantle remains still. It means reality is bereft, torn into factions that will never truly meet, binary ontological orders of mind and matter. This is a big deal, dear: home is either the taut, leathery staunchness of a slave-master's whip—and we must find our place in a predetermined hierarchy of things by giving our backs and dignity to the benevolence of tyranny—or it is a labyrinth of mirrors and, for all intents and purposes, we are starkly alone with ourselves, caught in the nuances of our own images, fundamentally estranged from the profound other.

If the world were merely a story or a complex of stories—just ideas rubbing against other ideas—then how do we explain the emergence of things that do not fit into our syntaxes? How is it that some events simply escape our sense-making, power-distributing, identity-perpetuating linguistic practices? What do we say about tsunamis and the devastation of floods? Can our story-sanctuaries accommodate the toxic prolificacy of radioactive shit, the resistance of errant winds and weather, the real and abiding effects of colonialism and rape on torn bodies, the fastidiousness of micro-critters breaching cell membranes?

It seems there is much more at work than our plots make space for—much more than can be beaten into the gauntness of alphabets. It seems the world also does things, also resists, also initiates, also produces and speculates and throws tantrums—and that narrative dynamics aren't the only things we must take into account as contributory factors in the world's emergence.

Untangling from the project of returning to Eden, or living with the Fall, means we have to rethink everything. Because modernism cannot account for the role of discourse in shaping the seen, and constructionism cements this bifurcation by positing that language is the stuff of the world, we need to meet the universe halfway—a way of bringing the world back in, without reducing it to dead matter, and a way of acknowledging the contributions of culture as well. Yes, we are still talking about "middles," or as Rebekah

Sheldon puts it, "a critical modesty from out of which [we may] seek to generate a realistic ethics attentive to the impact of human culture and also to the vivacity, vulnerability, and sometimes the surly intransigence of nature."[3]

One thing feels sure: we cannot pose the question of home without accounting for the manner in which we are beings among beings. We must consider Leviathan—forgotten beyond our fences.

Through the shrubs we catch a glimpse of the powerful monster partially submerged in water. In meeting his ferocity, in examining his dimensions, his breathing, his brooding aloofness, and his utter otherness, the faint wisdoms of God's response to Job begins to leak through: what could be better than an answer to a question? The gift of bewilderment. The incoming rush of something foreign to the linear logic of the inquiry. New air sucked into the nostrils and lungs. The terrain breaching the neatness of the map. Confusion—or better yet, con-fusion: a mixing together, a messy mangling of things. The motif of becoming generously lost.

✦

After I dress up, still quite shaken from the watery monster I have just experienced, I sit down for a while—picking up the blasted pieces of my body-soul. Geetha offers me tea. I haven't quite gotten myself together so I say thank you, wobble my head a bit, and smile. She seems to understand. I am hungry, but I want to go home. I can't wait to see you and Mama to tell you all about this crazy trip.

Kutti is done ironing his dress—the same one he wore yesterday. He folds the compact ironing board and slips it back into the tiny space between the two dilapidated Godrej cupboards in the room, just as Nandini stirs awake. Last night, the children had said they weren't going to school today, and Kutti feigned surprise—looking at me to contribute my own gesture of pretend astonishment to the emerging game.

Once he is done dressing up, he takes me out again, toward the water tankers, where he meets a friend and introduces me to him. The friend invites me into his tanker. I climb up the huge tires, first on its bolts, and then place my foot in the space between the tire and the rusting chassis, and then pull myself into a tiny space. The whole compartment has been modified so that there is a wooden plank behind the driver's seat. Kutti tells me, his teeth reddened with *paan,* that the driver's assistant lives inside this tanker, and this—the plank I sit on—is his bed.

Soon, we are moving through the city, passing motorists while honking a loud horn. We arrive at an estate for military personnel, stop at an underground tank a few meters from the guarded gates, and lower a green hose into the tank through an opening a few feet above the ground. I help the young boy pull out the hose when the tank is full, and—moments later—we are racing through the city again, scaring off smaller cars, making an old man walking his dog turn in fright.

We return to Kutti's neighborhood. I thank the driver for showing me a view of the city of Chennai I had not known. It is when we return to Kutti's shack that I find—just near a neat pile of pots and pans—two dark critters, sneaking past without a sound. Could it be? Kutti doesn't seem to notice as he walks straight past them and into his home to get the keys to his rickshaw so he can drop me off at home, as he had promised to do. He calls out to me from inside the house, momentarily distracting me. I answer that I'll be with him shortly. When I turn my head back to the twin shadows, they are no longer where I first noticed them. Dashing forward, I pick up a short stubby stick and poke gently at the pots—one-two-three taps. Four tightly spaced sighs. Then ... one-two ... there. The charcoal black slug-like things, no bigger than tiny mice, push out from behind the pots into full view. Hushes! Two of them, for that matter.

I look around me, suddenly conscious of my surroundings again. A young girl down the narrow walkway is standing out of a doorway, staring at me without expression. My hands trembling, I wave to her and whisper a "hello" only I can possibly hear. Then I turn to the hushes again. They are still there, but they could slip away if I don't do the prayers. So I place one nondescript piece of wood and a little steel container on both sides of the hushes. This is it.

I kneel down a respectable distance from the abominable things. Bàbá didn't exactly leave me with instructions about what to do next but, kneeling there, looking at their slimy rippling movement, I suddenly know what to do. My skin crawls as I consider it, while my heart, obviously in disagreement with what must now happen, threatens to tear through my paper-thin chest to kill me. *Heart! You will only kill yourself in the same way. We must do this together. You made a promise to Alethea. She needs her father now.* I stretch out my finger to touch the body of the first hush. It sluggishly recoils, folding into itself as it secretes droplets of a transparent viscous stuff along the length of its body. I touch the thing, and put the stuff on my tongue—squeezing my eyes as I taste the rank, disgustingly acidic thing go down my throat. While I am overwhelmed by a desire to vomit, I quickly do the same thing again—touching the second hush, causing it to recoil, taking a drop of its stuff on the tip of my finger, and touching my tongue. Don't ask why I did this. It just felt like the right thing to do.

The prayer is complete. At least with these two hushes. There are eight more to find.

I look up to find Kutti staring at me, just like that nameless girl had done a few minutes ago. I am not sure how much he has seen. Thankfully there are no other persons around. I offer an awkward smile as I walk toward him … a smile and a tap on his shoulder … anything to ease back into sane relations with another human being, who has most probably witnessed his guest perform the most outrageous thing ever. The slimy remnants and bitter-eggy taste of the hush secretions are lingering in my mouth as I say "let's go home." "Come," he replies through his teeth, his jaw locked up and gently moving at the insistence of *paan.*

Mornings have become my favorite time of day ... waking up to find you and your dad lying on the bed in a weird yin and yang curl. You somehow manage to snuggle your way into him, and fit perfectly in whatever pattern his body makes. You two have a relationship that makes me jealous.

But the best part of my morning is when you open those beautiful eyes, spring off the bed with the most beautiful smile, and run out of the bedroom, leaving your partner (since, a month ago, you decided to marry him and declared to all that I was now his girlfriend and you, his wife!) who is still asleep. You run right into the hall searching for me, and hug and kiss me when you find me ... as if you've been waiting to do this all night.

We then greet each other, and I ask you if you've had any dreams.

As a child I was a dreamer, always waking up in the morning with stories to tell about my dreams—which my mother would patiently interpret for me. From Chinese women riding giant mosquitoes to rivers taking the form of men to cross the street, my weird dreams always found a home in the careful embrace of my mother's wisdoms. When we greet each other in the morning, I always ask you about your own dreams.

These small morning moments that we spend alone are like my morning shot of coffee: they get my day going. But this morning is different. I wake up shortly before you jump up from the bed in sobs, and hold me tight. Tears are rolling down your eyes. I hold you, feeling your deep pain, wondering about what is disturbing you. As I rock you back and forth, embracing you in my arms, I ask you what the matter is, and you say—in between sobs—that you had a dream. "A bad dream," you add.

I'm shocked and upset that I did not protect you from your dream—as if I could. I tell you that I'm there and all is well and you try to tell me what happened.

You say you were in a forest and you were playing with a bunch of monkeys, climbing trees and hanging from them. When you and the animals got tired, the monkeys became hungry and went to get something to eat. Your head still buried in my chest, I keep rocking you gently and you look up at me and say, "Don't monkeys eat bananas, ma?" I say yes, and your eyes fill with tears again. You tell me you tried to tell your dreamy friends that monkeys eat bananas, not apples. But the monkeys, perverse, unnatural, monstrous, eat apples instead.

You are distraught. You say you tried to stop them but they kept eating apples and making fun of you in spite what you said.

I am confused. Part of me wants to laugh, the other part recalls the lingering memories of my own mother's gentle reassurances. But it's just a bad dream, right? Monkeys eating apples? So what? Could your three-year-old mind be forming figurative images of being different in a country where difference is a charged concept? Did some of your straight-haired Indian friends tease you about your curly hair, your darker skin? Am I a good enough mother to you?

I hold you tighter, offering no explanation for monkeys and their eating apples. Just a knowing silence. The kind that knows that the world often makes no sense. One day you will learn to live in a world where things don't add up neatly. A world constantly asking us to come to our senses, to new senses. To the unimaginable. I kiss your forehead gently, as your father, oblivious and lost, snores out what I imagine to be his agreement.

LETTER 3

HUGGING MONSTERS

Not to transcend this body, but to reclaim it ...

—ADRIENNE RICH

Dear Alethea,

Through the window on our left, the Pacific Ocean appeared in her turquoise gray glory, like the mysterious lady of the house—lately gowned—slowly come down a flight of stairs to greet her slack-jawed guests. I sighed. She was dazzlingly beautiful! Expansive and enthralling. A roar of nature.

I love the ocean. Maybe I love mountain peaks and mountain ranges more. *Those* often look like snow-bearded elders in conversation, seated with arms around folded knees. I marvel at the lithic intelligence of a mountain anytime I come across one. But primal bodies of water make my nostrils tremble and my chest expand. They look like eternity. This is why I elected that we meet here for these letters, for you are a creature of the depths too.

This ocean. Not only was she likely the most majestic stretch of water I had ever seen, but the way she beat against the edges of rocks and cliff confirmed her a vixen. Gorgeous and terrifying all at once—the embodied fury of things in their ongoing becoming. Her frothing defiance sent up huge milky waves against the coastal mudstone cliffs as we drove down West Cliff

Drive in Santa Cruz, California. Beholding the statesmanlike eminence of those serrated cliffs, the bangs of green flora that fell down their foreheads, and the silence of the irregular black rocks that dotted the undulating pocket beaches, I couldn't help but imagine both ocean and cliff as testy lovers whose spirited quarrels had shaped the majestic coastline. If you listened carefully, if you were silent for a little while, you might have heard the gentle spray of applause distilled in the electric air around us—as if appreciating the performance of sedimented rock and shifting water, thanking the titans for the spectacle of their tragic love affair.

Above her flat eternal spread, silhouetted against sun and azure sky, a bokeh of bright colors floated in the distance—barely noticeable.

"Paragliders and surfers, right? Must be a lot of fun," I noted. My friend Doug, driving, asked me if I wanted him to stop so I could take a picture. A mysterious fog was just ahead of us, and I, born, bred, and "buttered" in Lagos, Nigeria—having never been enveloped by a fog before—wanted to greet it, to be engulfed in the twilight of its passing, to perhaps eavesdrop on the whisperings of the ancestors within who straddled the line between being and nonbeing, and to say thank-you for the inexpressible gift I had just received from the elder Doug took me to. I considered Doug's offer a while, but I already knew my answer. "Let's keep going, brother," I replied. My heart was full. He nodded his agreement, his face stretching into a grin as the wind waltzed with his close cropped hair.

A day before, I had asked him to drive me to Santa Cruz to meet *the elder,* whose call came to me quite suddenly after I had finished giving a speech at a gathering of permaculture practitioners in Hopland, almost two hundred miles north of Santa Cruz. On this Wednesday morning, Doug had picked me up from the Bay Area after I had hitched a ride on a truck with a young man about my age, whose love for and knowledge of the cliffs was spellbinding. A Thai restaurant later, along with a soft education on the industrial economy of California, and many discussions about African music legend Fela Anikulapo Kuti, Doug and I pulled up to her home. It wasn't his plan to take me all the way to Santa Cruz where she lived, but I didn't know my way around the state or have enough money in my pocket. I was lost without his help.

The elder's home was just like she described it in the email she sent me: "Our house is midway down the block on the left, a turquoise (light blue) house between a red house and a yellow house." I felt like a kid arriving at the home of his idol. Was I appropriately dressed? What would I say to her or tell her that she hadn't already divined in the dark chambers of her sacred craft? Would she notice how smart I was as well, or would I need to speak with my jalopy American accent to appear "smart enough"? Gridlocked in the wide-open space between my waning self-confidence and my excitement at meeting this elder, I lingered in the walkway outside her home pretending to wait for Doug to alight from his black SUV. Then I marched up to the door, dragging the last morsel of esteem I had, and pressed the doorbell … wait! I can't be sure if I actually *knocked the door* (you know, three taps and all) or pressed a doorbell. Whatever. Remembering is hardly a matter of recalling facts as it is about embellishing traces of an inkling with bits of the plausible.

So, dear, whether doorbell or three taps, the door swung open to meet a familiar stranger. It wasn't *her.* It was her beautiful life-partner, Fern, who welcomed us both into her home with generous hugs, ushering us toward the living room. I stole a glimpse at the beckoning, homey interior. It smelled of tea, biscuits, and goodness. All the scene needed was fluffy balls of snow on the windowpane outside, a fireplace made of red brick, and a dining set with a red-and-white checkered tablecloth, and it would have taken me back to those televised visions of a "proper home" I was fascinated with as a child.

To the right of the room, as I had expected, there was a whole shelf of important-looking books in the hall. Something shifted: now, you see, I was clad in a blue and white Yoruba "indigenous-looking" outfit—just like the others I had at home, which I wore when I traveled to America or Europe to speak about my decolonial adventures. The clothes made me feel like I belonged to something important, and—perhaps more importantly—they made me feel comfortable to be black in the face of white scrutiny. But there was always a silent hypocrisy demon that taunted me when I attired myself in those Yoruba colors. They often felt like "performance clothes"—like a costume I got into to give the impression I was more "indigenous" than I really was, or that I had my feet on firm ground ... when I was really stranded in midair—lost and yearning for new settlements that touch the soul—like those who heard me speak. For one who was part of a lost generation, stolen from the soil by the highway, orphaned by the inhuman face of empire, speaking only the one-tongue of our white masters to our lands that were now mute, and without father, I was the Frankensteinian product of lord and slave, the silt between angry ocean and sullen mudstone—at home neither in womb nor away from womb. I was usually uncomfortable in my own skin ... keenly aware of the scandal in the court that had birthed me, but without a way to respond to my monstrousness. Walking into her home, Doug and Fern exchanging greetings behind me, I felt those pangs of vulnerable inadequacy—like I was being tested or examined again, as I had been throughout my conscious life.

And then, as if puncturing the suffocating bubble of intense self-awareness around me, the elder rolled up to meet us, her face beaming a welcoming, interested smile. She was in a wheelchair, her ankle broken in three places, as I would later learn. She wore a studious pair of dark-rimmed glasses and a cavalier green shirt beneath a black suede waistcoat. Her hair was short and whimsical. In her writings, she had taken pains to describe the way the void—the classical theoretical space some physicists insisted was empty—was filled with virtual particles conducting experiments with space-time. Her hair, flaying about in subversive curls, looked like an embodiment of that assertion. A carnival of silvery wispy tufts of wisdom.

"Hello, Bayo!" she said. I smiled, walked forward to meet her, and bent into her chair to embrace her properly, as she made to lift herself out of her chair to meet me halfway. I looked at her. I felt we had an understanding—a shared quest for the poetry behind the iron curtain, the sacred laughter stitched into the fabric of the ordinary. A keen suspicion that there was a more stunning home outside of the fences where we both found ourselves.

Like I had those years ago, she had only just lost her dear father—another thread of kinship that connected both of us as hauntees of abiding ghosts and present absences. As subjects of the workings of time out of joint. It was no wonder then that when we embraced, grieving child to grieving child, dad to dad (she refused the gender binary identification as a "woman"; her daughter called her 'dad') many worlds came in touch. She had called, and I was there. It was almost impossible to imagine: it was my thirty-third birthday, and I was in the home of Karen Barad—feminist icon, physicist, science studies scholar, and fellow monster.

✦

I rolled the petrified thing around and around, all my five fingers considering its strange textures and hard ridges. It had probably died a long time ago, curled up into an ammonite spiral, and assumed its prehistoric posture—frozen in its black silence for all time.

It was a hush.

The third hush out of ten.

I wasn't sure what to do with it, or what Bàbá would have wanted me to do at that point. But it really felt like the third one in the series I was looking for. It had, after all, found me under unique circumstances. In my mind, I was thus closer to answering the question of home, somehow. Karen would herself perform what seemed to be the accompanying ritual.

Karen had given me the lithified remains of the hush and a little light-green book she had written called *What Is the Measure of Nothingness? Infinity, Virtuality, Justice*. Both gifts sat in each hand as Doug drove through the fog on the way back to the Bay Area from Karen's home. Book and hush. Words and a thing. Language and matter. The postmodern retreat into stories that left the material world behind and the modern/colonial stabilization of nature that occasioned the retreat. Somewhere between, somewhere in the middle, the memory of Karen's voice and presence lingered.

Back in her home, as we sat together—a quartet of solemn inquiry—I mentioned that it was my birthday after both she and Fern had hosted us in conversation, told us about their backyard garden and children, and regaled us with the tale of how Karen had broken her ankle in Peru when she visited a mutual friend of ours, the good professor Frédérique Apffel-Marglin. There was no small talk. Just sunlight, a dog, the quiet purr of occupied sofas, and shared memory. We talked about children. I spoke about you—and my quest to "redeem" my fatherhood in an intentional pursuit of what it meant or what it could mean in a time like this. I talked about Bàbá's ritual of gathering the prayer items. I did not tell her those items were hushes. Doug talked about his career in publishing, and Fern, a rabbi, who gave me the impression that she was from an enchanted time of deserts, camels, traded beans, and shofars, spoke about her work and their children.

An angel passes by.

Karen turns to me and says, "You know, there is no time. *We have no time*—we are only here for a short while. So I wonder if you have anything to ask while we are here together."

At first, to my ears, it sounds as if she wants me to leave. *There is no time.* In Nigeria, that's the kind of thing you say to a guest that has outlived his welcome. But I can tell this is not what she means. This is the zeal of an elder, whose invitation has been honored, who sits on her short stool, who knows that the sun loiters in the heavens only as long as day is day, who wants to tug at one of her ears, call my name three times and ask me how many times she called it—just before blessing me. This is a sacred moment. This is meeting my father. He is here. Haunting this instant, begging me to toss a cowrie or my two hushes to ask a question before the portal closes. *There is no time.*

I have no prepared question. I feel a bit nervous when I consider raising a question about her thought project—agential realism—so I abandon the idea, and ask instead: "What is the most beautiful thing in the world for you, right now?" I think I notice her swallow with some difficulty—as if she is slain by the riddle. She bows her head, starts to say something but segues in another direction.

"This moment. This thick now ... this particular moment," she continues. "Because it is connected to all other moments."

Following Karen, Fern speaks about the divine play and sacred laughter that is the kernel of every object, every tick of restless clock hands. As both comment on each other's responses, I am afforded a private moment to imagine reality as a cosmic cackle, lingering and persistent, without some lofty purpose at the end of it—for there is no "end of it," no break in the giggling. Just laughter spilling into laughter long after the joke is spent.

When we knew it was time to leave, Doug and I started to say our pre-good-byes. Having learned during the visit that it was my birthday, Karen beckoned me, wheeling herself toward her shelf of books, leaving Fern and Doug again in a haze of polite chatter. I noticed a pristine version of her complicated magnum opus that had introduced her to me—*Meeting the Universe Halfway: Quantum Physics and the Entanglement of Matter and Meaning*—and watched with muted anguish as her hand drifted past it to pull out the small pamphlet-like book on nothingness. I had already read the pamphlet on the internet, but was too polite to tell her so. Then she said she had something else to give me. What could it be? She took it from a corner of her shelf—the small, irregular, and round body of a hush. When I sighted it, I might have choked on my own spit a little. Even as I write this to you, my dear Alethea-not-yet-known, I feel the hair at the back of my head standing on end: what were the odds that Karen would give me the very thing I needed to complete my ritual of prayer, my quest to understand what it means to build a home for you?

"You don't know how much this means to me, Karen," I said, with remarkable smoothness, "but where I come from, a child receives the blessings of an elder on bended knees—not standing up tall."

I fell to my knees, near the shiny bars of her wheelchair, and close enough to hear her whisper into my ear as her free hand rested on my head, anointing it with a queer oil of words.

She said, "May you find success in all you do." She continued to speak other words, her soft prayerful blessings reminding me of the gushing stream from the wound in the mountainside that Moses's staff had wrought: a crack in the presumptuous binariness of things.

I thought of all the things I wanted to succeed at: I wanted to love and be loved by your mother … to know her tearful smile as both of us shut our eyes for the last time, holding each other's hands—fingers interlocked—in the way we do; I wanted to meet my father somewhere in the fog, where he sighs in wait, his hair not a day older than when I saw it last on that fateful Wednesday; I wanted to know the intimate joys of living small, to relinquish my claim of ownership over myself and learn to play; I wanted you to grow up and remember me as one of your heroes, a good father, one whose trembling hands held you aloft every night, whose nostrils gladly accommodated your little farts, and whose shoulders gave you room to stand on to take in the majestic view of a wonderful world; I wanted to complete Bàbá's quest—*my quest*—to prepare a home for you, to know how to pray for your journeys.

When I rose to my feet, I caught Karen's eyes reflecting. She was *verklempt*. Her eyes were perhaps reddened by a memory, a feeling or some other emotion I might never understand. Had she found a way to eavesdrop on thoughts, and thus heard my faint yearnings? Had she caught a glimpse of her own father, skirting the relaxed boundaries between the now, then, and the yet-to-come?

"Thank you, Karen," I said. She nodded, her face speaking of an ongoing struggle with depths too deep for words.

As Doug's car ate up highway after highway, I thought about her teary eyes as I stroked the hush's frozen body. The mystery of it haunted me. Why did she cry? Did I remind her of someone, or did my kneeling down for her blessing trigger an unspoken sense of loss or grief about the harsh anonymity of the modern world she was immersed in? Was it the simple joy of a shared moment of intimate friendship? Or the curious peregrinations of a mind that had given itself too passionately to the rehabilitation of the body of the material world, and the articulation of a striking feminist ethic that repudiates racism, sexism, and colonialism. Perhaps she saw in me what she knew in herself to be true: a desire to inhabit a home that worked for all of us, not just a few above the many. Perhaps it was all of these and more—and not just one thing. Karen herself had written her book about the futility of seeking out a world populated by already made-up things, secret essences, or separate ingredients. The world doesn't work that way.

Whatever the reasons were for her tears, I had just been blessed by Karen Barad. My body tingled all over. It was like I was just from a revival meeting at a big tent gathering, and the whiff of the Holy Ghost still lingered like a stubborn scent. I tried to trace out the series of insignificant events that had brought me to the text of her work and, eventually, to her doorstep. Long before she pressed her fingers on my head, we had kept up a correspondence between us—emailing each other once in a while. I had initiated this traffic of mutual exploration when I expressed my fascination with her "agential realism," and she graciously responded, even when she was going through a difficult period hospicing her dear father. Out of the pixelated blue, her latest message arrived; it had the gravity of mysterious urgency—as if there was fire on a mountain and my meeting her was going to help put it out. She wrote: *"Bayo, I just noticed a post of yours saying you are in my neck of the woods, in Berkeley! Do you have plans to stay in the area for a bit? Any chance of you heading down this way? It would be great to meet finally. Peace, Karen."*

Okay, I admit that doesn't sound grave. Or urgent.

I'm allowed a few embellishments, aren't I, dear?

Nevertheless, there was nothing cavalier or playful about her summoning me. I probably would have responded with no less a sense of urgency than if she had told me the sky was collapsing on her head, and only I could save the day. In my mind, an elder had just called me to her side. Nothing was going to keep me from getting to her.

There's no surprise here. For a young African father, whose own father had left in him an asphyxiating quest for reconciliation, whose own lands were buried underneath the asphalt of a dead-eyed consortium of colonial propositions, and whose promise to his daughter textured his breathing moments, Karen's work was the structural equivalent of a gap in a steel wall. Or a crack in the perimeter fence, showing the wilds beyond it. There was something refreshingly generative and alluring about the ways she saw the world—a gritty vision of the real rooted in a rigorous and sustained engagement with the mysterious workings of the material world, and informed by questions committed to matters of justice. Her poetically textured writings honored the earth-affirming wisdoms of my people, sympathized with the life-denying elisions we suffered, addressed the ontological premises that occasioned those colonial encounters, and cleaved open new spaces of power and reenchantment. Hers was in fact a redescription of home that both challenged lazy notions of distant arrivals and finish lines, and recast the traveler in a posthuman saga of never-ending co-emergence.

I am hesitant to do so, but if I were to speak of the implications of her reconstructive work in the duration of a grateful sigh, I might say that Karen paints the portrait of a collective "coming down to earth." *That* redolent picture of coming to earth elicits imaginations of crumbling ziggurats and divine disruptions, as featured in the biblical tale of the Tower of Babel: in a bid to escape the diluvial fury of the gods, the children of Adam propose to build a tower so high that it would not only protect them against other possible flood events but reach the heavens where the gods reside. Anxious, the gods realize this undertaking of men might breach the established order of things, so they confuse the ears and tongues of the builders, so that even though they all speak one language, no one can understand each other anymore. This premodern fantasy project of human mastery and transcendent disembodiment is thus thwarted, and confusion—a meeting in the mangled knot of co-becoming—is the agential force that effects the humiliation of this postdiluvian civilization.

A coming down to earth. Leaving the certitude of oracles behind. Making do with this world of partial recovery. Reacquainting ourselves with dust. Meeting Karen in text and in person was an about-turn from my previous trail to heaven. If the taped sermons of Finis Dake were dispatches from a golden city of angels and gods above—coordinates to heaven, one might say—then Karen's was part of an earthly choir of agencies singing me down to land, urging me to notice the troubling yet surprising sympathy between all things ... all creatures ... a sympathy that weaved together mind and soil, sky and shadow, man and woman, god and dust. Father and son. A weaving so intimate that the connective stitches become indistinguishable from the fabric.

Her descriptions of the real weren't just intellectual exercises disconnected from the goings-on around the world. In fact, they were theoretically inseparable from her ongoing commitments to *feminism*. A *different* feminism, if I could put it that way. Not the one the chattering class in Lagos, huddled at a newspaper vendor's roadside kiosk showing various headlines about women contesting gubernatorial elections, learned to hiss at—wondering what was becoming of a world where women no longer knew their place.

Up till the time I started to encounter writings like Karen Barad's, the word *feminism* had meant little to me: it was yet another floating concern in the world out there ... mired in the background ruckus of the everyday, sometimes surfacing to cause furrowed eyebrows, only to sink back into the half-words, bleeps and crackles of the unseen long before those frowns became permanent.

I grew up with three sisters, your aunts Tito, Bimbo, and Wendy, and never considered myself at the short end of the stick for it—and though my teenage years were characterized by a desire to live up to Christian doctrine, the idea that men were one rung higher than women on the onto-divine ladder wasn't very attractive to me. No doubt I unconsciously imbibed the idea that the man was the head of the house. Why else would God create Eve from Adam's side? Was it not to say that women were to be submissive to men?

In our parents' house, there was a little sign that was hung on the wall that said: "A successful man is one who makes more money than his wife can spend. A successful woman is one who can find such a man." It felt biblical, like something that was written with the same ink, in the same fonts, and on the same page as "Honesty is the best policy." Not that my mother didn't make any money outside of what my father earned as a diplomat; she did— but there was an unwritten rule that dads came first in our consideration, that being a mum or a wife meant cooking in the kitchen and doing "mummy" things. All the pictures of the clergymen I revered growing up—the very popular ones and the upcoming ones—had their wives standing up by their side, leaning into the picture and resting on the shoulder of the "man of God," who was seated, suited, and fundamental.

Very early in my "evolution," the word *feminism* felt like another Western incursion. Another moment we could all sigh, throw our hands in the air, and bemoan the erosion of our values. "It's those white people again coming to tell us that women are equal to men." There was no talk of feminism in the church. The feminists were the rich artistes, the ones with rings in their noses, who probably were too rotten to have proper husbands and settle down like everybody else. As such, I learned to associate feminism with errancy, imagining women rising up early to go to work (just like their husbands), earning degrees (which wasn't bad at all), flinging off their tight bras in street protests (which was a bit troubling), or—most abominable!—not knowing how to cook at all.

My dear mother, your Bama, who was the epitome of womanhood for me, cooked like a water spirit intent on beguiling an unwary sailor man. Even now, well into her late sixties, she can make a hearty meal out of smelly socks and an abandoned shoe strap. I suppose "it's in her blood," as we often say in Nigeria. Her own mother made the best fried bean cakes or *àkàrà* in Èbuté Métta, a neighborhood in Lagos mainland. I might be exaggerating a bit, but I did hear that her bean cakes were so well done that the busy drone workers of the inner city money hives would often arrive at her stall for breakfast in the wee hours of the morning, skipping what was served at home. She not only made delicious bean cakes, she also made *ewa àgòyìn*—a local variety of cooked beans with an accompanying gritty sauce, which always went well with the stoic loaves of bread we ate, fondly called Agége bread. My grandmother's cooking sent my mother to school, and paid for an elite education that took her all the way to a prestigious nursing career in Glasgow.

So when my mum talked about food, we knew she spoke from her bones. Cooking was what she did best when she wasn't holding a syringe. She often hissed at food shows on television—when "oyinbo" chefs would boil leaves and sticks, and then have the audacity to call the plated rubbish "food," licking their fingers and "hmm-ing" away at nothing. It always made us laugh when mummy, while watching the shows, would exclaim to no one in particular: "But where is the pepper? Did he put salt in that fish at all? Is that one food? I'm sure it is horrible—he is just saying 'hmm-hmm' when there's nothing there!"

However, nothing perhaps made her more livid than when a woman didn't play her role. When she spoke to erring younger wives, her default position was that the man was the head of the home. Only in extreme circumstances of male idiocy did she take the side of the woman. She lived out her creed: she took care of her children with the ferocity of a mother hen guarding her chicks from street dogs. She went to work, kept the money books, prepared us for school, and had to look good doing it. She even knotted my dad's ties for him in the morning (he didn't know how to) before he stepped out—and, when he had to live without us in his diplomatic residence in Kinshasa, she would send knotted ties to him from Lagos by courier. Through all of this, she never questioned the gender role she was assigned and had grown up in; she never once wavered in her belief that this is what a good woman does. A good wife. She knew her place.

Then my father died and she was left alone, torn from her own flesh. Seeing her come undone might have been shocking enough were it not easily displaced by my becoming acquainted with her surprisingly fragile womanhood. All this while, she was "Mum"—fixed in place like a Kantian referent. She was the container in which my unwieldy human experiences were contained. And then … to see her torn apart.

There's no denying that I came to know my mother for the first time when Dad passed away—outside the rose-tinted hallways of my previous normal. I saw the way she struggled to make ends meet and feed us. The way she lost her cool when things weren't going our way, and then made up for it by scraping a few notes to take us to the local "Mr. Biggs" eatery. The way she begged my father's rich friends for support. The way she was made to wait in their living rooms to see them, where my father's presence would have brought them out of their proud chambers in less than "just a moment." She had the stench of a widow and the preexisting condition of being a woman. No one wanted that. Back at home, she would fall into the torn sofa, splayed out in a posture of abandonment, staring into the vacant distance. She often called my father's name in airy breathy sighs of longing. I remember hearing her cry again and again in the middle of the night. I would get up from the side of the bed where I slept, walk up to her side, and tell her, "Mummy, let me be your husband. Let me be your husband." For some reason, this would comfort her, and then she would sink into reluctant, troubled sleep—her veined eyelids trembling at the cusp of oblivion. But the pain—the dreadful pain lingered, and soon after, her sobbing would lash out against the blackest of nights. And morning would feel an eternity away.

Still, justice for my suffering mother and relief from a world that manhandled her did not take the form of an experimental feminism until you were born. With your appearing, a cycle was completed: her only son gave her a granddaughter. In your first days, you even looked like her. Everyone but a few believed you *were* her in some way. In a manner of mysterious returnings and cleaved lives. And for the first months of your life, she took care of you when your mother and I were teaching in our university classrooms. She taught us how to give you a bath, and how to put you gently on the shoulder and tap your back until you burped. She knew best how to sing you to sleep, shaking her upper body while singing a lullaby with the name she had given you: Joyinolá—a Yoruba name that means "I will yet eat the honey of my tomorrow." In this regard, you are my mother's prophecy, her stake in a more promising future. Her faith that the grievous hand dealt her with my father's untimely death would not slip by unaccounted for. In a familiar case of jumping generations, of the living haunting the living, her longing became your name. And your many names became my quest to find a place in the world for the womb that birthed me as a father and the womb that birthed me as a son.

As a young graduate assistant, however, my growing experiments with truth reinforced the very fundamentals I found deeply problematic: the same exclusivity that banished nonbelievers to an eternity of burning with sulfur and brimstone was the very framework that deified the male figure, rendering my mother a rogue planet in a fixed orbit of named or counted planets. I couldn't come to terms with a faith that was blind to the complexities of culture and context, treating belief as if it were a factory grade limit or quality assessment score, instead of the fragile, provisional, local performance of the sacred and of earthly questions. I couldn't relate with the judgmental gaze that looked upon the oppressed as victims of their own faulty mind-sets, instead of real conditions outside their control.

I remember writing in an essay a pastor had asked me to write that my footprints leading to church had dried up, long covered over by passing dust. The pews stabilized my participation in the exclusion of the other, my mother, beautiful cultures around the world that had their own keen senses of the sacred and ways of thinking through their finiteness. I had already torn away the front page in one of my many journals whereupon I had imprinted what (in my nerdish headiness) I had called my "life motto": "Magna est veritas et praevalebit," Latin for "Truth is great and will prevail." The idea of Conquering Truth stampeding the world on a noble steed might have made my colleagues salivate, but it made me shudder with irritation.

So, one innocent night, before I even met your mother, I lingered by the fence, the same one I had joyfully planted to stave off the uprising of the wilds, to cordon off the evil beyond. My mother's groans of sorrow echoed in the tempting distance, entwined with a feeling that other natures were indeed possible beyond the steely imperialism of Truth. I took one deep breath, and slipped through into rebellious frontiers lit seductively by a pagan moon, in search of the liberatory errancy rumored by the bodies of the paraphrased.

And you have more than one goodly heritage of fence-hopping debauchery in your collective story. Let me take you to another scene—one which you might recall:

Every Wednesday, over a hundred people gather into a six-hundred-square-foot apartment squeezed among other homes in the dense suburban neighborhood of Egmore, singing with each other. The music is rich, sewn into an exquisite tapestry of sonorous voices, shifting feet, and palms vibrating over the percussive surfaces of the South Asian tabla. Everyone sits on the floor, on clean mats, their feet tucked neatly underneath saris and *salwars* or jeans.

There is no dancing, as would be the case if this were a religious gathering in Lagos, but there is a gentle spirited swaying to the guttural *dum-dum* sounds that accompany the clapping and the heaven-bound whispering. They are singing about God and blessings and devotion. If you come in late, you'd have to tiptoe between glaring eyes and folded bodies to find yourself an unoccupied spot to sit. Every space is taken with children and elders, listening with rapt attention, laughing or singing when song breaks out.

In the middle of the room, a large woman in her late fifties sits on a lone chair set against the wall. She cuts an imposing matriarchal figure, like a mother oak tree in the center of the forest whose branches fan the length and breadth of the forest. Her face is stern, her brow sweaty, and her long woven hair falls behind her, snaking along the top of the chair then falling by its side. She is wearing a colorful but unassuming dress. There is no nail polish on her fingernails, no *pottu* on her forehead. She is animated, making a joke in Tamil that I do not understand, then seguing into the "word of God." She is the convener of this homey place of worship, a respected elder whose counsel is sought by the weeping wives of drunkards, by women who worry that their sons are wayward, by couples who must learn that love is not enough of an excuse to get married in India.

Her nightly speeches are often fulsomely peppered with words like "perfect," "holy," and "prayer," but you'd be mistaken if you thought this was merely some Christian gathering. This is a place open to all, even those who don't subscribe to doctrine. There is food and drink; everyone offers to help feed everyone else. The format of the fellowship actually allows for more conversation and less sermonizing, inviting play and games and troubling inquiries about the nature of faith today. The fellowship has become a home, open to all, discriminating to none. And at the reluctant center of it sits Syreena Dike, your grandmother, your Bama, whose life is a remarkable testament to the surprising generosity of errancy.

In 1983, the year after her Parsi father died, Syreena stood tall in her household, where seven other siblings were born to her father and mother. She was in her twenties, beautiful, and hardworking—with an eye for business and a dream to travel abroad. Her own mother, born of an English woman in Tanzania and raised into a stern Catholic who frowned on movies, rejected modern medicine, and required her children to say "Praise the Lord" as a greeting, founded a home fellowship—foreshadowing Syreena's own foray into community-building in the years to come.

The most prominent guests to those meetings were black students from Nigeria come into the country to pursue greener academic pastures. Nigerians had notorious reputations among many South Indians, some sustained by fantastical accounts about the body proportions of African men, and some steeped in the real. Some said these Nigerians impregnated their women and stole away to their own countries, leaving "half-and-half" children to their dejected mothers. Syreena would later work to connect some of those children, now grown and seeking, with their fathers in Nigeria—many times successfully. But for now, she—like everyone else—was wary of the black Nigerian students that populated her mother's fellowship, oftentimes out of necessity to fill their stomachs with the free food the fellowship offered.

One Nigerian student from the Hindustan Institute of Engineering Technology in Chennai stood out, lingering in the corner of Syreena's eyes. He was tall, princely, immaculately dressed, and with a halo of thick hair on his head. He was also a brazen fool, a joker of the highest sort, for he approached Syreena one day and declared, "I want to marry you. You will be my wife."

It wasn't just the manner in which he did it, or the fact that such interracial relations would have been cursed with bloodied teeth by her family and the network of families she was connected to, it was that Syreena didn't have the time for such nonsense. She was the fourth-born of eight children, the one in the middle with something to prove—the one with the boyish habits and a distaste for weakness. Her older brothers had left the house, and she had quickly risen into breadwinner status, taking care of the others, earning the little she could to help the others go to school. Her best friend was a young businessman; she couldn't stand the company of women or bear to hear the things they talked about. There was no time for love. This crazy black man would have to learn to keep away from her.

But Uzoma, of the Dike stock, whose people in Igboland were known for their determination and skill with medicine, whose mother was a midwife, and who was the first of his people to travel abroad to be educated, was not built to back down. He kept coming. In fact, the more elaborate story is that Uzoma, your grandfather you never met, was actually "fronting" for a fellow Nigerian friend and fellowship-goer who had entreated his support in winning the heart of the fair Indian girl who moved like a blur during sermons—the one they both observed with slit-eyed fondness while everyone else squeezed their eyes shut in devotion. Uzoma, like the alpha male he was, came for the kill instead. His friend fell to the wayside. Syreena was to be his wife, and he knew it. And nothing—not nature or truth or an army of machete-wielding Indians—was going to stand in his way.

He took a gift to Syreena, just before she set out one morning for Andhra Pradesh to accompany her younger sister to an exam. As he gave it to her, he told her that all the words within were the words from his own heart. And then he left. Syreena opened the gift. It was a Walkman music player. Inside it, a Ginger Williams cassette. Syreena listened to the tape. When she returned from Andhra Pradesh, her hustling slowed down a bit during fellowship. Her feet were heavier, her pace more measured. For she also had learned to look through slit eyes at the tall princely fool she had already fallen in love with.

But her family would resist, fiercely. To respect those who linger at the time of this writing, I will not tell you the terrible things that were done to your grandmother to punish her for her mutiny. Let it suffice to know that the wounds we often inflict on others have roots that connect oppressor and oppressed in a loop of shared unrequited yearning. Such is the ubiquity of trauma and the promise of leaning in farther than we are used to, if only to acknowledge that we are all collectively smitten—and that even evil has a story.

Uzoma was driven away from the fellowship and Syreena was forbidden to have any kind of relationship with him. But Uzoma, of the Dike stock, called his mother back home and told her he was getting married.

So, one innocent day, Syreena finished all her chores like she had done in the past, and then told her family she was leaving. She had been lingering by the fence, the same one she had planted to stave off the uprising of the wilds, to cordon off the evil beyond. Her lover's desire had echoed in the tempting distance, entwined with a feeling that other natures were indeed possible beyond the steely imperialism of Truth. With the aid of a certain "Brother Kumar," Syreena stole away to find her lover, the one she had once considered abominable. They would hide at Brother Kumar's place for a while after getting married at the Registry. A year later, they would hold the fruit of their shared sin, a cherub no less, the first daughter born to a proud Igbo man ... Ijeoma, meaning "safe journey," which is what we often say when someone is taking leave for somewhere very far. A scandal of departures. Your own mother, "Lali."

✦

I write these letters to you from a world where being a woman is an enduring scandal—never fully spoken, never fully heard, only eavesdropped on. The human male, in contrast, bathes in astral light, monumental and fixed—a chastising example to all other bodies. Most of our modern cities are built to honor the *idea* of the male—with towering spires and skyscrapers bursting out of the ground in a phallic opera that convenes our lives around this exclusive sentiment, this singular worship of modernity's patriarchal premises.

My initial endorsement of feminism took the form of an attraction to the "feminine," and I was happy your mother shared my preference for "girly stuff." When I met your mother (a story I owe you!), we knew we wanted a girl—two girls, in fact. It was an odd thing to wish for in both our cultures. When she eventually got pregnant, we were excited about finding out if our fondest hopes and prayers for a girl had come to pass. At the time of your conception, we were both working as lecturers in a Nigerian university. One day we drove out to have an ultrasound scan performed. I remember the technician in the later stages of his operation wiping the bluish gel off your mother's belly and then turning to me, saying underneath his breath: "Well, it's likely this is a girl." If you were in the room (well … you were, in a sense, but … well, you understand), you wouldn't have needed to ask him to speak a bit louder to hear the implied "I'm sorry" between the lines. It was the way he said it: in some needlessly reassuring and cautious way instead of as a celebratory declaration, as we would have preferred. Not surprisingly, he was visibly startled when I punched the air with a defiant "yeah!" while your mother-to-come—in her usual conservative way—simply smiled.

That same cultural hesitation for daughters prevailed in your mother's land, where you were eventually born. Here in India, the silent war against girls was so disturbing that in 2014 the government had to institute a law banning prenatal sex determination and other medical practices they feared might be deployed as sex-selection technologies. When pregnant mothers found out they were to have daughters, they would either seek to terminate their pregnancies or even kill their born children. An official of the Indian government, the present minister for Women and Child Development, Maneka Gandhi, reports that two thousand girls are killed in the womb every day. "Some are born and have pillows on their faces choking them," she noted on television.[1] Contrast this with the widespread understanding here that boys bring luck and prestige—a culture-specific issue that has recently become very real to your mother and me as we are now both expecting your longed-for sibling, and as people around us—well-intentioned friends and neighbors, mind you—pray fervently that we have the preferred gender.

It's not hard to see why daughters are a burden here in India's patriarchal and increasingly global-market-friendly society, or why women hardly ever become swashbuckling heroes as their male counterparts in film do. They are thought to be more intimately (and shamefully) connected to the elements, the purportedly blind forces of nature modernity seeks to tame in its pilgrimage of ascension; they do not bring money in to families as boys do when they later attract handsome dowries; they menstruate and lactate and bleed, and their unwieldy bodies melt and bloat when they get pregnant. In short, the tenderness and dramatic transformations that attend the female body do not make it amenable to the mechanical, take-no-prisoners, time-starved, disembodied imperatives of our progressively global economic and political contexts.

A patriarchal world order that functions by assuming the universal and making hasty generalizations will not long abide the excruciating particularity of the feminine. Today, to be female is to be a refugee in the very places that are conditioned upon its life-nurturing contributions. The Enlightenment may have gotten rid of pagan sentiments, and driven aground the remnants of vampires, werewolves, hoofed gods, priests seeking indulgences, and topsy-turvy carnivals of debauchery, but its flattened terrain bred its own unexpected monster: the female-identified body is the modern world's monster.

In India, many grew uncomfortable with the oppression of the female, and started to organize to address it. From the mid-eighteenth century, the European colonialists who observed some of the local traditions with contempt (like Sati—the custom that required a widow to take her own life shortly after her husband's death), made gender equality a central issue of their campaign. Like movements in the West—often delineated into thematic "waves" in progressive sequence—the rights of women to vote, to have equal access to health care and education and good pay, became paramount matters for preindependence and postindependence feminist groups in India.

In the larger world, women had been disenfranchised, denied rights, and treated as second-rate citizens along with nonwhite populations. Important victories for women's suffrage were won in Europe and then in the United States in the late nineteenth and early twentieth century, respectively. When fighting women and sympathizing men struggled, aligning the many-streamed feminist movements with the quest for civil liberties, other important legal victories followed that sought to protect women from sexual exploitation and marginalization.

Today, feminist epistemology (or the spectrum of theories of knowledge from a feminist perspective) is a wild forest of many life forms, a variety of value orientations about what should matter in theorizing feminist struggles and responses. There is no broad feminist consensus on what is at stake—whether equality with men or diversity—but, as I hope to show, and as I seem to have glimpsed in my pursuit of these hushes, the riddle *the woman* poses is our source of deepest hope in locating new existential settlements. The aroma of the home I seek for you drifts in the air, opening into a finer country—a home only to be found in the deepest woodlands, and for which a queer feminism of the monstrous is required. The story that follows about feminism trades in whispers and outlines. It is partial, broad, and too simplistic an account to even begin to touch on the intricacies of these cultural moments. Ultimately, however, I write of an exhilarating errancy that disturbs the kind of easy feminism I grew up with—the one that merely says women ought to have just as much. It is a material feminism that overturns "nature itself," leaps over fences or spills through, upends the logic of fundamental separation, hints at the inevitability of the grotesque in the regular, and cleaves open a politics that goes beyond equality to something more orgasmic: emergence. Indeterminacy. The preposterous.

$$\cdot \maltese \cdot$$

Mind if I go all nerdy for a while, my dear? Right. I'll assume you nodded an ecstatic yes—your mother's tolerance of my rantings hit zero years ago.

Following Descartes's clinical splitting of reality into a binarism—mind and matter, subject versus object, in here versus out there—the body became a "vexed object," a troubling obstruction in the way of the logical operations of pure rationality. Truth came to be seen as the unvarnished account of the universe, only to be accessed by means that were passionless and disinterested: to understand how the world works, the meaning of reality, the mystery at the heart of flight, the mechanics of light propagation, the pilgrimage of planets, and the strange monoverse that is the human mind, one needed to put away the flesh—the irrational, teenage, recalcitrant wildness of the body—and discipline the self well enough for the pure mind to perceive the faint signals of the truth. Like a Democritean orb, floating in bland emptiness, reality lived in an exclusive space that was difficult to reach. One needed a certain delicateness, a certain detachment to see the real in the midst of the fleeting. And men—white men, to be precise—were especially suited for the task.

Soon, this ontology of distance—this story that our own bodies betray us, that truth is far away, and that nature can only be truly known in certain ways that exclude the participation and contributions of the body and of anything material—became the bed and justification for a gruesome political configuration—a social architecture that preferred pyramids, with white men perched atop the structure and everyone else stuck in the quagmire beneath. Persons from other cultures were thus naturalized or stabilized (both euphemisms for "imprisoned") with some kind of biological essentialism, which supposedly determined their behaviors or explained why they deviated from particular (white) normative practices. The black slave was locked into perpetual servitude because it was their nature to serve masters. Women, seen as passionate, emotional, and weak, also needed the discipline of their husbands. They needed control, a strong hand, or a leash. Their regretful deviations and bodily otherness required the benevolent training and interventions of patriarchy.

A Caucasian gentleman named Samuel George Morton, an early-nineteenth-century "natural scientist" who was a professor of anatomy and earned degrees from prestigious universities, even went so far as to measure cranial capacity of Caucasian, Indian, and Negro skulls—inferring that blacks had diminished capacities for intellectually rigorous work, while Caucasians, created separately by God, were inherently superior to all races. Of course, that puts you—a child of an African father and an Indian-African-Caucasian mother—in a very confusing place, doesn't it?

Smarmy jokes aside, Morton's scientific racism has since been heavily disavowed and criticized for his bias in data collection, manipulated samples, and selective attention to those pieces of data that supported his deeply held prejudices. But even then, the point is not lost that scientific practices and knowledge claims are not immune to prejudice and fatal distortions of the sort that deny the contributions of blacks, of women, or of non-Caucasian balding men—thus perpetuating a power dynamic in the holy name of factual innocence.

Feminists saw how modernism helped produce the painful racial occlusions that were once endorsed by supposedly neutral scientific authorities, and justified disenfranchisement and oppression. When you assert a standard, when you draw a line in the sand, you simultaneously create the conditions for deviation and failure. "Blacks," whose customs and perspectives did not align with European philosophies, were thought to be lesser beings ... lower than Indians on a scale that ultimately and conveniently placed Caucasians at the top. Their shocking employment in the hands of their slave masters and colonial lords, who sought to capitalize on their labor, was legitimized by the ideas that this was what they were created for.

It may be hard for you to understand any of this, Alethea—and I hope that wherever you are, wherever you live right now, you never know that vacant sky to which many have offered a libation of tears, only to be told that the reason for their suffering and the injustices they feel in their bones is a just recompense for their very natures.

Understandably, feminists working in the academic world rejected this nature. They rejected matter, or at least placed more emphasis on the role of language in making reality. In their views, those perspectives that spoke of "womanhood" or moved painfully close to the body's workings were either complicit in constructing a social order that privileged some above others or, at the very least, dangerously at risk of imitating the same essentializing gestures that characterized chauvinistic paradigms.

As such, feminists took their enemies' arrow and turned it back on the modernists; they walked away from the universalizing schemes of modernism, insisting that we pay attention to the disciplining norms, cultural modes, discursive practices, and complex relationships that constructed bodies. In other words, feminists—especially those that latched on to the postmodern denial of reality—said everyone should pay just as much attention to the brushstrokes and the painters more than they did to their masterpieces about "nature."

These feminists described the manners in which long-standing institutions codified power and molded subjects into malleable shapes. They reclaimed emotionality and "irrationality" as legitimate forms of intelligence, and perforated the bloated myth of a "pure" rationality that wasn't already complicated by other forms of knowing. They hit at the fantastical accounts of self-determination and patriarchal permanence provided by modernism—attacking the idea of an essential self that wasn't discursively constructed. They critiqued the "generalized body," carefully developing insights into the particular ways one could no longer speak of "womanhood"—as if that were a single category where all women could be lumped together.

In short, they sought to castrate every phallogocentric ideological and institutional structure that claimed superiority over others on the grounds of nature. To their former lords who opined that nature makes us, they countered: "No, we make nature. And the nature you have constructed serves you to the exclusion of us." It's not difficult to see why there was (and is) a distaste for biology, for the empirical. Arguably the more popular feminist theories are the ones associated with postmodern sentiment and its characteristic abandonment of embodiment and the materiality of the world.[2] The biology of bodies and nature is the battleground evoking fresh traumatic memories of a time we suppose we have succeeded.

Many feminist theorists, seeking to "denaturalize" nature, advanced intricate arguments showing the many "discursive practices through which bodies and matter become intelligible." They placed the emphasis and the burden of causation on the discursive, on epistemology—not ontology. On language, not "material." It was our way of speaking about reality that was more interesting—not reality itself. "Reality itself"? No such thing. To return to ontology (or the study of "reality itself") was to yield ground to the idea that matter—the dead and mechanical thing of Cartesian imagination—had agency. That would be yielding too much. That would be giving in to essentialism and its blindness to context, to culture, and to the dynamics of political complexities—the equivalent of walking back to the scorched soil of previous battles and surrendering to the ghosts of your once-assailants.

None had forgotten how "women were associated with their corporeal reality"—a memory that hinted that "the road to their emancipation [seemed] to involve the removal of the biological dimension of the body."[3]

For the feminists of this epistemology, there was no body as such, nothing essential, just the "discursive formation of embodiment" or the particular ways certain bodies were made concrete. A particular kind of "somatophobia" set in—a morbid fear for the hot burning plate of the brazenly corporeal. And this because "biology all too often comes implicitly to mean an underlying bedrock, inaccessible to analysis ... often equated with unchanging essence."[4]

Frost writes that feminists sought immunity from the activities, processes, and dynamics of the body—and left it out of their analyses of the real.[5] It was either one or the other: either reality was "fixed nature," a machine whose effect was a biological (and behavioral) determinism that cast white males against minorities and women in a sadistic plot of masters and slaves, or there was no such thing as "nature" that was not already "made up" to look beyond reproach.[6]

These critiques, some might say, succeeded in shedding the weight of essentialism. Some might even say they succeeded too well. Today, "feminism" hardly resembles the organized coherence of resistance and the galvanizing concepts for critique that characterized older feminisms. A sort of aversion to grounding themes, to any sort of metanarrative, beats at the heart of the project. Actually, I don't think it can even be said that postmodern feminism has a heart, talk less of being a "project." It isn't one thing. It is this contradictory, pluralistic, antiauthoritarian, absurd "thing" that represents the shifting relationalities of femininity within popular, consumer, late-capitalist, neoliberal culture.[7]

Forged within a fervent consumer culture, held in place by fashion and media fluidity, and tattooed with a feverish individualism and subjectivity, feminism seems to have thrown off its "ism" to allow a form of "anything goes" milieu where empowerment comes in form of mobility, sexual adventurism, and cultural hybridism.[8] Perhaps this same "movement" without edges is partly responsible for the spiritual eclecticism that is inspiring migration to hot-spot sacred places like Tiruvannamalai, a town of many temples 120 miles south of Chennai, where you are very likely to meet white people with flagrant *pottus* on their foreheads, dreadlocks, and spirituality workshops promising clients the potential of summarizing enlightenment in six easy steps.

Identity is a construct—fluid, user-friendly, and multiple, manumitted from foundational moorings. Neoliberal economics actually thrives on encouraging people to change their identities as often as they please, to buy the virtual face of an avatar or remain hidden behind a profile picture. Additionally, there is an intolerance for the binarism implied in notions of struggle, a trend that might account for a "decreased interest in activism," except when it becomes fashionable to hit the streets or identify with a cause. One gets the impression that in unshackling itself from the prudery of modernist essentialism and universalism ... in throwing away the proverbial bathwater, so to speak—postmodernism-allied femininity also throws away not only the baby but the idea of baths as well. Everything is up for grabs. Whereas Rosie the Riveter might have been part of the appropriate iconography of previous generations of feminist struggle, the "new feminism" has no appointed image, no fixed cause, no poster child for its loose federation of concerns: the tongue-sticking-out, goth-nailed, nose-pierced selfie of a self-absorbed millennial is no less authoritative than the intellectual musings of an academic feminist.

One might wonder how postmodernism and postmodern feminism could ever be seen within the same universe as other antihegemonic paradigms, especially since it seems in cahoots with consumerist culture—celebrating everything from Beyoncé to the latest iPhone. How could something so airy and breezy, without heart and suspicious of structure or discipline, pose a threat to oppression? Perhaps the veneer of irony that postmodernism wraps everything with is critique. As Fien Adriaens notes, maybe the fact that postmodern feminism is without foundations, always paradoxical, and without fixed adversary or ally makes it "a potential breeding ground for emancipatory discourses." While she acknowledges that postmodernism can "extend and stabilize" neoliberal practices of elision, she notes that its amorphousness also grants it capacity to "critique and question ... a hegemonic neoliberal consumer culture."[9]

Postmodern concepts suggest we now live in a virtual world of our own making—a world of unequal power distribution, yes, but a world constructed from human comings and goings. There are shadows, but the world casts no shadows of its own. And if it looks like it does, this is only the ventriloquist behind the scenes, working the levers to gain power. Bodies are at the short end of the causal chain, without inherent meanings, and the mere backdrop for the inscriptions of culture.

What escapes postmodern discourse are the problematic stabilities it in fact produces—even when it claims that nothing is still. Even when it claims everything is flotsam, to be retrieved and discarded at will for our Crusoean ends. Falling squarely on its blind spot is a humanistic foundationalism that centralizes and privileges discourse at the expense of bodily contributions. It's easy to miss, but postmodern visuality betrays its deep anthropocentric commitments the closer one leans into it. You could imagine that with more sophisticated camera technologies, with zoom lenses, for instance, we have the ability to adjust focal length and depth. We can zoom in and out, traverse distances without taking a step—and with this focal changeableness it is easy to lose sight of the instigator behind the lens, the one afforded the luxury of permanence.

By centralizing human subjectivity, postmodernism effectively denies the material effects of the world that hosts us and shapes us. And that has real consequences. Perhaps the more visible effects of this "postmodern stretching" is that sooner or later, we face the retribution of the finite elasticity of things: the world snaps back and stings us. That sting is evident in the shadows of our cities, where the invocability of multiple identities and the denial of roots beyond the discursive are creating a feeling of homelessness, of tautological communication without depth,[10] and of estrangement. Young people cast about in the angst of abandonment, seeking belonging in the anonymity of the moment.

The "linguistic turn" from modernism is now being reworked and critiqued in a "turn" to materiality and its many agentic effects. The "new materialisms" embrace interdisciplinary work into the ways culture and nature can no longer be seen as separate; into the way identity and race are both material and discursive; into the way biology is already a matter of history and the discussions about it; into the manner concepts and meaning are material;

into the particular ways justice is not some giant supernatural arc spanning the globe like an ideal we can only ever hope to approximate, but shaped and born in topological openings and closures. And how the very concerns of feminist theory, the "old" anthems that draw us all into the gravitational pull of femininity, to the specificity of female-identified bodies, is also a cry for environment, for healthy economies, for ethically profound relationships with nonhuman others.

While it might be tempting to think of new materialisms as a successor to postmodern feminism, to do so would be to reiterate the dualisms that postmodernism claims to address, but fails to.[11] The startling "re/turn" to the material world that takes the shape and form of the many neo-materialistic theories is not some kind of fourth-wave feminism; neither does it follow from the postmodernization of feminism. Nor does it need to be tethered to a "progress narrative structure"[12] to make its vital contributions about "naturecultures."[13]

It is not post-postmodernism, not a "new" thing that dismisses the old or says, "We are the new philosophies in town, so back off." The popular sense in which we now speak of failing status quos and symptoms of underlying disorders, giving way to a more promising tomorrow or a better world, imbibes that implicit notion of progress and a dialectic of the new, where the previous is banished. In many indigenous worldviews, there is no new that is not old (which is often the reason why babies in Yorubaland are named after recently deceased grandparents, in a gesture that communicates returnings) and no old that is not inexhaustibly new—which is why many materialist feminists advocate we turn to "old" texts, work with the insights of modernism and postmodernism, hesitate to name monumental sociological structures as totalizing, and (perhaps) relinquish the idea that we will arrive at a situation or a world without shadows if only we learn to resolve the problems of today.[14]

For instance, Frost reminds us that:

Constructivism has been tremendously useful for feminist epistemologists in their efforts to denaturalize and politicize knowledge claims that disavow the historicity

*of empirical facts ... [and] as a critical project, constructivism has prompted the
exhaustive search for the mark and agency of the social in any knowledge claim,
a quest not simply to identify the social, linguistic, or cultural dimensions of
perception but also to specify the social and political relations, negotiations, and
practices through which both subjects and objects of knowledge come to be constituted as such.[15]*

If one could think of feminist postmodernism as a wave racing for the
shore in a game of who arrives first and who stays there, then perhaps it
meets an obstacle in the ocean itself, in all her ferocious turnings and twisting and playful involutions. Expansive and enthralling. A roar of nature.
The "material turn" isn't about getting to the shore, it's about obstacles and
finiteness and making queer leaps. It's about a world that snaps back, hisses,
obstructs, and objects. It's about being stuck, about emerging partially, not
fully understanding, not arriving, the rumor of a shadowy core at the heart of
brightest light. Coming down to earth is about being in the mangled middle.

✦

Before I go any further into this thrilling enunciation of a world stranger
than we can imagine—a world the hushes, the dots in my quest to connect
many dots to solve the puzzle of home, led me to revisit in new ways—let me
say a thing or two about obstacles.

When you were two years old, you took me by my little finger and
dragged me out of the house we were staying in while we were in Richmond, Virginia, with your aunt Ifeoma. You wanted to swim in the pool at
the center of the residential estate. That morning, I had made a conscious
decision to let you lead me anywhere you wanted to go. We waved good-bye
to your mother, and left the house—your determined gait pulling us in the
direction of the watery goodness ahead.

When we didn't make a right turn to the pool, I realized you had missed
the way. But an implicit aspect of my promise was to follow your lead,
even if that meant going in the "wrong direction." So you continued to run

ahead—in the direction of a nearby lake, while speaking animatedly about swimming in the pool.

As we approached the lake, you stopped dead in your tracks.

"Remove your shoes, Dada!" you said.

So I did. I liked to walk barefoot so it was just as well. But I didn't expect what was to come next.

"Wear my shoes, Dada!" you said, as if it were a very natural thing for a thirty-year-old man with size 45 feet to wear pink sandals that hardly protected his toes. But, as you already know, I did. And then you slipped your little feet into my own flip-flops, and reinitiated our journey. At this time, I could sense the first restless stirrings of the politics of adulthood, as I struggled with feelings of embarrassment.

Moments later, we were standing by the lake, at its loamy edges, watching the ducks, the faint ripples occasioned by their gentle retreat. We simply stood there. You, by my right hand, just stared at the serene body of water. Small innocent seconds rolled into uncomfortable minutes. At some point, I wondered whether this might be a good time to chip in a fatherly lesson or two, or to connect with you in a deep way—anything to fill the disturbing void of silence that had enveloped us. I tried to talk, but you shut me down. "Dada, don't talk," you said, with the cavalier eminence of a two-year-old. I had promised to let you lead, but I wasn't sure what the joggers nearby were now thinking of the queer voiceless figures standing by the lake.

Then, I heard birds. I am not good at identifying them, but those distinctly avian sounds came wafting through, bending and melting with the wind, ruffling the green leafy protrusions above us. A murmuration of sound, creature, and surprise. It felt sudden—like the arrival of a triumphant gestalt where there were merely bits and pieces of the puzzle. I noticed lichens crawling around a tree, the exuberance of the soil beneath our feet, the quack-quacking of the ducks intent on making themselves heard. It was a soft "a-ha" moment: I noticed that everything is alive. I understood in that very tactile and embodied way that the material world wasn't just a backdrop for human activity, wasn't just static being or template awaiting the ordainment of meaning.

You and I ended up playing after our unexpected libation of silence, decorating our faces and hands with mud, poking little twigs into the wet loamy soil, occasionally interrupted by the leitmotif of quacking around us. We walked back to our apartment like veterans of an exquisite order of things. Neighbors threw quizzical glances at us; I stammered out weak explanations like "she likes dirt" or something else to account for our very dirty appearance. Your mother was even less forgiving, and ordered us to the bathroom.

The stains of your lesson in silence were the only things that didn't wash off that day, and have lingered ever since. I am grateful to you for teaching me how to come to watery edges. Yes, you brought me here first. I am grateful to you for teaching me how to remain there for a while longer than is comfortable. For teaching me a tangential lesson about obstacles.

This is what I learned: that an obstacle is the richest, thickest, densest place in the universe. This is so because it is where things stop and often die, failing to continue on their way. It is where carcasses of hope rot into the ground, inadvertently fertilizing it. It is a place of desperation and longing and roaming ghosts.

This is my way of saying that I think it is not empty. This place—an obstacle—is bursting with activity, with microbial adventures, with dancing generativity, with experiments into dis/continuity, with playful meanings and alchemical shifts, with eloquent invocations and stuttered words. When you meet something fierce, too strong to overcome, too high to climb, too eminent to sidestep, too dark to enlighten, don't take it too personally—you have merely met an antibody, whose sacred task is to challenge you, discombobulate you, disfigure you, and introduce "you" to the strange vastness of your family. A larger commonwealth of becoming. Just as soils chastise seeds, and cocoons imprison caterpillars, obstacles are the universe's hubs of unspeakable creativity, redeeming us from tired victories, from the banality of crossing the finish line, from the soundtrack of getting everything we want, and especially from the hubris of thinking we are in control.

I am learning that a dead end is a beautiful place—partly because I have been there many times before I began these letters to you, as well as in the course of writing them. Dead ends are opportunities to reconfigure our notions of continuity.

In the resistance of bodies and the vibrant materiality of the world, new materialism theorists are heralds of edges. I like to think that some of them had been part of the pilgrimage of the never-ending story inaugurated by postmodernism and constructivism. They had fought back the stabilizing effects of modernist knowledge claims, reclaiming bodies as congealed conversations in an attempt to neuter their mechanized control.

But now at the Alethean edges, a silence brews—a thick silence sewn together with the protest of bodies, with the simmering intentionality and vibrancy of objects. With the stirring of the other-than-human. Among the congregation gathered by the banks, voices start to whisper like the pitter-patter of raindrops on the ground. Karen Barad, holding hands with the others, whispers to herself and to those within earshot: "Language has been granted too much power."[16] *Language has been granted too much power.*

The power of language is considered overbearing in its particular ways of explaining the world solely in terms of linguistic and social constructions. "New materialists" feel language has actually explained the world *away,* making invisible the ways the corporeal is also formative and agential in the world's emergence. Casalini writes that for these authors, it is necessary

> to go beyond the dualism between nature and culture, between the material and the discursive, and between realism and social constructivism. This is possible by imagining nature, objects and nonliving nature, not as static and ahistorical, but ... as agents themselves. Scientific activity cannot be explained on the basis of the separation between subject and object. It calls into question a network of relationships in which each actor (human and nonhuman) plays an active role. Nature and bodies materialize by emerging from an intricate web of interactions between actors and actants.[17]

There is much more at work in the production of reality than the processes and activities of language and politics. Matter also shapes the world; our bodies, dust, eyes, oceans and chairs have a logic of their own, and have effects on what is constituted as real. Casalini writes that we need

> *to go beyond the dualism between nature and culture, between the material and the discursive, and between realism and social constructivism. This is possible by imagining nature, objects, and nonliving nature not as static and ahistorical but ... as agents themselves.*[18]

The dead things around us are not so dead, which is why Alaimo and Hekman write that

> *Nature can no longer be imagined as a pliable resource for industrial production or social construction. Nature is agentic—it acts, and those actions have consequences for both the human and nonhuman world. We need ways of understanding the agency, significance, and ongoing transformative power of the world—ways that account for myriad 'intra-actions' (in Karen Barad's terms) between phenomena that are material, discursive, human, more-than-human, corporeal, and technological. Since the denigration of nature and the disregard for materiality cannot be entirely disaggregated, material feminism demands profound—even startling—reconceptualizations of nature.*[19]

This limits the unvaried application of discursive analysis to everything, and rephrases culture as an aspect of "co-emergence," not the warp and woof of it. A single radioactive heap of waste can have vast political consequences, in the same way a piece of paper is a thinly compressed material made from pulpwood, the microbial activity in heavy dense soil, climate characteristics, the discipline of a farmer, her partner's support, and even the presence (or absence) of particular governmental policies that regulate the felling of trees in their area.

None of this is metaphorical, even though these entwining linkages I have drawn might feel tenuous and overdone. In fact, given that the examples I just provided are hypothetical, I have hardly touched upon the world-implicating complexities involved in the production of a single object—in this case, radioactive waste and a single piece of paper.

The Yoruba people speak of *"ayé,"* loosely translated into the one-tongue as "life"—a poor translation, if you ask me, for what they try to articulate is a mode of causation that is unwieldy, surprising, diffracted, multilinear, ecstatic, and sensuous: where a single eyelash that unplugs itself from its socket and is stepped on by an oblivious human could curse that person with madness. Where a gust of wind contains not only dust and rushed air, but the charged cravings of a rebutted love-stricken admirer. For Yoruba people, especially those "uneducated" ones like Bàbá, one cannot draw too straight a line from cause to effect. Indeed, one cannot even draw a sure unidirectional line from cause to effect, since effect can flow into cause, and—even more startlingly—also because time is not conceived as a single stream flowing from past to future but as a cycle ... a muddy viscous puddle that means the past is amenable to reconfiguration. In a sigh, we—together with multiple others—are part of a web of life, not just stuck on it like a hapless fly-turned-spider-breakfast, but the very web itself in its fluctuations and rich complexity. And movement, the slightest gesture, sends tremors through the veins of our never-ending reiterative becomings.

Many new materialisms coincide with these ideas, and insist that the effort to pry ontology away from epistemology, or to think of matter as removed from the discursive, or to imagine mind as acorporeal, leaves us asunder and closes up interesting and promising new pathways for understanding the universe's multi-complexities.

This is why biologist Donna Haraway began to speak about "naturecultures"—no longer nature versus culture but the entanglement of the twain. Neither an ontology nor an epistemology but an onto-epistemology.

Karen Barad also coined her own neologism to explain just how intimate ontology and epistemology are: ontoepistemology. Neither an ontology nor an epistemology. The effect of that was telling us that ocean and shore are indeed "closer" than their intellectual history of gratings might suggest. Barad speaks about the material-discursive to highlight this entanglement between what we've traditionally taken as irreconcilable: our conversations about the material world (mind) and the material world itself (matter). With another profoundly disruptive formulation: "intra-action" as opposed to "interaction", she makes an argument for the intra-dependence of things. The latter presumes that the world is made up of linear causal modes and preset independent objects with pre-given boundaries, properties, and meanings—objects that later come to "inter"-act in an occasional relationship. Intra-action, on the other hand, turns that picture on its head, showing how relationships precede the objects in that relationship. Objects—be it a laptop, climate change, the idea of determinism, or what "home" means—only come to gain their "thingness" and specificity in the context of a relationship. And, this emergence doesn't happen in a once-and-for-all way. The world is not just an empty container for things, like this jar of toffee sitting on the water dispenser a few feet from me. The world is an ongoing relationship where "things" are constantly rupturing and congealing due to human and more-than-human practices. Intra-action presumes entanglement, not independence.

Take light, for instance. What is its true nature? What magic infuses this seemingly immaterial yet substantial "thing"? I often ask a question to people that meet with me on my teaching tours: is it possible to frame an intrinsic, independent, precontextual definition of light? To arrive at its essence in some final, unambiguous way? To describe what it *really* is as opposed to what it does or its effects? The responses usually range from the tautological "light is that which enlightens" to persons, grasping for words, trying to bodily perform illumination with widened eyes and spread-out fingers. And a quizzical gaze for good measure. Some science-oriented ones might say that light is a wave. Others say it is particulate.

Isaac Newton—the seventeenth-century English mathematician—was one of those who championed (in his book *Optiks*) the idea that light propagation was a matter of traveling particles, little corpuscles spilling into space. Newton was Western science's idea of royalty, so he went largely unchallenged in his views about the nature of light. But there were other notable scientists (such as Christiaan Huygens) who thought that light behaved more like a wave than like little balls. Up until the moment the nineteenth-century

English scientist Thomas Young conducted his inspired double-slit experiment in 1801, there was no one way to sort out this deeply troubling matter—to literally sort out the deep ontology of light. Whether wave or particle. One thing felt sure, though: light was *either* wave or particle. It couldn't be both. Such an idea would have been outrageous to classical physicists.

Young felt if light propagation was wave-like, it would behave like the ripples on surface of water, with opposing waves canceling each other out or reinforcing each other, creating interference or fringe patterns, and so on. His experimental apparatus consisted of a source of light filtered through a pinhole, directed at two slits in a barrier, and captured eventually on a screen facing the barrier. Young expected that when the streams of light from the two slits touched the final screen, if light propagation was wavelike, he should observe interference patterns or alternating ridges of darkness and brightness—but if the corpuscular theory was correct instead, he should see two bands of light directly in line with the slits.

When Young observed the final product, he noticed bands of light or "interference fringes"—confirming, after all, that light was indeed a wave. And that might have been the end of it were it not for the meddling interventions of Danish philosopher-physicist Niels Bohr and his "rival" of sorts, the more popularly known Albert Einstein. More than a century after Young showed diffractive patterns with his experiment, and in a time when the science of infinitesimally small things or quanta was all the rave, Bohr—some of whose philosophies are transposed[20] in Karen Barad's account of a queer world—proposed the abominable to a classically trained Einstein: light, or anything for that matter, has no inherent properties. Light is neither inherently a wave nor a particle. What it "is" emerges from the measurement performed. Change the measuring apparatus and the thing-that-is-measured will change as well. Barad writes up an engaging fictionalized account of the moment Bohr relates his hair-splitting idea to Einstein and, in fact, the rest of the sane world, who know that such things are nonsense:

> *Einstein is getting irate. Bohr insists that using a two-slit apparatus he can show*
> *that with one arrangement of the two-slit apparatus light behaves as a wave, and*

with a complementary arrangement light behaves as a particle. He explains that entities are not inherently "wave" or "particle," and that it is possible to produce wave and particle phenomena/behaviors/performances when the entity in question "intra-acts" with the appropriate apparatus.[21]

Bohr recommends a "which-slit" experiment, or a particular modification of the measuring apparatus that effectively allows an experimenter to observe which slit the photon (a bit of light) passes through. Moved by his quantum theory, he insists that the ability to make that observation will cancel the interference pattern on the screen, showing light to be particulate, not wavelike at all. He notes that under certain conditions light will behave like a wave, while under complementary conditions, light will behave like a particle. Each contingent arrangement excludes its complementary possibility from mattering simultaneously.

(Are you still there, dear? Your mum often rolls her eyes when I start to speak about Bohr and his thought experiment. Don't you abandon me to my devices!)

Einstein is understandably disgusted by the mere thought, because it presents itself to his mind as evidence of a world that is whimsical and mad. He had devoted his capacities to the description of a world that adhered strictly to elegant mathematical laws. Such a world required a fixed and stable ontology. But here, Bohr was suggesting some kind of "ontological indeterminacy" to reality, a weirdness at the heart of everything, a world without conservative values or immutable foundations. A spooky place. As the scene fades, Barad's dramatized Einstein reacts:

So what you are saying is that the very nature of the entity—its ontology—changes with the experimental apparatus used to determine its nature? Or worse, that nothing is there before it is measured, as if measurements conjure things into existence?[22]

Though Bohr and Einstein did not have the wherewithal to operationalize their thought experiment, hundreds of experiments have been conducted ever since demonstrating that Bohr was right. For example, in 1991, Leonard Mandel co-published a paper reporting his which-slit experiment.[23] The paper itself looks like the doodle-ridden napkin of a bored preteen in a diner, what with its equations and diagrams. Mike May cuts through its inaccessibility to write about the confirmatory observations of Mandel and his team:

In essence, they generated two beams of light derived from a laser and caused them to interfere, which is a wavelike phenomenon. But if they used an arrangement that allowed the path of the light to be determined, the interference disappeared, whether or not this determination was actually made.[24]

Let me put all of this another way, using objects that might be more recognizable to you. Balloons and balls have been some of your favorite things to play with—often to my irritation because you often leave them scattered about. Let's say we play a game when we both agree to dispose all these balls—a hundred or more—by tossing them at a freshly painted wall through the window. We do it blindfolded—just for the fun of it. When we open our eyes, we'd expect that most of the balls would have gone through the window and hit the wall. We'd expect to see the stain marks of the balls on the part of the wall that is directly perpendicular to the window.

The results shouldn't be markedly differently if, instead of one window, we threw away all the balls—all at the same time with a heave-ho!—through two windows facing our painted wall. Like before, when we open our eyes, we'd expect that some balls didn't go out of the room at all, but hit the doorposts. And we'd expect that those that made it through one window or the other formed twice the previous pattern: two clumps of stains on the wall directly opposite the windows. But what if instead of two neat ridges of stains, we find ten ridges showing an undulating pattern of stains, as if we threw the balls through ten windows? We'd conclude that something strange was happening—for how could discrete balls make wavelike patterns on a wall?

So what you might then decide to do is to throw each ball, one at a time, to see what happens. So we cover our eyes again, take a ball, and throw it in the direction of the two windows. We don't pick another ball until we are sure the previous one has made its mark on a surface. What if we did this, one after the other, each newly launched ball following the previous after a couple of seconds—and then removed our blindfolds … only to find the same outrageous pattern? If I know both your grandmas well enough, I can bet my dimpled cheeks they'd start to pray out of fright.

But it gets even stranger. What if—in a bid to resolve this fiasco—we ask one of your grandmas to stay by the windows, making sure she protects her face with a helmet or visor so the balls don't knock out her teeth? Her job would be to simply observe which window each of the balls are going through—and not to interact with them. We take the balls and start throwing again—all at once or one by one, it doesn't matter—and then we open our eyes. Your grandma is really praying now. She's spooked. We move closer to the windows and look at the wall beyond them. Now, instead of the many fringes like before, we see two clumps of stains where the balls struck. It's almost as if the balls knew grandma was watching, and then decided to behave differently.

Well, what Mandel saw (which Bohr predicted to be the case) with his "balls" was exactly this strange complementarity. When the balls—sorry, particles—are sent through without any knowledge of which slit they are headed through, their instruments measured an interference pattern consistent with a wave's rippling effects. But when a detector was added, a noninterfering detector designed to note which slit the particles go through, the registered pattern was consistent with particle behavior. The implications? Not that matter is illusory, but that matter is fluid, ontologically undetermined, and always co-emergent with the measurements made. The nature of nature depends on the measurements made. Nature is not natural.

Mandel's experiment is one out of many that sides with Bohr: ontology is nonessential. It's very strange, actually: "things" only emerge in the context of intra-acting relationships. This fact is demonstrably compelling for very little things, but it queers the line that supposedly locks away this strangeness to the quantum world, for if everything spills through, if bodies are not stoic mannequins with glossy exteriors and hard ontologies, then everything is entangled. Man and woman. Tree and mountain. The chemical secretions of a virus and the market price fluctuations of a commodity. The particular biological (and ghostly) incarnations of dinoflagellate *Pfiesteria piscicida* and the fishing economy of an eastern American coastal town. The world is a mangle of streams, a constantly unceasing, unfolding flow of co-emergent practices and co-enactments that does not privilege ontology over episte-mology or the other way around. It is only by virtue of intra-acting focal practices (which are not necessarily human) that things gain resolution and definition. We therefore cannot define a thing apart from the relationships it is part of, and to attempt to extricate a thing, to find its essence apart from the processes that make it, is merely to introduce different processes. Nothing emerges as a "thing" except within the stream of becoming.

Barad's notion of "material-discursivity" highlights the ways appa-ratuses produce material beings and intelligibility while simultaneously excluding other productions. This is a defining feature of Bohr's principle of complementarity as well: things do not come preinstalled with meaning. The meaning of a thing or its intelligibility is also constituted diffractively to the exclusion of other possible meanings. Computers, consumers, and capitalism only make sense because of the particular social-political-scientific-ethical-material circumstances that render them intelligible.

This is the hallmark of Barad's "agential realism," then: not only that everything is entangled—both matter and meaning, both subject and object, both inside and outside—but that things derive their meaning, material-ization, intelligibility, and physical characteristics from "agential cuts" co-enacted by human and nonhuman agencies. In other words, what it means to be human, for instance, is not set in stone in any final sense—as one would expect to be the case if we were living in a Cartesian universe.

To be entangled is not simply to be intertwined with another, as in the joining of separate entities, but to lack an independent, self-contained existence. Existence is not an individual affair. Individuals do not preexist their interactions; rather, individuals emerge through and as part of their entangled intra-relating. Which is not to say that emergence happens once and for all, as an event or as a process that takes place according to some external measure of space and of time, but rather that time and space, like matter and meaning, come into existence, are iteratively reconfigured through each intra-action, thereby making it impossible to differentiate in any absolute sense between creation and renewal, beginning and returning, continuity and discontinuity, here and there, past and future.[25]

As if possessed by my own ancestors, elders whose bonfire narratives about a universe too intricate to be at the mercy of humans were snuffed out by the arrival of ships and mirrors and gunpowder and Bibles, Barad's exposé on queer matter disturbs our commonsense accounts of reality, and speaks of the world as a gushing series of intersecting practices that spill into the supposedly "other," a breaching of boundaries … a world that strays from the Cartesian logic of quid pro quo causality. A world where relata (or "things") and their properties emerge from relationships, and not the other way round. A world of co-becomings so penetratingly deep that it leaves in tatters the Newtonian myth of independent objects, and the myth that proclaims humans to be ontologically unique, separate from animals and environment, and in control.

Depth after enthralling depth, we would not have "arrived" at the heart of the matter, that fabled "fountain" of truth—for reality is a hesitant allegory, a precocious child beholden to no particular tune, and with no final lessons. Even the manic search for meaning is itself a clever ruse, and the finding … a fool's convenience. The hole goes even deeper—and yet it is not the kind of depth that "arrives," it is a depth that presses on, loops up away from the ground, and takes flight into the air—its journey tracing out the majestic arc of a fathomless, uncircumcised circle.

What tugs at our strings is a reimagination of things, not as objects, but as participants. And what goes along with this resacralization of things is a redescription of the "human" as a "becoming," not a final product. A doing, not a noun. An embodied gerund in a sentence of gerunds whose final meaning is always yet to come. As such, *we* do not have language (language is not a property); *we* do not think except with others (intra-thinking!); memory is not a mysterious effluvium floating somewhere in the brain. Old scientific efforts to locate essential human attributes and functions within the "human person" fail to account for the incredible complexity and influence of what we like to call "the environment." Today, acknowledging that complexity, commentators write about "mangled objects," "flat ontologies," "a democracy of things," "intra-action," and "vibrant materialities" to hint at this rupturing at the heart of our ideas about the world.

Before you came into the scene, I had nerdish sci-fi fantasies of a posthuman future—I do hope you do not live there now—where different and bizarre assortments of man-machine assemblages are possible, and the meaning of the word *human* becomes radically different because of the combinatory agencies of life-sustaining technologies, perhaps due to an environment that is so hostile to life that one cannot perform simple biological functions we take for granted today. Taking the dreadful vision farther, I have often tried to imagine the legal ramifications of defining what a human is in this imaginary world: would their dystopian courts still consider a defendant human if he had all his legs and arms surgically removed, and if he depends on a metal bipedal frame? What if all his body parts but his head were biomechatronic? Could a robot crab that demonstrated sentience, humor, and all other frailties associated with "humanness" pass for a human? Is a brain in a vat—sustained by life-giving fluids—still human? Why or why not?

Where does being human stop and being animal begin? What impenetrable cosmic barrier prohibits one from the other? Where does the "self" stop and the environment begin? When does a man become machine or a cyborg? Is an old man with a pacemaker halfway to being a cyborg? Does Craig Lewis, a fifty-five-year-old amyloidosis patient in 2011, who lives without a heart and a pulse, and for whom Texan doctors built a humming "continuous flow" device largely from homemade materials, still have the right to rule so sharp a line between himself and his environment?[26] Between the calm smartphone device and the obsessed flurry of thumbs and glazed look of a modern teenager, who is the user and who is the tool? At what point is a fetus gestating in the mother's womb considered a baby? At what exact moment do a few grains of sand, being dropped to the ground one grain after another, become a heap?

Where do "we" draw the line in the sand?

Because we are immersed in *a world of doings*—where "things" are performances lacking central essences—raising such questions becomes interesting. I want to say that very carefully: we are immersed in a world of doings, which is to say that we are the world's doings. Again the world isn't a container of objects, but a differential flow of performative becomings. A stone has no "essence"; it is as much a doing as is a "human being"—a doing that tugs at the whole web. But again, if everything is entangled, does this mean there are no distinctions? What agential realism suggests is that the lines in the sand are constantly being redrawn, not fixed: differences between humans and nonhumans, between objects, between being at home and being adrift, are the constant productions of multiple "material-discursive" forces. Resolutions in the cumbersome tapestry of entanglement are locally enacted—that is, things gain their thingness in very specific intra-actions, but they never do this in a final way. Where Descartes cut cleanly through things, thus essentializing separation, we come to notice a lot more happening than empty gaps should permit. In a differentially entangled world, separation is never totalizing. It is not something to solve.

What new materialisms point to, then, is a different understanding of matter. A dynamic, vital, agential notion of matter that is far from the clockwork dormancy of Cartesian matter.

Let's breathe a moment.

Remember that feminist theory refused to cede ground to modernist epistemology because the theorists were (rightly) wary that such a move might allow the "body" to become a Trojan vector for essentialism, determinism, and their political corollaries: sexism, racism, colonialism, and ecocide. If matter, this reliquary of postmodern disgust, were allowed to gain primary status, if it crashed upon the shore first, it would undo the great advances feminists had made in undercutting the foundations of a political arrangement that justified suffering on the grounds of nature. So they swung their side of the seesaw way too high, propped it up so it never came down again, and nailed matter's side of the seesaw to the floor. What feminism's antiessentialism did not anticipate is a description of matter in nonessential ways—a description that ennobles matter with its own vitality and dynamics that are not derived from human culture. Frost writes that the "new materialists"

> *consider matter or the body not only as they are formed by the forces of language, culture, and politics but also as they are formative. That is, they conceive of matter or the body as having a peculiar and distinctive kind of agency, one that is neither a direct nor an incidental outgrowth of human intentionality but rather one with its own impetus and trajectory.*[27]

Feminist new materialists like Karen Barad are advocating for the reclamation of matter as agential, and the dissolution of the binary configuration of the world promulgated by Descartes.

That matter turns, beats, moves, wrestles, swaggers, resists, intends, persists, writhes, experiments, and summons might be a shocking thing to accept to the modern mind—because this suggests, rather rudely, that matter isn't as mindless or as banal as we think. As we *need* to think. Such a proposal is reminiscent of an old panpsychism, which postulates that some kind of proto-consciousness inhabits all objects, making even the most banal everyday item "aware." While some new materialists are willing to accept some kind of speculative panpsychic theorization about the vitality of the corporeal, others take this general curiosity about the inner life of things as evidence that the tide is turning: matter is coming "back" to reckoning.

We are used to thinking that the world swirls around us, that the quotidian movements of objects around us follow tedious empty laws while we gaze out from our passive sentience, free-willed and untethered. We suppose that to know the world properly we can assume some unmoving stance and gaze *out* at it, as if knowledge is gained in such static ways. We seem to have had plenty of success as a result of thinking of the world in this way too: we've constructed impressive cities; we've conquered the mechanics of motion and can move at terrific speeds; we've gone to the moon and back; we daily straddle virtual worlds, and reconfigure the fundamentals of hyperspace with the twiddling of restless thumbs; and, with scientific advances in biotechnology, it is now possible literally to engineer bodies and produce recombinant proteins and chemicals useful to our militarized consumer frameworks. We have proven time and time again that life is a matter of human achievements, an instance of teleological movements from the unsophisticated to the sophisticated. And the way we have done this is by applying vibrant mind to dead passive matter. So why this uncouth idea that the corporeal is more than it is, that the chair I sit on to write these letters to you is anything more than a dead mesh of atoms? Why say chairs are intentional? Why deny that the world's sole agency is human? That we are alone?

The next letters will dwell more fondly with these inquiries. For now, I hope it suffices to say that we are a companion species. The presumption that we can act or do act unilaterally, in any instance, can no longer be sustained given our troubling lack of independence.

It's simple, really. If I were to ask you what part of your body "sees," you might point to your eyes. And that would be true—but it wouldn't be completely true. There's more. There are preposterous connections to be made from there: for instance, your eyes cannot "see" if there is no occipital lobe at the back of your brain to process the trans-electrochemical signals relayed by your retinal cells. And the ensuing cerebral activities, shrouded in the dark, wouldn't be possible without the support your skeletal system gives to your brain. Neither would seeing or brain activity be possible were it not for the vertebral and internal carotid arteries that supply blood to nourish your brain. Furthermore, the blood transported through arteries is co-constituted by the foods we ingest, which are in turn delicately predicated on the health of the environment—which is always subject to and a shaper of politico-scientific matterings. Seeing is not a property of your eyes, any more than mud prints are a property of mud. "It," for the time being, is a product of material practices (and meaning-making practices) that extend beyond the conventional boundaries of our bodies or minds. A larger web of intricate relationships make seeing possible, and define what it means. And it doesn't stop there—but you hopefully get the gist of the matter, which is that the world is queer, a mangled, cat-cradling field of ongoing entanglements.

There are no easy "causes" or definitive "effects"; the line does not proceed unambiguously from point A to point B. Strayings, hidden plots, and spooky actions from a distance (in the words of Einstein) are part and parcel of this world. Not that there are normal things and queer things, but that all "things" are already queer, so that I wouldn't be incorrect to insist that the world is made of surprise.

The anthropocentrism that looks out on the world and says "*we* did this!"— including the more tolerable kind that looks out on the so-called Anthropocene (where human-led activity is so grossly consequential and disruptive for the planet's health that it rivals other geohistorical periods on the registers) and sadly mutters "we did *this*"—denies the significance of the other-than-human in the world's emergence. The closer we look, the more we find that we never act alone: every small gesture is a generation of the collective. Every small gesture is already cooked in a cauldron of many spoons, stirred by things whose names we can pronounce, and other things that are not quite nameable. Every small gesture is already a compost heap of a million critters. Little wonder some advocate that the humanities be renamed as the "humusities"—from "humus" (meaning "earth" or "ground").[28] The "human" is a carnival of nonhuman doings; it is, to use Karen Barad's term, a posthumanist performativity that shapes the world, allocates agency, and troubles boundaries. Like dust.

We are fundamentally porous and promiscuous. This is the world we live in—a carnival of the unexpected, of the irregular, the grotesque, or monstrous bodies—where the hard and cold lines that distinguish you from me, us from trees, trees from economics, and economics from whale shit are blurry, leaky, and wet. Our own bodies are populated by trillions of other bacterial cells in their own becomings, but these cells do not live "on" you, or with you, or through you. They *are* you: they are necessary to your body's ongoing survival. You couldn't be human without these alien nonhumans performing your body, or without so many other intra-acting entanglements that breach the fences between you and your environment. These overlapping bodies, pressed together in this strange material world characterized by a "horrifying kind of intimacy," make it impossible to make a once-and-for-all cut between where I stop and where you begin, or where life stops and death triumphs, or where matter gallops forward and mind allegedly tugs on the reins. It is in this sense we are monsters. We are one and many. You are only yourself through all others.

Brian Onishi concedes that "reason and science have done as much to conceal our relation to nature as provide insight into the working of nature." Monstrosity—our entanglement with everything—"is a story of borders and bodies that are open and fluid, a maddening insistence that we are always effected by the terroir of place. It discloses the mutual constitution of the material world by articulating nature as simultaneously an alien organism and intimate companion."[29] A dangerously beautiful movement of never-still edges.

As such, while we might say that the Wright brothers invented manned flight, a thicker account would want to draw our attention to the history of experimentation in aerodynamics, the flow of particular learnings and situated practices necessary to successful flight, the crucial contributions of materials for the plane, the impediments posed by geoclimatic effects, and the specific social milieu that made the possibility of flight an intelligible goal. In short, "agency is cut loose from its traditional humanist orbit. Agency is not aligned with human intentionality or subjectivity … [but is] larger than what liberal humanism proposes."[30]

Agency is acting. Agency is effects. The baker kneads the dough, but the dough organizes the baker's posture, disciplines his approach, conditions his body, and resists his advances. Where do we allocate agency, then? Who acts and who is acted upon? In the coordinates of humanism, agency is intrinsically a property of the human—the rest of the world is just mechanics. We attribute agency to human beings because we suppose we have curious things called "intentions" which precede action. However, this easy causality equation that traces out a firm trajectory from human intentions to concrete realities does not account for human porosity and immersion in a nonhuman world of multiple vitalities that also have effects. In the case of the baker and his dough, both act upon each other—in the same way today's smartphones are not just tools, but users. Neither needs intentionality to explain its effects. Our own bodies do astonishing things that do not fall within the domain of our control: we blink, break wind, burp, get tired, and feel a spectrum of affective states very often without intending them. It seems our bodies have minds of their own, and "we" are only along for the ride.

Is this a way of easing oneself out of responsibility for, say, the impact of industrial activity on climate and environmental well-being? No, it is a way of deepening it—because to so summarily assign blame and pin an entire upholstery of multiple events to a single factor, or an essential substrate working behind the scenes, is to further distance ourselves from the world's happenings and—intentions notwithstanding—reduce the world to separable parts where our technological mastery is its main driver. It is to strip matter of its own desire, will, intention, and movement so that it doesn't present an impediment to our concerns.

It is with this sense that we come to some understanding that to say "We placed a man on the moon" or "We have built a city" or "Humans are the major cause of climate change" is to centralize the human, and to deny the material-discursive contributions and conditions that make such statements even comprehensible.

Barad's contributions to feminist theory—especially as they emerged from her engagements with Bohrian physics-philosophies—show how very little things, quantum things, speak valiantly of a carnival world. A world of hard facts, yes, but a world that dances. *Waltzes* would be better to say. This is not the arbitrary world of postmodern lore, or the mechanical world of modern fantasy, but an emergent world that presents real constraints and real limitations—and yet is never closed to emergence. This material world isn't the one of Democritean wet dreams. We live in, and are produced by, a celebratory, orgiastic, festive, teenage, promiscuous, and downright perverse world that offers no safe grounds for those that propose an essentialized nature as their ultimate reason for lording it over others.

When Barad wrote about Thomas Young's nineteenth double-slit interferometer test to determine the nature of light, I imagine she must have

gasped ... for what she saw wasn't a clunky assemblage of things following previously decreed laws in a blind zombie-like fashion. Something else
is going on: something that calls into question everything we think we know
about how the world works. And indeed *something is going on*. Other feminist materialist scholars like Donna Haraway, Rosi Braidotti, Susan Hekman,
Vicki Kirby, Elizabeth Grosz, Myra Hird, and Stacy Alaimo contribute various
ways to rehabilitate our notions of matter—effectively decentering humanist
notions. But what does any of what they say mean for my mother, mean for
your mother? Mean for you? How does this address the initiating question of
home and place? I think the grander message is that the world is now open
for play, and yet closed off seductively ... and that in this playground there
are mysteries and beings and other presences (and absences) that totally reca-
librate the logic of our quests so that the questions to ask about the future,
about our lives, about living well, might not even be here yet for the asking.
There are hints of an invitation here in this ecstatic redescription of feminism:
to stand still in the face of a monster, warts and all, and recognize ourselves.

✦

Taking the plunge off this cliff, from the classical vision of a Crusoean pilgrim marooned on a brute pile of oblivion to a vision of shared vitality where
the pilgrim realizes he isn't alone and has never been alone, is not only difficult but fraught with troubling implications for our quest for home. Things
aren't suddenly okay because we are coming to see—with help from feminist new materialisms—that the room is crowded with others. Others who
can resist, object to, and disrupt our plans to seek out new worlds. Others
who can stand in the way of new homes and new ways of thinking about the
rising sun, the yielding ears of corn, and the sleepy-eyed gaze of the moon.
Entanglement is the milieu of monsters.

In the course of the years since I visited Bàbá, I have learned many
things—some of which did not want to be learned. I still remember the
mischievous grin on his face as I left his shack—the mask of a trickster,
whose frozen grin could have been a blessing or a wordless curse. However,

underneath the mask I sensed an elder—in the same way I came to know Karen Barad as an elder—who truly found it fascinating that an old Christian boy had come to him to consult with the shadows of his ancestors, and who wanted me to succeed on my quest for new ways of thinking.

But there were many moments when, I confess, I felt the urge to give up on this quest. It hasn't been neat, swift, and tidy, as I had hoped it would be—something that might have been over and done with in the time of a week or a month. It hasn't played out that way. I am not finding answers as such—just new questions. Traces of questions. I still do not know what it means to be at home—or even how to ask the question in a way that makes my heart beat faster.

To be sure, I still continue to see hushes occasionally—terrible new species of the repulsive critters. Flightless ones, horned ones, smelly ones, and some that look like the stain made by a nylon bag filled with ink and dropped twenty feet to the ground. No one talks about them still, even here in India. However, coming across a trail of hushes isn't the same thing as encountering the ten that Bàbá asked me to assemble for the ritual. Once, I tried to pick up four in a row: these ones looked like pink fairy armadillos. They followed each other snout to rear-end along the side of a rough and uneven sidewalk outside the only barbershop I patronized in Chennai. They were black and featureless, with some fur running along their sides. They were too small to be rats and too big to be roaches, but a thousand times more repugnant for reasons I haven't learned to examine yet. It had been a while since I saw a hush, so I rushed at them. They didn't even increase their pace or scatter across the street as ants in a food line would do when they sense an interruption. I got two, as many as my trembling hands could carry, twice as many as my sudden embarrassment could accommodate. One wriggled in my palm, the other was just eerily still. I might have stuffed them in my jeans pockets if they were large enough. They weren't. And my repulsion was steadily rising past my bodily threshold of disgust. It was no use. I placed them on the ground, wiped my hands on my jeans, and walked away—swearing to my misfortune.

So far, I have five out of ten (how I caught the fourth and fifth hushes—in the space of writing this letter—is the subject of the next note). The ritual is its own force, and will not be hurried or rushed or bullied into the plot points of my tender convenience. There is no other way to explain it except to say that I feel different ... *called* ... when the right hush slithers my way—or is handed to me, as was the case with Barad. And then, a question becomes lucid—and sort of pierces the tranquil surface of the familiar, presenting itself to me as a mermaid would do to a sailor lost at sea. Still, I do not fully understand why the ritual requires hushes: my theory is that they are bringers of questions related to my petition at the shrine. Maybe the last hush, the tenth, will bring the answers to questions I do not even know how to ask yet—or, at the very least, coincide with a deep discovery that will help put this journey into context. For the time being, these letters to you—taken up soon after I licked the first two hushes at Kutti's slum—are the one way I can make sense of this strange journey and reach you across perplexing space-time.

Do you remember the Bath Monster, dear? The gruff-voiced towel-clad figure that waddled around the bed like a penguin, and took you to the bathroom on many mornings—and sometimes just before bedtime? Every time you scowled at the invitation to have a bath, I'd summon the Bath Monster, who would conveniently appear when I was "missing." All I needed for a complete transformation was a towel, a limp, and a lisp. When I puttered into the room, your eyes ... they would chuckle, in that way that told me you knew it was me underneath the towel but wanted to play along. I knew this because I peeped out the side of the folds to see how you were reacting. I would pick you up, giggling and squealing, and then balance you on my shoulder. You'd be quiet, your face frozen into a heartbreakingly beautiful smile, as I gently put you back on your feet at the bathroom's entrance. I'd ask you to close your eyes, count to ten, and wish the monster away. As you did, I'd hastily toss away the towel, then turn to meet the merest of joys in your face. You loved the monsters I created, but you liked that I came back when they outlived their welcome. In the years to come, I would teach you how the monsters never did go away, and that when one got to the heart of the matter, we all are monsters too. The dragons that breathe fire in the distance are no less monstrous than we already are. To put it differently, a monster is not the exception to the rule; a monster is the rule without exception.

You didn't go to school like your cousins and your friends, but your mother and I took your education seriously—especially your education in monsters or in alterity (the state of being different). I remember being so proud of you when you—just three years old—went up to an old lady who lived on the Chennai street outside the barbershop where I got my hair cut, and talked with her, eventually bowing your head a little so she could touch you and bless you.

For us, it was important that you learn to respect the outcast, the broken, and those rendered inappropriate by particular regimes of power; we hoped you'd learn to notice the "other" within, and that everything touches the other—in unholy matrimony. In striving to make you a home, we sought to introduce you again and again to a sensuous world, a mischievous world that is full of surprise, a troubling world nonetheless—a realm where the monstrous was a signal that there was something else at work ... something calling for attention. Even now, with you here at this sandy threshold, I encourage you to pick up a pebble, a rock or the remnants of kelp littered about. Anything will do.

Look how things sprout from other things. How nothing is itself all by itself—or without the contributions of other things. When you happen upon a flower, especially one whose otherworldly beauty and feminine fragility contrast sharply with its less endearing environment, you might immediately treat it as this localized "thing," as an object—one deserving of admiration—but an "object" nonetheless: removed, unique, separate, and even audacious. What our linguistic conveniences blind us to is how that very flower is no more distinguishable from the dirt, the erratic weather, the traffic of pollen bearers that come from far off, the blazing sun, and even the occasional imprint of a boot worn by an uncharitable tourist, than a wave is distinguishable from the sea.

In this sense, we couldn't even say that the flower is "part" of the environment—that is admissible, but it seems clunky and mechanical, and more importantly, it lacks aesthetic appeal. We need a different metaphor. Perhaps we could say that the flower is the environment itself in rapturous dance; that the flower is a symptom of its ecosystem, or that the environment "flowers" (treating the noun as a verb—as surely Mr. Watts would have delightedly approved of). And all we would be hinting at is a "new" paradigm of thought—one that inaudibly recognizes how everything is connected; how nouns are "verbs in masquerade"; how the "other," the "strange," and the "alien" are a sibling emanation of the "same" process constantly exfoliating from the ineffable; how truth is impossible, and sincerity, insincere; and how what we "really" are defies notions of size, hues, grades of quality, origin, and destiny.

The world is mutually infectious, an orgy of touching. Like turning on the light to see the darkness better, or changing the nature of a photon merely by peeping at how it interacts with obstructions, you cannot approach any one part of "the world" and walk away intact. You cannot witness it without being stained by it. There is no privileged perspective, no lofty body afloat over the mangled reaches of her carnality. But there is more: it is not that we can avoid being in touch; we can't—for we ourselves are produced in this ungodly ontology of irreducible compromise. This is the red-toothed, Pan-horned, cloven-hoofed, lava-forked fear that haunts our present practices within nature or our institutions of escape: that we are the seething mass of pungency we have quarantined away from view. And that even perched atop our whitewashed steeds of superiority and moral nobility, we never really left the ground.

Like unruly children in a classroom, no "thing" stays still and as disciplined as we would like it to be. Hard at work creating the world, God inscribes an irrefutable equation for multiplicity on the bodies of all living beings by causing everything to appear in twos: a creature and its less prestigious helper companion. The binary is thought to be locked into the scheme of things; you are either male or female. It's an Aristotelian law: a thing cannot be itself and not-itself at the same time. One stands at an irreparable distance from the other. And like east and west, never the twain shall meet.

Once in a while, however, it seems the twain do meet in the middle, with perverse combinatory effects that bewilder the careful taxonomies of the modern tinkerer. A woman sprouts a six-inch-long beard; a young man becomes pregnant by artificial insemination; a five-thousand-year-old male yew tree, old enough to be quite set in its ways, undergoes a sex change and begins sprouting berries; bdelloid rotifers, microscopic leech-like organisms (too small for human eyes to define) and *Timema* stick insects defy the sex modes altogether—remaining both sexless and prolific—or swinging into whatever sex mode they want. In other cases, things do stuff they "shouldn't"—stopping us in our tracks with the ponderous eminence of a gasp: monkeys mating with dogs; sea slugs producing chlorophyll (as only plants *should* do); brittle stars intelligently responding to environmental threats without the use of brains; orcas conducting experiments on human scientists; the future affecting the past; or, in the study of very small things like electrons, particles *speculating* about what it means to be at home. I suppose it suffices to say that the world seems to be replete with things that stray away from fixed categories, things that appear to go contra naturam, defying the supposedly immutable laws of reality.

When things melt past their assigned boundaries, when they touch each other across the wide ontological canyons that divide them, we name those resulting things "monsters." Monsters are the stuff of nightmares. Monsters are a queering of categories, a disturbance of purity. There is not a greater scandal to the modern thinker, who is still faithful to the Renaissance's quest for pure universal categories, than when a thing—supposedly tranquil in eternal light and beyond reproach—*moves*. Our many social, political, and literary histories are replete with things moving into things, things doing perverse things, becoming the occasion for yelps of horror and hysterical recapitulations of doctrines of holiness. A once-man reconstructs his body with estrogens and antiandrogens, and transforms into a woman. Splayed flesh meets bone fragments and metal and coursing electricity and wild ambition and thus becomes Frankenstein's monster—angry and seeking; the Yoruba playwright Ola Rotimi absolves the gods in his play *The Gods Are Not to Blame* when Odewale, the tragic protagonist, commits the ultimate abomination and, unbeknownst to him and everyone else (save an old messenger), kills his father, marries his mother, and becomes a father to four of his own siblings.

In response to accounts like these, we recoil in horror and repulsion—spitting out the aftertaste of the revolting stuff on our tongues. We fortify our foundations and raise the walls a few more inches, installing soldiers and searchlights at the tops. The alarms echo through the neighborhoods, the gong sings in the village square as we ship the decadent ones to faraway killing fields to be ended. Within our fences, we start to sigh: we have driven out the heathen from the Holy of Holies. Now we can relax in our consanguineous spotlessness.

Except that alterity (or radical otherness) has never been successfully excluded or mastered. Sooner or later, we will notice yet another demoniac infiltration, another monster sprouting from the cleanliness within: our searchlights will burn with greater ferocity, its sweeping gaze scanning the grounds for a speck that shouldn't be there. This time, the light will settle on the least expected place: us. But even more scandalous than the fact that we are vectors for the monstrous is the observation that monsters are not occasional anomalies that appear when the moon is blood-red, or when a crazy scientist retreats into his fusty enclave to debauch the holy order of nature. Something deep and troubling is happening at the very "heart" of the world. Something that is not merely occasional or frequent. Monsters keep the world fresh; to the one who supposes that things are settled, that forms are given, that the road is clear, monsters spring a surprise—opening the new in the belly of the old.

Indeed, Lovecraft's Azathoth is the all-powerful monster whose sleep dreams up reality itself. In turning to the edges, to madmen, and to "the invisible," I supposed I might learn how to meet the universe halfway, and how to answer the call of Leviathan—the ecology of monsters beyond atom and story. I suppose the same might be true for you. Home lies in the direction that strays away from the logic of fixed answers. You will have to learn how to walk off the beaten path that snakes into the dark forest—the one that safely leads out. Meeting the "something that calls" cannot be on your own terms. You might walk a whole day, or spend a lifetime entangled with thick bushes and tree branches without anything to show for it. If you wait there, if you are "still," she might approach you. This "other woman." I speak of the mother of monsters, the one who calls, or Leviathan—who, according to some, also goes by another name: Lilith. *The other woman* whose ghost leaves traces across the length and breadth of this letter—nodding gently to the expositions on entanglement. The mysterious lady of the house—lately gowned—slowly comes down a flight of stairs to greet her slack-jawed guests.

✦

Take a bow, Lilith. Or don't. In any case, meet my daughter.

Perhaps no other mythological character has exerted such an influence on popular culture in my time as the purported first wife of Adam, Lilith. She is a product of many cultures, harking back to early Sumerian and Babylonian tales about demon-lovers, wind spirits and evil temptresses, whose breasts are filled with poison, not milk. She wanders across arid plains, also not yet at home. In the matrices of rabbinical imagination, her feet are not at rest. Talmudic references to her are few and sketchy, echoing earlier Babylonian images of her as an embodiment of unwholesome sexual practices. But an abiding interest in her story bemoans the inadequacy of text and the poverty of orthodoxy. She appears in fleeting traces, showing up by name only once in the canon—yet exerting enough of a force to disturb its storied eminence and confound the neat storyline of redemption. She is sprinkled in anonymous satirical writings (like the Alphabet of Ben Sira, circa 800 CE), and she takes on a legendary status in the Zohar, the foundational book of Jewish mystical thought—Kabbalah (the concealed part of the Oral Torah).

Stories about Lilith predate the Judaic accounts, harking back to Sumerian and Mesopotamian figures of a venerated goddess of fertility, who was worshipped, prayed to, and celebrated when there was a rich harvest. Jewish rabbis writing in the Zohar and the Ben Sira books, however, tell a strangely negative tale about Adam's first wife. They first begin by implying that Eve wasn't the first woman at all. That honor belongs to Lilith. Fashioned from dust (or more specifically, grime and muck—a notable distinction that is, in some quarters, influential in the telling of the legend), much like Adam, Lilith is described as abusive and needlessly contentious in matters that should be without controversy. She and Adam get into numerous fights—like who should lead or who should be on top during sex—and Adam has a hard time bottling up the volcanic rage of his wife. One day, her rebellion erupts and she leaves Adam—sprouting wings by some unnamed power and sailing away from the Garden of Eden like a winged serpent, just after uttering the hidden name of God. Adam, broken and dejected, cries to his maker to help him revitalize his dead marriage. God gives in to Adam's irritating pleas, and sends three angels to retrieve the erring runaway bride at the eponymous Dead Sea. Lilith, refusing to come peacefully, chooses to become the mother of demons, the primal womb of the inappropriate. She is cursed by the angels—who vow that one hundred of the demonic children she will give birth to will die every day. Lilith strikes back by swearing she will hurt the seed of Adam, killing his children (except those protected by an amulet engraved with the names of the three angels) to avenge the death of hers, and beguiling men.

These mystical traditions therefore portray Lilith as the one who steals the semen of men when they sleep at night, coming to them in their dreams as a succubus. She is a child-killer, possessed by the devil (whose evil light made its way through the mud and infected her during her creation), and a monster of the first order whose perverse rebellion against the established order is directly responsible for the subsequent Fall event. The kabbalistic text of the Zohar identifies the seditious serpent that comes to Eve—God's second take on womanhood—as a woman scorned. Lilith herself. She is the temptress that throws the spanner in the works, the sex addict who asserts her place as her husband's equal—an act that probably inspires God to make a bolder statement about the inferiority of women by making Eve from Adam's rib, not dry dust.

She is the mother of the monstrous. The matron of the occluded.

Even after seeing a bit of her backstory, it still doesn't fully explain why Lilith becomes so hideous. A monster of monsters. At the level of the text alone, the stories about those who become monsters seem to suggest their transformation is an effect of the carnal ... or ontological failure of the deepest kind. A fall from grace. An opening up to the wilds. A glitch that ruins the program. Lilith rejects the biological determinism of the master creator by destabilizing the establishment and its naturalizing effects. She will not be under. She contests that. Her grievance seems framed in oppositional subjectivity, a contentious feminism that hates men for being men. But then she suddenly sprouts wings ... and takes off. We are not told how this happens. And this is the thing with monsters: an explanation is not necessary or helpful. The logic of the previous or a full disclosure of their backstory is not enough clarification about the surprising emergence of the monstrous. The monster demands sensuous causalities and reprimands the linearity of answers or the confidence we repose in the intelligible. It resituates oppositional subjectivity without dismissing it. When we come to the monster in the story we come to the preposterous; we come to a generous place (the menu becomes larger) where the logic of the story is not superseded or dismissed but queered.

Monsters are reminders of particularities—children of a world too complex to be spoken of in terms of the universal. They can be mediums of democratic expansion and forbears of new cultural modes of relationality. They can be creatures of reenchantment (I consider the effects of transgender politics on our sterilized and binary notions of gender). But I am hesitant to attach instrumentality to the monster. I feel it defeats monstrosity, making it less alien so we can accommodate it. While there is no general monster, the particularities of each will not be reduced to discursive analysis. The world is keener than neat form, correct answers, linear causality, social agency, or right responses. Something the body is doing needs to be met, and something about the co-emergence of the material and discursive seems to suggest that we must allow for a world where everything is not possible. Where things happen and their causal path is not open to scrutiny.

In the monster, we do not come to the end of critical analysis; we meet its queering. We come to touch the silences and gaps that our discursive grasps cannot comprehend.

Our usual response to monsters is to curse them even further. They are unpredictable. Our survival is at stake if we allow them to multiply their perverted bodies. So we contain, medicate, bracket, paraphrase, and lock them away. But considering that the gift of the monster is a glimpse of our mutual porosity, other responses are possible and perhaps summoning both of us at this time.

If you've been following the soft themes flowing between the lines in this letter and previous ones, you might already know what I might say next: yes … you got that right. We need Lilith; we must seek her out. Some say she still roams in desolate places. This much was told to me by one of the Yoruba priests I met with—not Bàbá, but another: "You have chased away the spirits with your roads and development and projects. They hide in the thick forests, and it is there we must go to in order to understand what is happening." Toward the wilds beyond our fences, where Lilith dwells. A winged serpent cursed to fear the footfalls of Eve's offspring, she slithers into dreams, makes her bed in blind spots, and tends to the eggs in her belly. If you stray from fixed paths, my daughter, you might meet or you might be met by a ring of dancing tricksters. Vampires. Werewolves. Succubi. Demons and fallen angels. Wild uncivilized people. These are all Lilith's children. And every night, she mourns as a hundred of them are slain by righteous angels. Her crying echoing in the dark forest, causing everything that moves to huddle closer to each other in trembling embrace. But Lilith's tears do not linger too long on a soft, broken face. Like Kali of Hindu mythology, whose urge to destroy overcomes her again and again, she is refilled with an abominable rage, and she seeks cocksure men and their children to assert her place in the world.

Why must we seek her out, you ask? Why would anyone seek out an ancient monster, talk less of the mother of monsters? It is perhaps no coincidence that Lilith is at once a goddess of fertility as well as a monstrous entity. Maybe we can infer that the monstrous is prolific, or that fertility is a matter of embracing monsters. That nature itself—the appropriate order of things that God and his righteous angels seek to preserve—is not a stable location, neat, neutral, or without controversy. That the generativity of the world is premised on its deep-seated monstrosity. That the closer we lean into the world, the more we are inspired to sympathize with Lilith and her abandonment of things-as-they-should-be. That in the grotesque, in the anomalous, in the scandalous, we glimpse not a fall from grace but a deepening of its work.

I imagine that when Lilith visits Eve's children at night, her eyes still stinging with rage, there is a deep compassion that speaks as well. I imagine she curls up to our ears, tucking her mangled colubrine body that has been cursed and maligned and stepped upon by patriarchal righteousness into the folds of our pinnae, and then says:

> *Hearken unto me, fellow creatures. I who have dwelt in a form unmatched with my desire, I whose flesh has become an assemblage of incongruous anatomical parts, I who achieve the similitude of a natural body only through an unnatural process, I offer you this warning: the Nature you bedevil me with is a lie. Do not trust it to protect you from what I represent, for it is a fabrication that cloaks the groundlessness of the privilege you seek to maintain for yourself at my expense. You are as constructed as me; the same anarchic womb has birthed us both. I call upon you to investigate your nature as I have been compelled to confront mine. I challenge you to risk abjection and flourish as well as have I. Heed my words, and you may well discover the seams and sutures in yourself.[31]*

So why do we seek Lilith? Why must we heed her call? And how does this have anything to do with homecoming or finding our place in the world? We must seek Lilith because we come from her—because we also are born of the rage of a world astray. Because she is the mother of monsters; because she is our mother. We must seek her because she seeks us too. I must seek her because she stands in my way, and she is trouble. Perhaps to stay with this trouble, to pray to her, to hug this monster, is to learn—very faintly—that what stands in our way is also part of the way home.

I sing you to sleep ... my belly swollen with the life of your little brother who now comes to join us. Your long legs sprawled across my lap, your spotted head resting in my arms and then moving to my chest. I sing you to sleep. I can hear your soft troubled breathing—the way you rub your head hard on my breasts, anything to relieve the itching. I can feel your pain, but I can't allow you to scratch. Let them do their work.

Put your arm around me. I will lock it under my armpit. Let the devilish things blister and pop and swear. No matter. Let them burn. If you scratch them, they will leave splotches on your skin; they will mark you as one who did not listen to your mama.

Close your eyes. I will hold you with one arm, and use the other to comfort the one who rolls and kicks under this pimpled hill ... the one who has made my navel his footstool. With my other hand I will pat my belly, and take deep breaths.

Don't mind that the floor is hard. It is what our bodies need now—hard places, not soft warm places where these things can hide and taunt us later. This is what our aching bodies desire.

Your father stands limp. His eyebrows are turned outward where they meet. His face is sad. If he could take away these spirits from your body, he would. He doesn't know what to do. There is nothing to be done. Sometimes things have to be done to us. Your father has been visited too—long ago when it came and made his body a large kitchen of many boiling pots. He says he scratched every one of them until he became fire.

I worry that if he moves too close to us, these devils will possess him too—even though that is very unlikely. Moreover, I will not allow him close—there are urgent matters at hand. He is writing letters to you. He is speaking about home and community and why you must now sleep. Tomorrow will dawn and the sun will bring you closer to the time when these will take to the wind and bless another body, in another time. In another place.

For now, listen to the sound of my voice. Go to sleep. Let them do their work.

LETTER 4

LIBATIONS AT THE CROSSROADS

He took me by the hand and led me into the spirit world.
I did not speak Yoruba and he did not speak English. Our only
intercourse was the language of the trees.

—SUSANNE WENGER[1]

Dear Alethea,

I'm "just black." Your mother is "yellow, sometimes white." And you? You are *"brown"*—conveniently situated somewhere in the chromatic middle, where extremes meet and forgive each other. And *this* you decree—again and again—carving out our humble places in your gently expanding world of colors.

You first made this austere announcement about our skin colors one Wednesday while I toweled you dry. Mama and I looked at each other, not a word said in response, and then we fell on you tickling you—and then each other. If there's one thing we like doing, it's collapsing into a single pile of giggles and flapping limbs. It was yet another moment when we—your mum and I—felt ourselves in awe of the fact that our little Alethea, who only a while ago was a yelling-crying-blustering bundle of surprise, now could form a meaningful sentence about the beautiful colors this very material world bequeaths us for a while.

And—speaking of toweling—even though your mama now frowns at the thought of me writing this to you, I thought you should know that I am the official bath-giver in our home. Apparently, I do it better than anyone else (and yes, there are many people that bathe you ... your many mothers—your aunts, your mother's cousins, your grandmother—with her long flowing hair folded into a neat bun behind her neck, and—sometimes when I have to travel alone and go away—your mum).

Mama used to give you a bath, but I was more vigorous in my bath-giving. When I really got into it, everyone began noticing that you sparkled—so I took on the noble calling.

No matter the circumstances or the menacing urgencies staring down at me, it falls on me to take care of you this way. To give you a bath. Bathing you is a ritual that has purposes deeper than self-care. Deeper than purpose. Greater than you and me. The world steals into our little bathroom in these precious moments, dripping through the louver windows with sunlight and curiosity and the yelling of children playing down our street, gushing through the bronze tap in an exuberant column of partnership, as you—our soon-to-be four-year-old girl—shed your skin and remake yourself. During these daily ablutions, we sing aloud, both of us—making up songs about teeth and tongues and scrubbing. And, of course, we take many liberties with the well-known nursery rhymes— like the time Little Bo Peep lost her goats, or when the bear went over Sanju.

Sometimes you get some soap in your eyes, and then throw a titanic tantrum that slices through the humidity in the bathroom—leaving us both moody and testy. But most times we come out singing—not before you tell me you are going to scare me, and then—after I have gone to get you a towel and returned to the door to pick you into it—you jump out from behind the door with a loud "Boo!" I feign shock, trembling as best I can while you stand there studying my reaction, seeking signs that I am genuinely frightened. Convinced that your scare tactics have worked—the same one you use after every bath—you say "Surprise!" And then I pick you up in the towel as we both discuss how good a "scarer" you really are.

When I began giving you baths, mama taught me how to mix turmeric powder, coconut oil, *besan dal,* and hearty helpings of patience into a small, dense emulsion, which I would then vigorously rub into your skin after scrubbing you with a soft sponge and lathery soap. I once watched an old Indian woman (whom we simply called Patti-ma) bathe you in a similar way with this same grimy mixture a few days after you were born. A grandmother and local midwife who sustained herself traveling from county to county within Tamil Nadu, helping new mothers take care of their delightful bundles of horror, Patti-ma would sit down on a tiny stool, lock her ankles together, and expertly slide you into the cradling space between her legs—where you seemed tranquil, until the washing began. Even so, her fierce care always left you with a noticeable glow about you.

Patti came every Wednesday, always delighted to help out for a few rupees. She couldn't speak any one-tongue, but she let me know (with your mum interpreting her Tamil) that the mixture was to help make you fair. "What's wrong with black?" I'd ask, possessed by an old sensitive spirit. It often took your mum a few moments to assure me that Patti didn't intend to transform you into a Caucasian; she just wanted you healthy and bright-looking.

But there were spirits that churned and curdled whenever the intense scrubbing began. Old wounds. I often felt that the hint of darkness that pigmented your skin in certain areas was seen as a stain on your beauty, and that the daily regimen of applying turmeric and dal was intended to chase out my claims to fatherhood. In my defense, there were other prevailing cross-cultural circumstances that made me feel this way, but I wouldn't want to write about that now.

No matter how vigorously she scrubbed you, however, your complexion always blossomed somewhere between beige and a desert-sand brown hue. Right now, at three going on four, with a mouth that spills wise things, with a generous heart that beats out rhythms for those around you, and with little feet that tiptoe across the floor—as if at any moment you'd sprout wings like

Lilith and fly, you are a rainbow-colored bodhisattva, at whose feet I long to sit. You are not pitch black like your father or the off-white ambiguity of your mum. You are not one color; "brown" doesn't quite cut it. You are neither midnight nor bright sunny noon. Just the rambunctious ground that steadily observes the antics of the skies above.

However, I often wonder if that would spare you—for this town, with all its joys and colors, seems to bask in the fleeting hospitality of bright sunny noons, leaving out those like me with an affinity to midnight.

When I started to visit Tamil Nadu in the months before mama and I got married, I noticed a fondness for whiteness and a cultural apparatus that ascribed beauty to persons who were on the lighter side of things. This giant hidden hand, rarely visible, produced billboards advertising "Fair & Lovely Skin Lightening Cream," and selected the distressed damsel for their local movies. The girl to be rescued, the one who sang her undying love to the swashbuckling hero, swinging her hips on a hill, teasing him from behind a tired tree, or pouting at the camera, was always, almost without exception, light-skinned or (if not fair enough) heavily plastered with makeup to look lighter than she really was. Beauty didn't come in shades of black, and I wondered why.

I would walk down a street, or linger at a bus stand as people looked outside their windows, or literally came within a few inches of me to stare at me like I was some fascinating variation of a familiar beast.

Of course, I didn't like any of it, but—to be fair—I didn't feel like I was at the receiving end of some kind of racism down here in the South of India. Your mum helped me understand that their ways of performing curiosity were merely strange to me, and that they meant no harm. Up north, however, in the more populated cities of India, it is a different story for Africans that have migrated there. There are reports of Africans being abused, beaten up by violent mobs, denied basic services, or called names to their faces for not having straight long hair.

Recently, a Kenyan woman was dragged from her cab and beaten by locals in Greater Noida; African men (mostly Nigerian men seeking business opportunities) who have moved into urban areas in South Delhi are frequently assaulted, followed into dark alleys, and beaten with sticks until they die. A wrong gesture could land one into lots of trouble.[2]

Being a frequent traveler, I have often met immigration officers at Indian airports who, upon realizing a black man is next in line to present his passport, put on a disheartening scowl, while I do my best to smile from ear to ear, echoing a loud "Good morning" or "Good evening" in exchange for a muttered icy acknowledgment. They would flip through my passport, and then their eyes would almost jump out of their sockets when they see that I have an Overseas Citizen of India card, which means I am—for all intents and purposes—Indian. A female officer once sized me up many times, unable to comprehend how I was in possession of such a document. She asked what I did, if I was married to an Indian. By the time I answered that I was a professor of clinical psychology, author and speaker, and that—yes, I was in fact married to an Indian—she had darted off to show her colleagues in neighboring booths the wonder of an OCI card tucked neatly in a Nigerian passport—the horror of it.

My mother often wonders why we decided to move to India. "There are other places you could go. You both finished summa cum laude—you could get well-paying jobs here in the UK," she would say again and again when she calls. It's probably true. But that is not the life we want to live, not the deep lesson we hope to bequeath you. Moreover, I love India—its wild geographic splendor, its unctuous sensitivities to the texture and ecstasy of bodies that lurk behind a studied (and perhaps colonial) prudeness ... as if any second the thin veil of decorum would burst and release a delayed orgasm. How else could one explain the gasping abundance of culinary delights, of endless colors, of sacralized objects—from knickknacks to huge ornate statues baptized in milk and touched with powders and mixtures? And how could one reconcile this culture of excess with its seemingly pervasive shyness, this inclination to fold into oneself, to tuck in the shirt, and put on an administrative uniform of homogeneity?

When your mother and I made the choice to come back to India and live here in its coastal south, we did so not merely because both of you were born here, and not merely because we have strong communal support here, but largely because we believed the life we want—small, intense, and intimate—could be provided here. Yes, I do find myself falling to worry when I read Indian dailies about arrested Nigerians, or watch a Tamil movie about an overpowered deified policeman, whose villain is a Nigerian drug smuggler that he refers to with a snarl as an "African monkey." I hate to think that we moved to a beautiful and sacred country so attuned to the sensuous materiality of the ordinary, with people whose blue and wondrous gods are fashioned in the figures of animals, and who know how to boil a bucket of milk into a soft cube of edible ecstasy—only to find a politics of complexion and a fascination with white people.

So I sometimes walk about stiffly when your mother sends me down the road to the local store. I would put on an affected Americanized accent, or say I was from South Africa when people ask me what part of the world I was from. It's true. I hardly feel at home in my own skin—which seems like a necessary prerequisite to fashioning new settlements and new ontologies of home. If your own skin repels you, then where might you live?

Now I tell you all this because it seems that the world has favorites—and one's skin color has a lot to say about whether you are well off or not seen at all. Whether you are shown a seat at the table, or shown the door. Bàbá's quest has taken me on journeys across the Möbius strip of my days to find a way to pray for you, as a ritual to bless the world you will live in. And though I haven't found all the hushes yet, I know well enough to say that I want you to be seen, to be embraced with the many colors your skin takes on. I wish for a world that loves you the way I do, that knows something the world I now live in doesn't know.

I began to think about this world you will grow in—wondering whether your brown skin and frizzy hair might find room in a world thickly textured by fair and white skins. Who would hold you when I am gone? Who would see you, in your diffractive splendor, and love you just the way Lali and I do? Is there a place for those that fall between the binary, mired in the morass of the middle? Or were you cursed from the moment you leaked through the matrix, drawing in air that was reserved for the proper born ones?

In Nigeria, where I grew up and where your mother's father was born, in the cities, the air is thick with a forgetfulness and a busyness. With a preference for white ontologies. Everyone rushes about with a "skeptical pout," fulfilling the prophecies of a forlorn myth, the sides of their faces nailed tight to the phones in their hands, singing the lyrics of a song that has no rhythm or sway.

We speak development and progress and GDP. We endorse their standards of excellence. We tell ourselves that the white man knows the way forward, and we curse and spit at ourselves because we do not add up to the cherished figure of the foreigner. Because our airports don't have functioning carousels or operating air conditioning units. Because blackness often feels like an unfortunate deviation from the default of whiteness. And we shake our heads when the television screen lights up with images of yet another building or engineering feat in the legendary West. There's even a song for those moments when we feel there's something wrong with us and everything right with "them": "Come and see American wonder! Come and see American wonder!"

It is said by those among us who seem to know better about our own nobility that we have lost our own stories, our own histories, our own senses of fortitude and worth. They say, in effect, that we have potholes in our roads, not because we are laughably inadequate to the task of tarring our highways, but because something in the soil resists the finality of the industrial order, and potholes might very well be the orifices through which other potential political imaginaries breathe.

And in other places, the veil that shrouds our painful loss is just as thin as the space between the red earth and asphalt layers. If you press closely, you might hear the interrupted strokes of tunes that might have been sung. You might hear hooves and equestrian stirrings, ghostly laughter and merrymaking, and the prosodic invocations of the *kalengo* drum attending every step of a legendary king.

You might hear stories spoken by moonlight of when Portuguese ships pulled close, in 1485, docking at the shores of a mighty kingdom and the mighty people of Old Benin. The tragedy of those arrivals not yet foreseen, and the magnificence of the courts—now filled with Manila hemp, clothes, and the guns the Europeans brought with them—blinding them, they opened their gates to the British travelers who came afterward. Our chiefs sold ivory, gold, oil, and slaves to the coastal settlers, whose explorers and mapmakers then ventured inland, proposing to save us from our original sins and teach us how to read and write.

Those coastal enlightenment settlers, transacting by the waters, remaking our children, unearthing our dead ones and closing up the pagan places, never did leave—even when they made a great show of leaving and bequeathed us with a new word, *independence*. The white cloth had already been soiled; the cowries had already been cast to the ground. And there, in the divining of their smooth bodies, were the stories of dispossession and curious inflections of the familiar.

I speak of loss and dislocations. Of futures interrupted. Of dances halted by the crack of gunfire splitting the night into a strange duality. Of strange poisons buried in the land so that the ground no longer recognized the once intimate footfalls of my fathers and mothers in their comings and goings.

Achebe's Okonkwo hung himself on a tree because he no longer knew the ground he had always made love to, the womb that had given him sturdy yams and kept him aloft when he threw "Amalinze the Cat," the wrestler that he beat at the opening of the book *Things Fall Apart*. This violence, this pain of being estranged from one's ground, of losing a sense of gravity, also haunted "The Man" in Ayi Kwei Armah's *The Beautyful Ones Are Not Yet Born*, a meditation on postcolonialism in Africa. Armah writes of the nameless man: "Outrage alternated with a sweaty fear he had never before felt. Something, it seemed to him, was being drained from him, leaving the body feeling like a very dry sponge, very light, completely at the mercy of sly toying gusts of wind."[3]

He might have been speaking of Okonkwo. He might have been speaking of those among my fathers that pressed their ears close to the earth to hear its vibrations and could no longer hear them. He might have been speaking of Bàbá, who lives away from a proud modern highway—the poisoned black stuff that scorches the ground so that cars and their newly minted owners can drive faster to hell.

He might have written of the Osu people of eastern Nigeria.

✦

Your grandfather—your mother's father and my other-father—was a proud Igbo man. He came from a respected line of Igbo men. His father was a chief and his mother a midwife. I have already written a little about him, and would write more if I knew him ... if I had the honor of prostrating before him for his daughter's hand in marriage.

He was Nwadiala—which in the Igbo language means "sons of the soil," a designation for the freeborn that only makes sense in the context of what it excludes, those born of the weird, the Osu.

One can either be born of the soil, to the Nwadiala, or to the "accursed" Osu people. The Osu are considered untouchable, unclean and abominably alien to their communities. The Nwadiala neither marry them nor do business with their children. In fact, if a member of the Nwadiala wants to get married, the family of the intending one conducts thorough investigations to make sure that their own does not get entangled with an outcast. On the off chance a headstrong cross-caste couple insist on love and get married, certain measures are taken to quickly end the marriage or, in some aching instances, end the couple:

> *A human rights group outlined the atrocities meted out against the Osu in Igbo-land. They include: "parents administering poison to their children, disinheritance, ostracism, organized attack, heaping harvest offering separately in churches, denial [of] membership in social clubs, violent disruption of marriage ceremonies, denial of chieftaincy titles, deprivation of property, and expulsion of wives, etc."*[14]

After one of Achebe's fictional characters is told by his son that he is about to get married to an Osu girl, he lectures him about the deeper import of his proposed action: "Osu is like a leprosy in the minds of my people. I beg of you my son not to bring the mark of shame and leprosy into your family. If you do, your children and your children's children will curse you and your memory ... You will bring sorrow on your head and on the heads of your children."[5]

There aren't many written histories of the Osu that one might refer to, but there are some oral histories that have been passed around. It is believed by some Igbo historians that the Osu caste system came into existence six centuries ago. The ones referred to as Osu emerged as a priestly class to administer and perform—on behalf of the community—a series of rituals to appease the gods of the Igbo indigenous cosmology, many of whom took on "the form of major topographical landmarks like streams, rivers, lakes, caves and mountains, or maybe trees, animals and famous ancestors."[6] It was part of the worship of these powerful deities to be attended to. Some of these supreme beings were ranked so high on a hierarchy of power that their proper care required "a retinue of high priests and attendants on full-time basis. The high priests' attendants were responsible for performing intricate religious rituals, which were taboo to the average citizen, in the shrines of the deities."[7] The special ones who took care of the deities' needs and loved the shrines were known as the "osus" of the deity in question.

In short, the Osus were sacred in precolonial Igbo communities; they were not to be touched, and only to be approached with reverence. They were a people apart. Untouchable only in terms of the power they wielded on behalf of the community and their "living sacrifices" to the gods.

However, when the British made their way inland, they disrupted the order of things. Intent on gaining political and economic control over the Igbos, but lacking the manpower to effect this radical transformation, they adopted a system of rule by proxy, indirectly stirring the pot of local life through the familiar visage of sympathetic chiefs and rulers. With missionary outposts and newly built schools, they began supplanting indigenous wisdoms and values with the Christian faith and with the promise of a better life if they learned the one-tongue. As adherents grew, the lands where the Bible reigned supreme shriveled up into a stark binary of those who believed versus those who didn't. The offerings to the shrines dried up; the deities no longer heard the prayers of their people. Buried deep within the symbolism of the cross, which now dotted the new landscape, was a deep antagonism that rejected the now pagan claims of the Osus. In one fell swoop, a people apart became a people *in part*—their ontological inadequacy now arising from an abhorrence and deep-seated hatred for the animism and lecherous materiality of the Osus. There was no room for their practices of care.

The changing conditions of respectability required new frames of seeing and new motivations to forget one's connections to the nonhuman world. With new aspirations, people moved into the big cities, where many others also gathered in floating congregations, left unmoored by the universal promises of white modernity. The Osus had, like Okonkwo, suddenly become unwitting subjects of a new power and of a new Future; their eyes became vestigial, no longer serving their visual negotiations with thick places. Their memories? The fabulations of superstitious minds needing the "benevolent doses of the real" only white people could provide.

I tell this story of the Osus because we are living in times of a deep forgetfulness, and because the subject of home cannot be dealt with without thinking of homes we've already lost. And because you are born of people who have been (and are still) considered a people in part. You are the first fruit the Future forbade, the child of children who were not meant to be and which society had no place for.

As a black man—probably "blacker" than the current diasporan descendants of the young men and women our ancient chiefs sold off to traders heading for the so-called "West"—I know the numbing cramps of dangling feet. The unbearable lightness of having no ground, no lasting support for one's claims to identity.

It's an itch, really. An existential itch right in the middle of one's back. People like me are constantly trying to reach it, to scratch out a deeply ingrained idea, supported by the political-economic structures of our time, that we are inadequate. A people only *in part*. Not fully matured to take on the mysteries of the world or the challenges of being alive. And so we struggle with our mottled manacles—our full-mouthed accents, our inferior cultures, our pouting lips and abrupt hairlines. Any bodily manifestation that deviates from the default requires correction.

My mother once told me about the time she and my father stood outside a hospital in Germany—looking for a nurse to attend to them and help wheel her in. No one came to both of them. It took my mum's grabbing a nurse that was about to ignore them by walking past quickly before they were paid any attention. But it was too late: my sister's head, your Aunty Tito's head, could already be seen between her thighs.

For me, the feeling of not being at home has always been tied up to the color of my skin and its associations with backwardness. Well, not always per se—but since I came to realize I was a citizen of white normativity in my own land. As I have probably mentioned in a previous letter, I was beaten in school for attempting to speak my own language, by teachers who were most probably beaten for attempting to speak their mother tongues. I was trained to think of the world as a dead place I could eventually plunder. Trained to find myself in universalized homogeneous time. Our countries are categorized in terms of their proximity to the edge of the moving hands of this giant clock. While Europe and America are ahead in the first realms of this race, Nigeria and India—two countries that lay their claims on your body—are known as "Third World" nations or developing nations/emerging markets—as if the most important thing that can be known about a country is how well it does on the development scale. Lately, India has been doing better than Nigeria, and its leaders are doing what they can to ramp up the nation's potential to become a global superpower. Left behind in this quest for a seat at the global table is India's richly embroidered history and cultural wealth.

We are all in a race, heading toward the Future. But being black—being a nonwhite human being—means one is already late. There's a tongue-in-cheek name for our lateness: it's called "African time" (and its cross-cultural equivalent: "Indian time"), and rightly refers to the cultural tendency to be less than punctual, but may just as well be a comment on our second-tier or third-tier status as humans. We are all late. And you, my daughter, like me, and my father who haunts me, are late too. Turmeric and dal be damned.

So then, when will the shofar blow, announcing our exodus toward lands flowing with milk and honey? How do we respond to these exclusions, these Manchurian transactions that leave us without help, without a past, without a history, without a seat at the table? Is there a place where it is safe to sit in our nonwhite skins without being considered *in part*? Without being paraphrased or encapsulated? Is it too much to imagine a world that embraces my difference, and recognizes my wealth?

These questions have been airborne long before those new slaves that had traveled across the Atlantic walked off their vessels and into cotton fields. They were alive when Martin Luther King Jr. sang the lyrics of a powerful hope for a postracial America, standing on the steps of the Lincoln Memorial monument and at the cusp of a civil rights movement's yearnings for peace; they were alive when Mandela punched the air with his upheld fist, walking out of Victor Verster prison and his twenty-seven-year incarceration for challenging apartheid. Those questions are especially alive today in America—where the old apparition of racial violence screams through the easy domesticity of the American dream, shocking its mostly white settlers, who thought race was just a thing of the past, "a problem still found here and there, in the outback of Idaho or in the imagination of the academy."[8] These racial tensions are most pronounced when a black man is shot dead or manhandled by those supposed to protect him on the streets, or when a colored person is treated differently, objectified, or italicized as a strange occurrence in the otherwise normal flow of a sentence. They are certainly alive here in India, still struggling in the schizophrenic twilight zones between its ornately wealthy histories and the colonial infractions of a singular Future it must now adhere to.

In my queer journeys for hushes, I have had the good fortune of meeting very sincere people—white, black, brown, yellow, you name it—who care about countering white supremacy, racial prejudices, sexism, and the out-moded claims of environmental patriarchy. They are forming neighborhood groups, joining rallies, printing T-shirts with "Black Lives Matter!" boldly emblazoned on the front, calling out deeply entrenched patterns of seeing and talking and behaving that are insensitive to minorities, and writing elo-quently about the social structures and institutionalized power dynamics that militate against people of color. In the face of those that deny the shad-ows of the past and would rather say, "All is well—there's no such thing as racism … if you work hard enough you should make something of your-self," they are countering with troubling questions, conjuring memories that most would rather bury under the cavalcade of the modern present. They are pointing hard at the embroidery of a modern-scape that is already tex-tured in ways that notices some and dismisses others—no matter how hard they work or try to prove themselves just as humanly variable as the noticed ones. I am thankful that I met these beautiful feet; their unseen practices, hidden behind a blitzkrieg of entertainment news, are part of an insurgency of hope for a world of justice.

I am, however, meeting the traces of a strikingly different reconfigura-tion of the kind of questions we pose to the world about race and justice. A different ethos, one which I will … with great hesitation … christen as "transraciality" (being fully aware of my hubris)—not to be confused with "transracialism." I'll tell you more about this as you read on. I started to think differently about race when I met a forbidden child—someone who came forth from a hard-to-swallow union of bodies. An outlaw. Yes, yes … it seems this crazy, seemingly improvised journey to meet strange creatures has—so far—been about meeting strange women as well. This "forbidden child" … she met me in a queer time and place, and gave me the fourth and fifth hushes[9]—bringing me closer to my destination.

Meeting this forbidden child in the time that I did has afforded me an opportunity to look around, to survey the vexed ideas about race and iden-tity, and raise interesting questions that I would not have considered if we didn't (already) meet.

In 2015, a black American civil rights activist, professor of Africana studies and president of the National Association for the Advancement of Colored People (NAACP) chapter in Spokane, Washington, grants an interview with KXLY 4, answering the questions of a reporter outside the frame of the camera that is trained diligently on her facial expressions and responses. Clad in a white blouse that is imprinted with a motif of graphic black squares (which is perhaps a figure of the shocking revelations about to be made), she speaks emotively about her history of being victimized, and about one of her black sons—thirteen years old at the time—feeling so terrorized by a "package" her family had received that he now sleeps next to her in bed. She talks about hate crimes perpetuated against her and her two black sons, and the police modalities for identifying hate crimes. She falls silent sometimes when she considers the seriousness of racism in America, the images of lynched black men she has come across, and her work fighting for racial justice.

"I would love to live in a world where hate crimes didn't exist, and I can assure my children that we are safe," she says, her voice almost drowned out by the heavy traffic of vehicles, trucks and people to her left, in what seems like yet another run-off-the-mill interview with an eloquent black woman about prejudice.

When the reporter goes off topic a bit and asks whether her father could make it for an event in Spokane, she smiles and tells him her father has bone cancer and was not able to get cleared for surgery. She looks down to something fluttering outside the frame, out of our sight, apparently a picture the reporter is holding in his hand. There is a palpable shift in her countenance. She looks worried.

The reporter asks, "Is this your father?" She nods hesitantly. "That's … that's my dad."

"This man right here is your father—right there?" the reporter presses further, with a tone of managed incredulity that now spells a marked and awkward segue from the earlier focus of the interview.

"You have a question about that?" she asks, visibly ill at ease.

"Yes ma'am, I was wondering if your father is an African American man."

"That's a very … I mean … I don't know what you are implying."

"Are you African American?"

She stares at the reporter, her fried brown coiled hair shifting in the wind as her forced smile drains away into a scowl. She is barely able to keep this up much longer.

"I don't … I don't understand the question of … I did tell you that yes that's my dad … and he wasn't able to come in January.…"

The reporter, Jeff Humphrey, starts to ask if her parents are white, but his subject—Rachel Dolezal, who is to become the eye of a stormy scandal about the politics of race and racial relations in the United States and the unloved poster-child for the contested notion of transracialism—has already walked away.

Thanks to that interview, Rachel Dolezal, a blond white woman who identified as a black woman, and had built a comfortable career on the back of that co-opted identity, was outed as a phony. A hailstorm of studio music and flashy graphics streamed across television surfaces in the nation as journalists and show hosts capitalized on the scandal of her transformation. Not since Clarence King, a nineteenth-century "blue-blood society type who lived half his life as a well-known explorer and Manhattan man about town—and half as a black married man with five children in Brooklyn and Queens,"[10] had anyone else reportedly crossed the racially charged divide that runs through America, and lingered on the other side for so long.

Riding the crest of the controversy to the shore of public outrage, Rachel's father and mother appeared on television in their Caucasian glory, denouncing their daughter as delusional. Members of the NAACP felt duped, including the preceding president, who believed Rachel when she said she was African American. Rachel's adopted brothers, both black, announced that Rachel had taken them aside and told them she was going to adopt a new identity, and asked them to keep a secret. "She grew up privileged," one of her brothers said. "She had good intentions but she didn't go about it the right way."

Defending herself, Dolezal released a statement identifying herself as "transracial"—this in spite of the fact that she did not grow up in an ethnically ambiguous household, had Caucasian parents, and reportedly lived a privileged life like most white people in her town.

The seething rage from both black and white communities felt justified. Why would a white woman want to "pass" as a black woman? In earlier times, fair-skinned black women often "passed" as white women or were often mistaken as white. But they used this to reduce the crushing existential load of suffering that they—and people like them—had to endure. Rachel Dolezal's curious reversal of identity roles felt like the perpetuation of a certain brand of American anything-goes-ism, a state of affairs that applied more to rich white people in the upper echelons of society than to minorities in the doldrums of exclusion.

This much was clear to Ijeoma Oluo—a writer who has your mother's Igbo name and who, like your mother, is multiracial with a Nigerian father and American mother. I recently came across Ijeoma's article, which she had written following a visit to Rachel Dolezal, or—as she chooses to be called now, after a Nigerian Igbo man had given her a new name—Nkechi Amare Diallo, following the latter's recent publication of a book recounting her ordeal as a transracial person.

Oluo's opinions about Diallo were already rock-bottom; she had been part of previous conversations about the white woman who pretended to be black, and was exhausted with the topic. However, taking an offer to interview Rachel in her home, Ijeoma flew out to meet her—perhaps hoping for a glimpse of someone she might come to sympathize with. She didn't find that person.

Her report—widely praised and celebrated—was scathing and full-toothed in its in-depth analysis of Nkechi's apparent malaise, pointing out that Nkechi's colonizing adoption of black identity was yet another unfortunate instance of white privilege exerting itself.

There was a moment before meeting Dolezal and reading her book that I thought that she genuinely loves black people but took it a little too far. But now I can see this is not the case. This is not a love gone mad. Something else, something even sinister is at work in her relationship and understanding of blackness.[11]

Oluo sniffed out what came across as a critical lack of awareness about whiteness: Diallo, seeming to compare her early childhood experiences to chattel slavery, appeared to have fetishized blackness, unaware of the enormous privilege and power she wielded to be able to co-opt the experiences of black people in her personal quest for redemption. Oluo's point—that she treated blackness like a plaything, while enjoying the security and access her white skin granted her—amounted to an egregious erasure of black people. Her forays past the drawn lines of racial memory did nothing to dismantle the furniture of white exceptionalism—in fact, as Oluo noted, Diallo shifted the fence a little bit more, taking a chunk of the little ground blacks had left:

I am more than a little skeptical that Doleẓal's identity as the revolutionary strike against the myth of race is anything more than impractical white saviorism—at least when it comes to the ways in which race oppresses black people. Even if there were thousands of Rachel Doleẓals in the country, would their claims of black-ness do anything to open up the definition of whiteness to those with darker skin, coarser hair, or racialized features?[12]

Oluo was right.

In so far as Diallo's adventurism left white dominance critically unchallenged, shifting the burden of hospitality and moral nobility to the victim, it was a denial of the power inequities that exist between white and black people. Black people—especially black women like Ijeoma Oluo (who, ironically, would have been labeled "white" or "oyinbo" back home in Nigeria, because of her fair skin and obvious "mulatto look") do not have the liberty to cross lines or jump fences the way Diallo did. Black people cannot look away, or change their robes in telephone booths (I'm sorry if these references are lost on you, dear!). They are locked in. But power can: power can look away, can take your skin … where to turn would be the death of you, and where if you could exchange your skin for a loaf of bread, you might have done so a long time ago.

Oluo stopped short of calling white Spokane woman Rachel Dolezal—turned–Nkechi Diallo crazy. Like others, she chalked it up to the familiar fluctuations of white supremacy. Nothing strange was happening. Blackness was once again saved; its virginity restored. Oluo's article was a furious anti-body dispatched to eject the viral element from the bloodstream of black-ness, an invasion that might very well have weakened the black cause for justice, for reconciliation, for equality, for reparations, for safer streets and friendlier cops, and for the same socioeconomic privileges of normalcy white people enjoy that black people need to be exceptional to attain. For the right to sit at the round table. For a piece of the Future promised everyone regard-less of creed or color.

And yet, when the dust settled, I felt slightly unsettled. I found myself asking questions the Forbidden girl had taught me: is this all there is? Is there no more surprise? Isn't there something yet unexpected in the experience of blackness—or is this it? This eternal dialectic with whiteness? This quest for equality? This closed settlement and barricaded steel walls of secure identity?

✦

Growing up in Nigeria, I didn't think of myself as black. Sure, I was darker than midnight and all my siblings were fairer than I; this was just a matter of genes and too much beans. In fact, I felt more white than black. White people were fascinating to me. I loved watching "movies"—which, for the sake of needless clarification, always meant movies made in Hollywood. Most of my friends (if not everyone I knew that was my generation) disparagingly called our own movies "films" or "homemade videos"—in our eyes a lesser cate-gory of quality, since our products didn't have the magical special effects and awe-inspiring wizardry that attended Bruce Lee's gravity-defying leaps, or Steven Seagal's blustery martial tactics that allowed him to take out an entire mob of gangsters with his lanky limbs. Or Robocop.

You didn't find white people walking down my street, as they might have done in Johannesburg or Pretoria in South Africa. The white people who came into my country were mostly expatriates, some of whom earned brief-cases of dollars working with oil companies, banks, and global conglomer-ates. They lived on Victoria Island, in the poshest parts of Lagos. If a white person came to my area, everything would have stopped. Bus conductors would have danced merrily while hanging precariously on the sides of their *danfo* buses—pointing at *"oyinbo pipu."* Women who made *àkàrà* and fried yams like my grandmother might have blushed if a white person came by to patronize them.

Everyone dreamed of "going abroad" someday—and those that got visas after prayerful fasting and spiritual vigils and then squeezed their way into airplanes flying to Europe or America often came back, a few weeks later, with the most disingenuous accents you've never heard. They would say "wanna" and "gonna" instead of "want to" and "going to," deforming their faces and twisting their lips to approximate the elusive sound of a schwa, just to prove to everyone that they'd been there. Done that. We didn't mind. We let them have their time. The comedic value of watching someone try to speak like an American or with the cockneyed abandon of a Londoner was always dampened by the soft internal reminder that we ourselves hadn't been "there." The Western world was a dream, a story everyone wanted to tell. And every story deserved embellishment.

We looked up to African Americans too. I certainly did. To us—to my friends who lapped up every fashion trend propagated by the hip-hop artists of the day—black Americans had it good. From Notorious B.I.G. to that Reid guy that played a professor on the TV show *Snoops*, African Ameri-cans were just as "other" to us as the white people that liked to jog down the streets in the rich residential areas, their pale pink and sweaty bodies brazenly exposed, to the mild irritation of our mothers. Somewhere at the back of our heads, in vague recollections of history lessons we hardly paid attention to, we knew black Americans were the children of old slaves—connected to us across watery miles of savagery and maltreatment—but, at least, they lived in a country with constant electricity. They had good schools, good trans-portation, and white people around them. We had none of that. We were late, living in a world that was never on time. We envied African Americans, and considered them "oyinbo" as well.

I remember my father used to amusedly say the f-word sometimes when he was younger. They were few and far between, and hardly ever in the context of abuse or heightened emotion. In fact, his usage lacked the caustic sting of his "black" sideburn-totting brothers in the diaspora. He mostly learned it from blaxploitation movies, for he too—like his own generation—thought of black Americans as an avant-garde culture.

So while there was "black," we sometimes felt "black-black": lower than our better brothers whose fathers couldn't outrun the trade ships.

But the antagonistic response to whiteness—we didn't have. Only in small academic circles of those who read Walter Rodney, you know, the professor kinds whose wives would roll their eyes when they started to speak about the ways Europe underdeveloped Africa in the company of friends, and who never made enough money to cajole their spouses to allow them be their quirky selves, did such talk thrive. We didn't have the immediacy of a ready villain, just the traces of their ghostly presence and a desire to piece the puzzles together so we could get to heaven one fine day. All our agony was reserved for "the government"—those *buba*-clad politicians that promised us we too could look like London if we elected them into office.

I didn't know the pain of dispossession or dislocation. Not directly. I didn't lose a language, since I was born into the one-tongue. I didn't miss out on bonfire tales by moonlight, since the fires had already been snuffed out by tarred roads long before I was born. I was born in exile—after the dust had settled into a maze everyone was now told was our new reality. To one born in chains, confinement can look like a privilege denied others.

Eventually I became one of those "professor types," reading Fanon, Baldwin, Achebe, and Soyinka. And yes, Walter Rodney too. It felt like an awakening. In the context of my critical surveys of the damage that had been done to our lands, to our psyches, and to our futures, I began to recognize my whiteness and the white halls of power I had been born in. The music stopped, and the world felt like the scratching sound the turntable makes when the needle has skated off the record: the music extinguished, my days were spent pondering the loss of my identity. Where was my original blackness that had been taken from me? And how was I to restore it? My questions took me to an angry pan-Africanism in search of innocent pasts and black essences, and then to a postmodern pacifism but no less agonistic reappraisal of identity and culture—both of which left me in some sort of stable and unproductive blackness ... a fugue blackness that sort of hinted at the heritage I was supposed to have, the feelings I was supposed to feel, and the attitudes I was supposed to adopt to be properly "black," without the satisfaction of the actual thing.

I want you to know, dear, that I hope the world you live "in" is a beautiful world, and that you never know the scowls and rudeness and exclusions I have known for being a certain color—not to mention the pain and suffering our mothers and fathers knew in order to find us a place to plant our feet. I do not know what such a world might look like or what racial justice even means, but I hope to share some of the questions I have been asking as I bring together the pieces of the puzzle of home.

The issue of race is a vexing thing, escaping full articulation. In a time of tearful losses and oppression suffered because one is not the "right" color, much rides on the particular ways and particular thoughts we employ to think about blackness.

The painful memories and whip marks inflicted on black bodies, the intergenerational trauma of chattel slavery and lynched families hanging from trees, the dislocation and disenchantment from one's own wisdoms, the effacement of the vexed past and the Euro-American appropriation of history, and the influential figure of civil rights activists like Martin Luther King Jr. have inspired a generation to seek to preserve the black experience. The justice-seeking claims and hopes for equality rest heavily on the survival of blackness as a pure category to itself. This is probably why Dolezal was severely criticized by the black community—because her foray into blackness threatened the integrity of the identity and diluted its power to lay hold on the kind of restorative future black communities seek.

At the same time, fetishizing blackness is hardly productive in generating new ways to think about our changing contexts and the complex burdens a changing world places on our identities. Such a strategy invites the risk of subsequent exploitation, and locks blackness into adversarial coordinates.

Another view of race denies there's even such a thing. There's no such thing as a black race or a white race. Race is an illusion—or better yet a mirage of power. The closer you get to the shimmering surface, the faster the apparition disappears. Because race is viewed as genetic reductionism, this postmodern interpretation and its distrust of the metanarrative of blackness seeks to denaturalize race, and expose the interests and power dynamics that are stitched into biologically deterministic notions of race. The effect is a rejection of the body entirely and a dependence on what we know, or epistemology.

What this inquiry provides is powerful insights into the politico-economic negotiations and identity-shaping influences that teach us to identify as black, white, yellow, or brown. Yet, it maintains a hostility and fear of the body (and thus negates from the get-go any possible exploration of the agency of the material world in race and identity), and leaves its analysis within the orbit of humanism—centralizing human thoughts and discussions on the matter.

Whatever we posit as the "real story" of race behind the scenes, most of us seem to experience it in its manifoldness—as an economic sorter of persons, as a phenotypic distraction away from the waltz of power that is inscribed upon every frolicking molecule of space in the world. But trying to arrive at the "essence" of race is to obfuscate the intra-active effects that are at play in merely talking about it as an "it." We are not allowed the luxury of speaking from nowhere—we can only settle with a partial view, one that inexorably excludes other complementary views.

There could therefore be no complete appraisal of white privilege or fully adequate synthesis of all insights about racial oppression into a single unified theory. Things—including concepts and bodies—are inexhaustible; they show up only partially. If you can see everything, then you've already missed a spot.

Thinking this way affords us an opportunity to ask the question: What are we missing, then? What are we occluding from the picture in our particular descriptions of blackness and white normativity? What new insights can be generated in particular modes of inquiry and action that could heal racial divides—and possibly conjure a world for your skin to breathe in?

If we must seek to understand racism, then we can turn it this way and that, entangling ourselves with its multidimensionality—however, not with any hope of arriving at the surest, most universal way of thinking about it. There isn't one. By engaging "it" differently, however, new meanings and modes of action are made possible.

✦

Reading about Susanne Wenger, the white woman who had come to Nigeria with her linguist husband in 1950, proved not only to be a counter-story to the Nkechi-Dolezal-Oluo account, but a soft expedition into the first stirrings of a different way to imagine racial relations and responsivity to white normativity. Susanne Wenger not only became "black" in the eyes of the community that adopted her but eventually learned the customs and language of the people of Osogbo so well that she became a priestess—accepted by no less than Yoruba deities and their priests as a sacred intermediary and interlocutor for Orisha worship. She renounced Christianity, divorced her husband, adopted black-black children, rejected formal education as a form of colonization, and was believed to have saved the traditional beliefs in Osogbo from extinction with her work to preserve the forest. Better known by her adopted name, Adunni Olorisa, Wenger died in 2009, in the home she loved and with the people who called her their own. It is said that the day she died a midday rain began and ended abruptly, and then she died—surrounded by her fifteen adopted children, some of whom were revered chiefs in Osogbo, Osun State.

Revisiting Wenger's story recently, I started to wonder about Dolezal's (or Diallo's) claims to be transracial and the intense animus this generated in black communities in the West, contrasting this with Wenger's relatively celebratory reception and welcome into a Yoruba community in Nigeria.

Both incidences are incommensurable in many ways: Diallo is perceived as disingenuous and deceptive in her adoption of an identity that served her particular career and professional choices. Her critics insist she could walk out anytime from her blackness—simply uncoil her hair into its "original" blond look, and no one would bat an eyelid. Wenger, on the other hand, was an Austrian artist who arrived in pre-independence Nigeria with her husband during a time when being white in Nigeria afforded you the highest privileges ordinary citizens didn't enjoy. Instead, she forsook that identity, and decided to live with a people, eventually learning their language and culture, and becoming a strong advocate for the preservation of those traditions. She didn't take the identity of blackness; it was offered to her, in a sense.

Many in my time might detect a hint of white saviorism in Wenger's story and scoff at the familiar story of redemption from abroad—but if one is to be cynical and dismissive, then one must also simultaneously diminish the capacity of the indigenous Yoruba people and rubbish their traditions and rituals for adjudging authenticity.

But there is more to be learned—something that troubles popular accounts of blackness and resituates (not displaces) analytics of racism, white privilege, or antiblackness. Something that rekindles my hope for a racially sensuous world.

Responding to a French documentary maker in 2005, who was inquiring into her remarkable journey and her eventual acceptance by the Osogbo people, Wenger said of her sacred mentor: "He took me by the hand and led me into the spirit world," adding that "I did not speak Yoruba, and he did not speak English, our only intercourse was the language of the trees."

The language of trees.

There have been many insightful analyses of blackness and whiteness (such as Oluo's), many descriptions of microaggressions in racial relations, and many inquiries conducted into the real and horrific injustices that white supremacy occasions. And yet racism persists. As Jerry Rosiek notes:

> *The persistence of institutionalized racism despite the sheer scope of the suffering*
> *it causes, its resilience in the face of multigenerational organized resistance, the*

way it adapts to and subverts every political and intellectual intervention, sug-gests that we are dealing with more than a mere conceptual mistake. It suggests that empirical research on the phenomenon of racism, white supremacy, white-ness, anti-Blackness—whatever our theoretical suppositions lead us to call it—will ask more of scholars than adopting alternative epistemologies and practices of description.[13]

What more is demanded of us?

Perhaps we find in this "language of the trees" the interesting proposal that the racializing agent is not singularly human or just a social construction but a flow of material-semiotic practices that engulfs/shapes/constitutes humans together with trees, stones, stories, concepts, and the world. Per-haps the world around us, the environment, pulses with the question of race. What happens if we reconsider blackness, the strictures of identity, and white privilege within a world that is porous, constantly unmaking and remaking boundaries? What if the lenses with which blackness is seen—in agonistic tension with whiteness—are just as much a product of white colonial ways of knowing—an epistemology that does not take into consideration the racializing effects of the material world and thus situates the source of racism in the human? What if racial identity is not a property of persons, but a flow of becomings—of post-human becomings—that challenges our claims to ownership? What if we all are a becoming-each-other? And that even in the sham of pretend-blackness or pretend-whiteness lies the shamanic gestures of an art that speaks an unsuspected truth? A possibility that we are transra-cial as a matter of fact?

Speaking at a town hall event in Sonoma County in California, after being invited to share some of my understandings about racial justice, I began the meeting by inviting the audience to envision a world where racial justice had finally "happened."[14] What would that look like? The responses traced the contours of a familiar social justice imaginary: no one gets left behind; a cop sharing a thumbs up with a black driver; no one has to live in fear; equal rights. I might have said the same things, including reparations; designing policies to help at-risk people of color, especially black men who have a higher probability of being incarcerated than white men; and seeking the forgiveness of those who were decimated, chained, and eventually cordoned off in reservations in order for nation-states to rise.

But I wonder—as I did in that meeting—about the paradigms of responsivity that make these contributions meaningful, and—more to the point—what they exclude from our collective gaze. How are we responding to white privilege, white normativity, and racism? The imaginary of racial justice and its juridical implications in a sphere of rights posits a directionality … a "there" in future time we are supposed to reach. To climb this pyramid, and claw our way to the top of modernity's pointy summit in a gesture of arrival, is the suggested route of resolution. The driving ethos is equal access—access for the many races. Access to prestige, to educational opportunities, to career fulfilment, to fair representation. A level playing field. Open doors to white, brown, and black alike. And racial identity—often circumscribed in the caul of accusation and distanced away from the "other"—is the beating heart of this imaginary.

I have said that my journey of decolonization took me to a pan-Africanism and an Afrocentrism that insisted on seeing the world through the unique contexts of the "African." I even wrote a book called *We Will Tell Our Own Story!* with the much-respected scholar of Afrocentrism and elder Molefi Asante. Inside me, however, the call to African centrality felt like a call to arms, a call to proliferate many other centers in defiance of the previous monocentrality of Euro-American thought. To crouch behind sandbags we had erected to keep the creeping hordes of the white others away. Postmodernism seemed sympathetic to this political project of reengineering history and of calling attention to the processes of elision that underlined the institutionalization of physical and social sciences as white knowledges. I began to fill my bedroom wall with lists of things black people had done—the things written out of history or muted by the status quo, like the silent p in *psychology*. From dustpans to potato chips to the carbon filament and traffic lights—and even the internet, which might not have been possible were it not for the calculations of one Philip Emeagwali, an Igbo man like your grandfather, which allowed microcomputers to communicate with each other simultaneously within what he called the Hyperball International Network of computers[15]—the items black women and men inventors created became my coordinates to a black heaven.

But, as I may have said, I noticed the constant need to assert my place, to hold up an objectionable finger in gatherings—where I found I was (once again) the only black person present—just to point out Africans "had done it first." And like a coconut forced open with sweat and toil only to serve a few drops of its tender fluids, asserting black identity felt like doing so much only to get so little.

Not that I was against confrontation. Even now, I understand that there are situations where confrontation is already built into the dynamic of things, where anger must be allowed its troubling passage as one must allow the mysterious night masquerade to dance and scream its frightful secrets in the tight corridors of the village. Confrontation, anger, and pain have their place. But in asserting my voice, in being naturally suspicious of the white subtext in the sentence of the everyday, in being prickly about what "that white woman" or "some other white person" *really meant* when she suggested that audiences listened to me because I was "exotic"—a young black man that sounded articulate, or why that immigration officer held me at his booth for far longer than the other travelers had been held, I slowly came to the realization that even victimhood could be oppressive. Power shows up in ironic ways. In fetishizing my blackness, I was perhaps "guilty" of some kind of conservation of victimhood and polishing of enemy figures.

What began to give way was my firm grip on identity. There had to be something beyond the stark proliferation of gated communities of racialized bodies, each staking a claim for itself in the flatness and scarcity of modern life. There had to be a different notion outside these lines bloodied fingers and half-broken fingernails had anxiously scratched into the earth to demarcate "them" from "us"—a line white people were barred from crossing, and which most blacks seemed content to preserve.

Bill Maher, white liberal American comic and host of the political talk show *Real Time with Bill Maher*, learned the hard way about "crossing lines" as he bandied words with his guest, U.S. Senator Ben Sasse of Nebraska, while filming on set in May 2017. Midway through their conversation, Maher, in response to a phrase from the senator that had the words "work the fields" in it, responded by saying he was a "house nigger." A collective groan reverberated across the United States: the joke, most said, was not only in bad taste but was an affront to black people. How dare a white man—even one who had had black female friends—utter the word *nigger?* The backlash was swift as black celebrities called for Maher's head to appease the gods of the line—the same line breached by Maher's presumptuous bravado, the wrath of which even his liberal cred and brand of political incorrectness could not save him from.

When legendary hip-hop artist and actor Ice Cube appeared to film a subsequent *Real Time* segment, Bill knew what was coming to him. "So I know you are here to promote an album," he said. "I know you also want to talk about my transgression. What do you want to do first?" Ice Cube, probably the fitting figure for the angry black male, laid into him almost as soon as he had the chance to start talking.

"I love your show, you got a great show," Ice Cube noted. "But you be bucking up against that line a little bit," he added, just before upbraiding him for sounding like a "redneck trucker" once in a while.

"I have two questions: what made you think it was cool to say that?" Ice Cube asked. Maher noted that he had given it no thought; it was a comedic reaction in the moment, one that was begging to be made given the ready premise Sasse had inadvertently set up with his own "work the fields" phrase. Ice Cube accepted Maher's apology, but proceeded to try to get to the "psyche" of the matter. "There's a lot of guys out there who cross the line 'cause they a little too familiar ... it's a word that has been used against us; it's like a knife, man," he said. "It's been used as a weapon against us, by white people, and we are not going to let that happen again, by nobody."

As I watched the clip, I tried to bring myself to imagine the pains of growing up in a black neighborhood, in "the projects" constantly surveilled by white policemen who saw black bodies as threatening. I tried to imagine the anger immortalized in the lyrics from one of Ice Cube's popular tracks, where he and other members of the rap group NWA write:

A young nigga got it bad cause I'm brown
And not the other color so police think
They have the authority to kill a minority[16]

I tried to hold close the trauma of watching one's family lynched by fully faced white men who knew that the law was on their side and their extrajudicial killings would sink back into the texture of things. How could one not be angry when white men passed around the body parts of their hollowed-out victims, and smiled for the cameras as they held those parts like souvenirs? The word *nigger* scorches Negro backs in the heat of its fury, lands on one's face like auburn spit through gritted teeth, and turns the ghosts of those memories—whose spectral bodies still bear the marks of that painful label.

I could identify with Ice Cube. I may not have agreed with his position, but I could honor the scowl beneath his remarks on *Real Time*—for, make no mistake about it, white people *did* name black people. I am no hip-hop lyricist, but in feeling with Ice Cube, in churning those transgressive memories of bodies elided, I imagine that early white slave owners, colonialists, and even present day authority figures say:

I name you nigger. I name you black.

I serve you this dish with a side of repulsion and disgust.

The black I name you is not the innocent absence of light, the tide of night in its ebb and flow, but an abominable vacancy, the depthless stretch of your bodily ineptitude and moral profligacy.

I name you monster, you blight on the glorious order of salvation—perverse and evil in your imaginations. I reduce your many hues to the one color of your sin, Dark Continent.

I name you wretch. And the burden of my days will be to yield to the benevolence
I shall exercise in finding ways to save you from yourself. To redeem you into the
original score your cacophonous sounds have fallen short of.

I am sorry, dear, if this doesn't sit with the terroir of your times—all
this hate and agony and wounds. But I suspect that whatever world you live
in can only be a bit more mature to the extent it has learned how to honor
even hate, how to hold space for its passing, how to hold the urgency of its
yearning without dumbing it down under the Band-Aids of forced positivi-
ty—a point that brings me to the other half of those hastily contrived lyrics
of mine, the black response:

You know that thing you did with us? Naming us and all that jazz? Well, I do it
to you too. So, here: I name you white. I call you out. I name your pale-pinkness,
your aversion to colors, your fragility in the face of difference.

You brand my body with your empire; I name you plague.

You cut me off from the ground and hoisted me in unwilling branches—my limp
body suspended in midair a figure for your own longing to fly. Your own longing
to escape these rufous curls of earthly matters. But you are no angel, so I name
you deluded.

This word you force on me to own me, nigger, let this word be our own shibboleth,
but a constant reminder of your twisted benevolence. You will never cross this line.
You will always remember your guilt, and speak with deferred words that will not
come. For you yourself, in your pale-faced whiteness, will never arrive.

And these words, if faithful to the universe of interracial relations Ice
Cube inhabits to some degree, show how blackness is a phenomenon of
white arrangements. Much in the same way postmodernism derives its angst
from modern foundationalism, blackness is a white construct only made possible by the industrial conditions that assigned dark bodies on a ladder of
proximity to power. Blackness is a spatiotemporal allocation of bodies within
the logic of modern ascendancy. It is forcing the posthuman polymorphism
of bodies into the single teleological track of "American hierarchy." The line

Cube warns Maher and Maher's audience never to cross, the line that preserves black power and the integrity of our identity—guarded by the reverse engineering of the word *nigger* and forged in trauma and pain—is the same line that locks us in, keeps us immured to a threshold that delineates possible power to the exclusion of other places of power.

To the degree that white supremacy valorizes, organizes, and directs attention—in an orchestra of bodies and stories—toward the summit of the pyramid, it denies other places of power. It denies the agency of the world around us, the enchantment that sews all things into a quilt of co-becoming. The structure that allocates identity and fixes it in place also befogs the ongoingness of these "identities," blinding the eye from noticing how spread-out we are, how the many colors we take on bend with the play and openings and closures of topographical shifts, climactic changes, and biological matterings. To speak of blackness as if it were an essence or whiteness as if it were a fixed other is to ironically extend the reach of white normativity.

Ice Cube, in conversation with Maher, notes that black people can use the same word that white people are absolutely barred from using. He suggests that the context doesn't matter—so long as you are white, you are prohibited from using the n-word. Of course, this essentializes whiteness to estrange it from blackness, which is in turn a move of "white power."

As a rhetorical device, I might make the claim that prior to the colonial moment, there was no such thing as "blackness." Except perhaps as an occasional description, "blackness" and its charged theo-psychological undertones of backwardness and biological monstrosity did not emerge except as a substitute category within an industrial order of limited allocations and privileged recipients. This is the same industrial order of the American homeland that situated whiteness as a

> *homogeneous identity offered to newly arrived European immigrants in lieu of their own peculiar peculiarities. The myth of white sameness [in turn anchored] African slaves and aboriginal savages [to] a fantasy of colored difference and a fiction of natural inferiority.*[17]

Here, in these modern wastelands, blackness is perpetually hidden away behind the polished figures of its own trauma, behind sensitive walls. Locked in. Waiting. Accusatory. It sees the same vision of power that whiteness coaxes it to adopt: food security as access to shopping malls; prosperity as more dollar bills than one can spend; the self as an atomized individual that knows no community or treats community as the proximity of estranged bodies, not the strange we-ness that precedes I-ness; and the Future—that imaginary of techno-utopian supremacy—as the only possible timeline.

A shamanic perspective draws upon shapeshifting ontologies, cosmologies of dust and threadbare boundaries, and other visions of power-with-the-world. Within such a worldview, one cannot be "black" or "white." Not for long. This is, however, not an ethos that is blind to colors or seeks to synthesize them into a general all-color neutrality. Instead, it is potentially an approach that emphasizes racial differences and peculiarities only to the degree that it stitches those identities within a quilt of mutual entanglement. Only to the extent that the "other" becomes the condition for the one's existence, and vice versa. This entanglement ropes in not just human contributions to race but nonhuman contributions as well. In fact, one is not only black but green and blue and yellow-spotted and red-hued. That is because human bodies are the workings of both human and nonhuman agencies, or should we say "non/human" agencies. For example, the role of climate change intra-acting with melanin, and congealing in color-polymorphic bodies and phenotypic plasticity and new genetic adaptations, is just one instance of the way the environment has racializing effects,[18] and why whiteness (or blackness) is not simply a state of mind, a moral choice, or social construction.

Our manners of explaining race hinge on tracing ancestry and examining historical matters in terms of the legacy of colonial infractions and the tragedy of contemporary occlusions. We tend to think of blackness as stable, making it the unit of analysis, holding it constant as factors around it change. That reading does not account for the breathtaking intra-activity of the world, where time itself is not a mere container for the goings-on "in" the world but part of its reiterativity. Being part of an ever-changing, ever fluid, open-ended material-discursive universe means the past is not fixed and is often resituated;[19] that though the intergenerational trauma of racial violence marks our bodies and inhabits social structures, trauma is not to be summarily resolved but is often "practiced into relative stability"; and that the work of decolonization or of addressing these issues are not uniquely human—since race is more-than-human. In short, black bodies are not the products of black ancestries traced back, but the intra-acting negotiation of bodies and climate and economic power and theological categories and the modern will to purpose, direction, and power. In a manner of speaking, blackness (like "whiteness"), to be generative and prolific, needs to be "reimmersed" in the stream of mangled and co-emergent colors it was extricated from. We are not black or white: the interface between bodies and worlds is continuous and ceaselessly flowing so that race is not a property of individuals or something we are "in." It is the world in its many doings. That of course is not to say race is a separate ontological category of its own, hardboiled into the scheme of things, and oblivious to fluid power dynamics and class constructions. Such demarcations are no longer tenable. I mean to say that being black or white is not just about social arrangements —even though that is an important point to make—it is also about movements in the world. It is material-discursive. And what race means, and how we make distinctions between being this or that, is ever-changing—due to human and non-human forces.

In short, Shiva—the god of dust—stands at the door and knocks. The ground is giving way. He melts through "the line" like it wasn't even there, and he challenges our claims to identity. For healing to happen to both white and black, to address white supremacy, a new ethos is demanded. A quantum leap from keeping the other at bay to noticing we are already the "others," already entangled in palimpsests of trauma and possibility and co-becoming. New concepts disturb the rigidity of "identity" and help us see how already entangled we are. How prolific, promiscuous, porous, and potent our becoming is. And how this can inspire a different ethos of responsivity.

✦

In many African cosmologies, a call-response dynamic is built into the ways we see the world.[20] In Yoruba music, for instance, you are very likely to hear the singer only within the ecology of many other voices, who seem to attend to his or her singing, answer his questions, or emphasize a strain or lyric the singer seeks to expound upon. It is something different from the dependent relationship a band has with its lead singer. The act is premised on this in-betweenness, as is more apparent in juju music and highlife. Sometimes the background even comes to the foreground, switching places in a fluid rejection of static roles. Such is the rhythm that imbues our world.

It is not only present in music, but in how we dance (in dyads) and in how we communicate. I have often found myself more willing and more able to wax poetic when speaking before a crowd, when that crowd "hmm-hmms" or vocalizes presence in some way.[21] Recently, I have begun incorporating the call *"aló o"*[22] before I speak, asking the audience, European, Asian or otherwise, to respond by shouting *"aló!"*—oftentimes to comedic results. In retrospect, the many pastors that preached in the churches I attended, who would punctuate their sermons with "Can someone shout 'Hallelujah'?" ad nauseam, knew in their bones that they were only permitted to speak to the degree the so-called audience also did. To speak is to speak-together-with.

When Yoruba people respond with *"asé"* to the proclamations of a king, in greeting, in praise of another, or in libatory moments, they perform this call-response betweenness. *Asé*, usually paraphrased as the Christian "Amen" or "So be it" of Hebraic etymology, means more than a granting of affirmation. In Ifá tradition, it is a philosophy that imbues everything, that makes change happen, that motivates the earth to breathe and the skies to regurgitate rain from their bellies. While some scholars define *asé* as "a coming to pass; law; command; authority; commandment; enjoinment; imposition; power; precept; discipline; instruction; cannon; biding; document; virtue; effect; consequence; imprecation,"[23] Imhotep writes that *asé* is extraordinarily complex, a polysemic word that "does not signify anything particular, yet it invests all things, exists everywhere and as the warrant for all creative activity,"[24] and suggests that its underlying theme is "power."

In other words, *asé* is the sound of the euphoric "participatoriness" of all things. The tonality of the gathering. The premise of change and the signature of hope. It is the cosmology of middles, one that hints that power is not contained in this or that, hidden away in a trope, or found at the distance. The divine is sprinkled in everything. *Asé* might very well be aligned with the performativity of dust.

Worthy of mention is that *asé* is seen as a vital force kept by Èsù, the trickster-deity of the Yoruba pantheon—who in the abracadabra of colonial inflections became Satan, the devil required to satisfy the Christian thirst for duality. But Èsù is something more than devil and is not to be replaced by the ghost that haunts Christian notions of embodied evil, as Funso Aiyejina intones:

> *The definition of Èsù which has, however, persisted in the popular imagination is the Euro-Christian one which maligns him as the devil/Satan. This definition was midwifed by Bishop Samuel Ajaiyi Crowther (1806–1891) who, in his pioneering translation of the Bible into Yoruba, had chosen Èsù as the Yoruba equivalent of the Christian Satan. In A Dictionary of the Yoruba Language, published in 1913 by the Church Missionary Society Bookshop, Lagos, Nigeria, Èsù is defined as the devil, a definition that would be repeated, albeit alongside other more traditional Yoruba definitions, in the 1958 University of London's Dictionary of Modern Yoruba.[25]*

Aiyejina goes further to read out Èsù's incredible roster of accomplishments, his cosmic résumé:

> *In Yoruba philosophy, Èsù emerges as a divine trickster, a disguise-artist, a mischief-maker, a rebel, a challenger of orthodoxy, a shape-shifter, and an enforcer deity. Èsù is the keeper of the divine asé with which Olodumare created the universe; a neutral force who controls both the benevolent and the malevolent supernatural powers; he is the guardian of Orunmila's oracular utterances. Without Èsù to open the portals to the past and the future, Orunmila, the divination deity would be blind. As a neutral force, he straddles all realms and acts as an essential factor in any attempt to resolve the conflicts between contrasting but coterminous forces in the world. Although he is sometimes portrayed as whimsical, Èsù is actually devoid of all emotions. He supports only those who perform*

prescribed sacrifices and act in conformity with the moral laws of the universe as laid down by Olodumare. As the deity of the "orita"—often defined as the crossroads but really a complex term that also refers to the front yard of a house, or the gateway to the various bodily orifices—it is Èsù's duty to take sacrifices to target-deities. Without his intervention, the Yoruba people believe, no sacrifice, no matter how sumptuous, will be efficacious. Philosophically speaking, Èsù is the deity of choice and free will. So, while Ogun may be the deity of war and creativity and Orunmila the deity of wisdom, Èsù is the deity of prescience, imagination, and criticism—literary or otherwise.[26]

Èsù, as the trickster fiddling with the cradling strings from which everything emerges, is the personification of *asé:*

Èsù is the Divine Messenger between God and Man. Èsù sits at the Crossroad. Èsù is the Orisa that offers choices and possibility. Èsù is the gatekeeper, the guardian of the door. Èsù safeguards the principle of freewill. Èsù is the keeper of asé.[27]

I am especially delighted to know that Èsù sits at the crossroad—and where else would he sit, actually? If *asé* is borne in response, in the riddling middle of reality, in the betweenness of things, then the one who keeps it has to be a phenomenon of the crossroads. And the fact that Èsù sits there finds a conceptual playmate in the notion of diffraction—the optic phenomenon that "troubles the very notion of dicho-tomy—cutting into two—as a singular act of absolute differentiation, fracturing this from that, now from then"[28]—as put forward by Karen Barad. This concept of diffraction figures in a decolonial notion of self and identity that Barad echoes when she quotes Trinh Minh-ha:

Identity as understood in the context of a certain ideology of dominance has long been a notion that relies on the concept of an essential, authentic core that remains hidden to one's consciousness and that requires the elimination of all that is considered foreign or not true to the self, that is to say, non-I, other. In such a concept the other is almost unavoidably either opposed to the self or submitted to the self's dominance. It is always condemned to remain its shadow while attempting at

being its equal. Identity, thus understood, supposes that a clear dividing line can
be made between I and not-I, he and she; between depth and surface, or vertical
and horizontal identity; between us here and them over there.[29]

The concept of self and identity, redescribed in the queer materialism and diffractivity of *asé*, cannot conceive of the "other" as "negativity, lack, [or] foreignness"; it repudiates the idea of identity as "an impenetrable barrier between self and other [that is set up] in an attempt to establish and maintain its hegemony."[30] In other words, just as you find bands of darkness in light, and a heart of light in the blackest shadow, the self and the not-self are not separate, and difference—though real—is not fixed, but dynamic and co-emergent.

Èsù sits at the crossroads. The crossroads is not the place that lies ahead, a one-time occurrence. All roads are crossroads; every highway a junction of intra-sections. Matter-mind ... reality ... every "thing" is already a quilt whose sewers, human and nonhuman, are scattered across space-time— every object a node in the cosmopolitical, material-discursive traffic of things crisscrossing, cross-hatching, crossing-out, bleeding-in each other.

Asé disturbs the idea that whiteness is an "other" to blackness, but sees "both" as arising from the same matrix. It does not deny difference; it queers separation. It dispels the myth of unilineal oppression or independent victimhood, tying both the powered and the disempowered in a call-response ambivalence. Power does not flow from them to us. Dominance cuts both ways, injuring the colonized and reinforcing the strictures of the colonizer, but even that dynamic is not locked in place. The past we often mourn in our intellectual projects that seek a "returning to Eden," to reclaim a sense of indigeneity, were never coherently indigenous, harmonious, or without shadows. Modernity is not essential evil come destroy our havens of communal living and well-being.

Èsù, like Shiva, fritters away the tough edges between us, calling us to inspect our claims to victimhood, to lean into nontarget populations. To learn to pour libations at the crossroads. One cannot easily condense Èsù's nebulous character into well-polished morals-of-the-story or principles or even underlying themes, a situation that ironically informs a different ethos of racial justice: that in the game of sides, the greatest loss suffered is the other side.

✦

I make the case, my dear—as a black or rather a "black-black" man looking through the lenses of agential realism and my own indigenous cosmologies— that blackness is a phenomenon of white normativity or of a modern spatialization project that occludes the material vibrancy of the more-than-human world, snuffing out other places of power and hiding away the language of the trees, if you will. Blackness is a product of white power—a response made possible and meaningful within preset frames. In asserting the purity of our identity, in essentializing the other and fixing power in this modern logic of hierarchy and ascendancy, we are blinded to ways of being "otherwise" with planet, with people, with generations to come, and with power. Only within the binary sterilization of modernity, only within a settler epistemology of fixed Newtonian bubble identities, only within a world shorn of its vibrancy and agency, does blackness become naturalized as inferiority and become associated with backwardness. "Outside" of the quests for equality or reconciliation, there is a sensuous, richly generative, luxurious intra-activity of bodies ... a stream of becoming and movement that disrupts the hard edges of our claims to blackness or whiteness, and engages white normativity and privilege from a place that is simultaneously compassionate and generative— without turning a blind eye to the oppression suffered.

The way the British colonists took over Igbo settlements and gained adherents for Christianity was to reverse the roles the Osus played. The Osus' untouchability, once a mark of sacredness, became repulsive distance. They had hitherto operated within a posthuman cosmology, which allowed them to think of themselves within a community of other beings. A web of life that connected them in vital links with their environment. *A fish is not wet inside water.*

They offered sacrifices and paid homage to the gods, who were in turn embodied performances of their environments, peeping through the stories the people shared, stirring in renegade gusts of wind, dreaming with the soft breathings of every dust-infiltrated surface. The lifeblood of the community they served hinged on the balance between the mundane and the sacred. As such, to be human was to be in debt to other actors, seen and unseen. To be human was to be immersed in a sensuous world that did things to you.

By displacing this posthuman sensitivity, the colonialists downplayed the agencies of the nonhuman and more-than-human world around them—and not just for the Osus ... this is how colonialism took place and still does: a shrinkage of the wide, wild, nonessential, nonteleological vitality and abundance of the world into a grim binary, a bitter modernity that reifies the human being as orphaned agent and the world outside of him as tool. Draining all the agency away from the material world, wrapping it into an essentialist bundle, and stuffing it into the human being as a natural category meant that the world was reduced to a machine.

Education was now to be gained in isolated, suspiciously standardized places called schools, and not in the immediacy of a moment or by learning from the environment. The free-flowing gift cultures that coincided with the values of Ubuntu—the idea that I am, not because I think, but because you are—were undermined by a new economic milieu defined by artificial scarcity, greed and pyramidal quests for ascension. A new universal metric for evaluating wealth displaced the abundance these cultures had known. All that was left for the lords to do was to rapidly convert indigenous artefacts, lands and these cultures into commodities.

In order to help this world-eating machine of capital globalization grow more tentacles, a universal time and singular future was pressed upon everyone. A linear notion of time—one that flows from past to present and to the future—helped foreground the discourses of development and progress as the engine of a Future-yet-to-come. That same clock, floating disembodied and static over everything, has shut down the way time was negotiated between plant and ear, between moon and tide, between the bulging saccharine sweetness of a ripe fruit and a farming family. The rituals of attending to what the world is doing are displaced by new modern rituals of trying to escape it.

Blackness—at least to some of us black-black people—is a "passenger concept." The class divisions on an airplane—first class, business class, and coach—only make sense within the airplane. The plane's architecture organizes its transient airborne society according to those categories. Could it be said that our black identities speak more to the particular social architecture we inhabit, haunted by worlds elided and practices forgotten, than to some essential identity within?

Modernity, the mapping project of locating bodies (whether female, environmental, object, animal bodies) within absolute categories like "space" and "time,"[31] shaped blackness within an enlightenment settler humanist ontology. As such, white normativity is the heartland of blackness, for it was fashioned not only as a class tool for creating wage-free slave populations, but by the new "blacks" themselves as a rejection of the material essentialism of their bodies by which they were stabilized into servitude. Blackness became their existential struggle to transcend the new spatialized territories, or a rejection of the fixedness of the "nature" exploited by capitalism. Where being black might have been an issue of complexion, modernity's cubicle ontology predesignated it as "lack."

If a word is only understood within context—deriving its intelligibility within a stream of other words—then modernity is the gridlock that separates words away from the umbilical cord of sentences. Within this framework, the goal of synthesis—or two separate things coming together—plays out. Justice becomes about black people having just as much economic and political access as white people. However, if blacks finally transcend their unfair placement in white settlements, I would argue that this would be the greatest triumph for white normativity—because even though winners would have changed, the game still abides. When black people fetishize blackness, white settlements are reinforced.

If white normativity is agential, then its purpose is to continue to find intelligent and resilient ways to organize society in a hierarchical way. Its effects are to valorize difference as separation and enforce closures, to lock the "I" away from the "not-I." By maintaining a harsh cut between black and white, male and female, dead and living, animate and inanimate, modern ontologies obstruct an appreciation for the unending traffic between mutual borders—the intra-activity that insists, quite rudely, that black and white are co-constitutive. Even more critically, and this point needs to be emphasized in the context of the conversation about "other places of power," the dissociation of the "human" figure from the environment creates relationships of power that emphasize exploitation over nature, not partnership or co-becoming *with* nature.

This colonial logic of identity—whether black identity, white identity, female identity, or male identity—rigorously denies that spillages are possible, that our bodies are actually doing something that undercuts the rigidity and confidence of our passionate discussions. It nails down identity by settling for an anorexic pixel in the stead of a screen, and for a morsel of the canvas—still life—where the portrait is still being painted by a sympoiesis of bodies. An *asé* of bodies.

This is all to say that we became black when we were surgically removed from a stream of many colorful becomings, and positioned in a rigid table of categories … when we were stabilized and naturalized as citizens of a globalizing status quo. That status quo is characterized by an emphatic focus on the sole agency and supremacy of human beings above communities of nonhumans, the erosion of multiple pasts, the occlusion of the abundance and gifts of the world, a mechanistic ontology and the fostering of a single Future. To address racism and oppression, one must notice the materiality of the social conditions that hold us in place, in suspense, while occluding other ways of being in the world. In preserving itself, what this complex of oppression invites us to advocate for is equality. The ideal of a world where blacks are finally equal to whites (or even the prospects of black domination) is as unsatisfactory an ethical response to patriarchal domination as is taking a child's playthings away—and then rewarding the child with the promise not to beat her too much if she stops crying so loudly.

Why be equal? Why abide a metric of equality that pays no mind to the ways we diffractively enable and disable and permit each other? Why do we gather and mourn at the race track, in a stadium filled with other games to play? It is an underwhelming compensation—one that pretends that blacks—and whites—are really bound by a phallic system of value, and that the only way to be relevant, to be useful, to be real, is to ascend a pyramidal structure, the estranged pinnacle of which is the source of power.

Is there a universal black experience, a policed line that should not be crossed? Is my blackness still subject to the elements, or do I betray it by furnishing you, Alethea, with a "white argument" that betrays the experiences and sufferings of people who look like me? Am I a sell-out? Or is there something in noticing that even this blackness will go the way of other colors: in the compost heap that disciplines everything?

Even right now, like spent charcoal in a dead bonfire exposed to the air, I flitter away in soot and pieces. The closer I come to my identity, the more I see that it is diffracted, dispersed, and unevenly distributed across time and space, so that to say I am "black" is to cut a chunk away from my inexhaustibleness.

You, for instance, are a shocking palimpsest of colors and bodies.

Your mum lies now on the bare floor a few meters from where I sit. Her beautiful body is riddled with chicken-pox rashes and scars, as she is halfway in her recovery. It has been a tough seven days taking care of her. To blame the varicella zoster virus as the culprit here would be to forget its entanglement with other agencies. This is to say that your mother's chicken pox is itself a movement of other bodies, environmental configurations, biological events, and situated cultural practices of taking care. The diffractive becomings of chicken pox are a good figure for identity. Like the wind on its way, identity is never still—a point Maxine Sheets-Johnstone makes in her book *The Primacy of Movement* when she affirms that movement forms the "I that moves" before the "I that moves" forms movement.[32]

In the absence of a DNA test and a family history from my side of the family, your mum wanted to impress you with just how convoluted your identity is—and just how much she is proud of your heritage. So, weak and exhausted, her face yellowed with turmeric and her body spotted with a neem leaf emulsion, she traced out your maternal web of others. I reproduce it here for you to see:

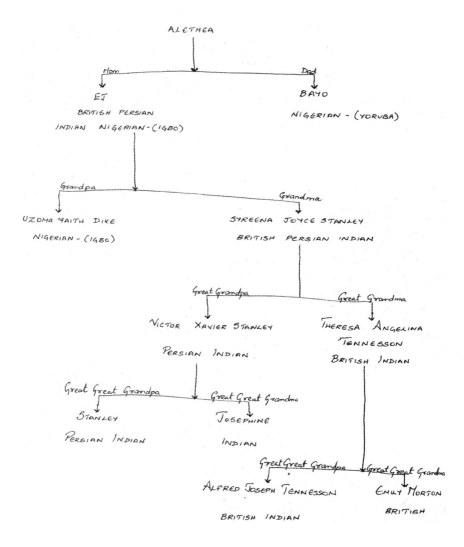

I really don't want to bore you with commentary on your lineage, so I hope your mum's handwriting is clear enough to confuse you about your "true" identity or your innocent appropriations of brownness. There is no essence here, just movement—connecting colonizer and colonized in erotic mixtures. Somewhere down the line you have an English great *great* grandmother and Iranian parentage, an African grandfather, and Indians all the way down. But even this does not capture the complexity of your heritage: not only is each person here not a stable Newtonian mix of already static identities, their identities—even though most here are dead—are still being rewritten.

Family trees are fundamentally structured to represent identity as a stream of past events congealing into the moving present. In that time conception, the past is done with: if we could capture all the elements of your ancestry together, or find a way to trace your heritage "back" in the record of races that have contributed themselves to you, we can theoretically form an aggregate of these individual identities and squeeze out what you really are—as we would squeeze out juice from an orange. That proposal falls in the face of a different notion of time, one that modernity chases away to make room for its homogenous universal clock, and one that is at the heart of racism, anthropocentrism, sexism, and speciesism.

In many indigenous non-Western cultures, time is circular—not flowing forward from past to present then future, but entangled together in a thick now, so that the past is still accessible and the future can be remembered. Or as Karen Barad puts it, "the past is yet to come."[33]

Do you remember the double-slit experiment I described to you in the last letter? The one with the sticky wall and one of your confused grandmas? Where the very nature of reality is called into question, and where we find that only a relational ontology could possibly help us make sense of the queerness at the heart of things? Well, it gets stranger. A modified version of that experiment challenges our conceptions of time. It's called the delayed choice quantum eraser experiment. You could just call it the "Grandma waits to look at the balls" experiment.

In the original double-slit experiment, if you bring a source of light near a barrier with two slits in it, on the far side of the slits you'll register fringe patterns, or undulating ridges of shadow and light, on a screen. If you were to use particles, sending them flying toward the barrier with slits, you still register a fringe pattern—even when you send each particle one by one. When you try to find out which slit the particle went through, the pattern on the screen changes back to what you would expect for particle behavior. As soon as you stop observing which way (which slit) the particles went, the interference pattern returns. Right.

Where we left your grandma the last time was near both windows, recording which particular window each of our hurled balls went through. Because we aren't so sure that grandma isn't meddling with the thrown balls before they pass through the openings—even though she swears on her life that she has nothing to do with the queer results we are obtaining—we decide to move the poor woman outside the house, in between the windows and the freshly painted wall (I know this is stretching the metaphor but stick with me). Her job is like before—only this time—she is to carefully observe which windows the balls are coming through, after they've already come through it. Her eyes are wide open as the balls sail through either of two windows. As they land on the wall, the two ridges of stain marks (not the diffraction pattern) emerges. She shouts this out to us—telling us there is no diffraction pattern.

But alas, the thing we most feared happens: one of the balls hits grandma in her head, and she staggers away, calling it quits with our nonsensical game. We were blindfolded, so we couldn't tell where the balls were going through—and now, the only person that can tell is out of whack. We remove our blindfolds. Instead of two ridges—we see endless rows on the wall. Remember we had established an order to this madness before: when we don't know which window the balls go through, we get the endless ridges of ball stains. When we know, we get only two. Now we effectively "switched off" our ability to know after the balls had already struck the wall, and even though two ridges formed, they disappeared after grandma walked away—it is as if they were never even there before. As if the moment grandma walked away, the balls went back in time and altered their behavior, exhibiting the diffraction pattern.

In nongrandma terms, what these experiments show is that even after the particles have hit the final screen—showing a pattern that tells us they are "particles" because we have information about which slits they are going through, the results can be "reversed" when we remove our ability to gain that information. We see a diffraction pattern when detection is turned off, consistent with the fact that we are dealing with waves. What is downright queer is that the particles behave as if they were *always* waves—as if they went back in time, altered their history and rejoined us as waves. A case of a future event causing the past? An instance of time travel? Or a queerer story?

Karen Barad offers some thoughts:

> *So the point here is: how do physicists interpret this? The way physicists interpret this is by saying that we have the ability to change the past. Because I am chang- ing how it went through the slit after it has already gone through the slits. So there is a talk about erasing what already was, restoring the diffraction pattern, and basically moving the clock backwards or changing how the particle went through after it has already gone through: the ability to change the past. Now I want to suggest, though, that that is a very convenient kind of nostalgic fantasy. I cannot blame physicists for engaging in this. I think this is a very seductive fantasy. Perhaps at one time or another all of us wish that we could change the past and the marks left on bodies, and change the ways in which we materialized the world, especially when we are not being careful, that we would like to undo what has been done, that we would like to go back and do it differently. But is this really what this experiment is telling us about what is possible?*[34]

She then offers insights diffractively gained from feminist theory and cul- tural studies that what is happening here is not a simple return of a previous diffraction pattern, but a new one. The deeper implications here are that time is just as indeterminate, and not the parameter that matches forward from past to present to future. It is constantly reiterated in the now.

> *What we are seeing here is that time is not given, it is not universally given, but rather that time is articulated and re-synchronized through various material practices. In other words, just like position, momentum, wave, and particle, time itself only makes sense in the context of particular phenomena.... The "past" was never simply there to begin with, and the "future" is not what will unfold,*

but "past" and "future" are iteratively reconfigured and enfolded through the world's ongoing intra-activity. There is no inherently determinate relationship between past, present, and future.[35]

Temporality is co-constituted and reassigned in the particularity of each moment. Bodies don't move 'in' time or through time; bodies and time are configured together. *Asé* means that even time must come to the crossroads, not linger above it. Memory and remembering, for instance, are not about latching on to an already-done-with past, but are about recreating the past each time memory is evoked. But does this mean we can singularly change the past? Does this mean we can erase the traces of different iterations of the past and impose the ones we prefer? Remember the diffraction pattern does not return when the detector is "off"; a new one is created that is haunted by the memories of the "previous."

The past, like the future, though, is not closed. But "erasure" is not what is at issue. In an important sense, the "past" is open to change. It can be redeemed, productively reconfigured in an iterative unfolding of space-time-matter. But its sedimenting effects, its trace, cannot be erased. The memory of its materializing effects is written into the world. So changing the past is never without costs, or responsibility.[36]

Indigenous worlds resist the idea of universal homogeneous world history. The identities of our forebears, seemingly locked in the past, are still being remade. Time bends and dances and jumps from here to there—or, following Barad, makes "here" and "there" by jumping. The idea that "the past is yet to come," that the Future imposed by the developmental models we subscribe to, and that causality is a lot more than mechanical bodies bouncing off each other, undermines the totalizing regimes of homogeneous time, which—it is possible to argue—was one of the foremost tools employed by colonial forces to estrange communities from their own wealth, from their own intimate partnerships with nature, from their own anticipatory disciplines, and from other places of power.

This moment here now is alive with the dense seeds of other times and spaces—pasts/futures in constant reconfiguration. That the past is alive (not rooted in a singular universal Futurism) challenges the emptiness of enlightenment time. It is not about erasing the tears of oppression that once landed on anonymous barren earth—the sorrows of our mothers and fathers. It is about the constant generativity of what is supposedly done but not forgotten. It is about what the past can yet become, what the tears falling to the ground might yet fertilize. It is the queer idea that we cannot allocate these lively marks on our bodies to the category of "history" (leave it there or bury it, for even the dead are active).

To truly honor the past is to admit it moves—and to admit it still speaks and haunts diffractively through our current specific contexts and circumstances is to do the difficult work of revisiting our standpoints and finding new questions to ask by lingering in the silences of what we don't know.

The point I stress is that we are haunted by what we've repressed. Given insights generated by indigenous traditions, quantum physics, and feminist materialisms about the queerness of temporality, the collective intelligence of the world around us, the intra-connectedness of all things, the agency of materiality and its entanglement with discursivity, we have to rethink racial justice vis-à-vis the rhizomic emergence of identities. If becoming is an "open, nonpurposeful, contingent process," characterized by a "becoming-with" (or sympoiesis), then racial justice is not necessarily a race for races but might (yet) be a slowing down—to a complete stop if necessary—to consider the tracks that urge us on.

It's not that there is something conceptually inadequate about our descriptions/actions for racial justice; it is that our engagements are themselves fashioned within an apparatus—namely, modernity—that thrives on those charged distinctions between black and white and absolute notions of separateness to work, while leaving out the contributions the world is already making to our realities.

We are situated in an architecture of racism. Racism or prejudice is not a human attribute any more than humans are themselves independent, self-contained, and separate from the unspeakable material-spiritual goings-on. This architecture is not entirely conversational or discursive. It is biological, material, visceral—implicating not just our communicative transactions or knowledge-creation practices.

Perhaps, then, if the holding milieu were any different, Diallo's claim to blackness might have been investigated with different lenses. With the sensitivity of an "Osu," who knows that fathers often "come back" in form of their children, who understands that the whisperings of one's ancestors are often mistaken for madness, and who knows how to consult with other agencies. But under modern circumstances, each "side" is locked in. An Osu's blackness generously opens up a world of crazy dreams, ancestral connections, queer pasts, posthumanist performativity, and the connections our bodies are making that we moderns do not see because we are trapped in our castles of identity politics. No one is essentially black or white; we all are a becoming-black/white. Race is not biological determinism, or linguistic absolutism—not fixed or arbitrary; it is emergent. It is not even a thing of human ancestry alone, since the human is a matter of the nonhuman becoming.

Race is a gerund.

This is not to say that we should just hold hands (whatever that means!) and walk into some future, forgetting the whispering of our ancestors and the tender wounds inflicted upon us even now. Entanglement is not submission to a hive mind or an effacement of differences; it is instead, as Trinh Minh-ha reminds us again, noticing that we are inescapably interconnected—and this is tragedy and hope.

Who knows? With an Osu cosmology, Diallo's infiltration might have been an opportunity to meet our notions of identity as if for the first time, to ask weird questions, and to examine the historical, technological, material, geographical and colonial conditions that situate blackness(es) and whiteness(es). I tell this story of the Osus because we are living in times of deep forgetfulness, but the point is not to see that pasts are never remembered—pasts are re-membered. Reconfigured over and over again. Not erased. But manufactured from the threads of this very moment.

In so far as our colors abide on this single track, on this trajectory of progress and anthropocentrism, within this space-time cartography of whiteness—the same framework that once colonized and still colonizes white people too—we might never know other places of power.

Blackness is the figure of being late and the pressure to be punctual to a time that is not ours; it is this Sisyphean striving to arrive early to a party that started long before we were told about it. And for so long, we have stood at the gates, and we have stammered out excuses for not being punctual enough, and we have fought for seats around the table where the juiciest plates are being arranged. We have demanded to be seen, to be heard, to be invited, and to be served. But therein lies the thick Faustian plot: in these moments of angst, for which our loud protests are christened a form of justice-seeking, and which are inscribed with a dense forgetfulness, we do not see that there are other clocks, and that there is no single universal homogenous world history to adhere to. The world does not careen toward progress, and human improvement and well-being are not matters owned by the practices of economic development and growth. There are songs that trees know that we haven't heard; there are alliances that termites and the pheromones they secrete forge that we can learn from; there are wild things that do not know the moral discipline of purpose or the colonizing influence of instrumentality; and then there are murmurations—the waltz of wind, sky, starling, and ground—which are not meant to be spoken about but merely to be seen and appreciated. In short, there are other powers, other agencies, and other clocks. And, perhaps, we release ourselves not only to the performance of our many colors, but we free those in the posh parties that have somehow denied us entry from their secret fears of losing their own seats at the table, when we say "there are other clocks, and we will not be on time."

✦

We are in the marked time of a global socio-economic order that hinders us from noticing our sensuous connections to each other. We are in a convoy of exhausted traffic blind to the expanse of wealth on the sides of the highway leading to an enlightenment Future—the future premised on the assumption that humans are alone, that nature is dead, that you and I are separate from each other. I refuse this premise. This repulsion at the heart of colonial truth. I am not separate from you. My father is not separate from me. We are not alone.

But how do we find our time? One might say that a different feminist ethos of racial sensuousness, an *asé* of racial justice-making, or what I call "transraciality," brings us initially to a notion of self and identity that are posthuman, diffractive, and intra-active. It invites us to see that racism does not sprout from racist human bodies containing ignorance and hatred but intra-active relationships that are always yet-to-come.

It slows us down to see that power is not only never complete, not only partially realized, but shared—so that victimhood can become an ironic vocation of maintaining problematic orders of things. In the same vein, it tells us that there is no perfect victim, no innocent past or coherent indigeneity that was lost and which we have to regain. It disciplines our edges and teaches us that every moment is a reconfiguration of identity—and that we do not ease gently from one second to another intact. That we will not solve racial injustice, and that our inability to do so is not a function of our inadequacy or a want of ideas, or because racial injustice is sewn into the very nature of matter, but because we—the once coherent selves of humanist imaginations—are not at all central to the equation of the world. Asé forbids this. We are not complete. We are not in charge. Our best exertions will never totally embrace everything there is to consider, but will ripple out into the crossroads, touching here, excluding there. Far from being an invitation to despair, or to abandon efforts in service of racial justice, we are "called" (so it seems) to resituate ourselves within the mangle of other forces and to think of ourselves as co-participants with a world that never was inferior to us; a world that is also embroiled in material explorations and experimentations in the questions of justice. This "transraciality" is the very fabric by which all things matter, and by which things show up only partially. It does not dismiss the imaginary of equality, but it tells us how this is framed in an anorexic, neoliberal apparatus that obfuscates our multiple connections and potentials of partnership "with" nature.

If we frame racial justice within this apparatus—and there are specific contexts that demand this framing—then our victories will be dependent on the enactment of laws and operationalization of policies that address economic, political, and scientific exclusions of people of color. However, other justices are possible. Other ways of meeting each other. In a wide open space, in a world dislodged from its neoliberal coordinates, what racial matterings might look like are yet to be seen—and we may not be prepared for what wants to come next. Since there are no resolutions, no points of firm arrivals that are not already takeoff points for other kinds of emergence, each of our ideas and practices are what the "whole," or a movement of bodies that precedes us, is doing. Each of our projects are yearnings performing a provisionality. Each of us pours a libation at crossroads.

Perhaps an *asé* of racial becomings can gain ground in a politics of possibilities thrown open by this commitment to entanglements. Perhaps this is what whiteness can do: to ally with colored bodies and learn to develop "affective muscles"[37] with which they can serve as generous conduits of rage—letting screams of "I hate white people!"[38] be held not as evil or as something to be repressed but as the trans-affective flow that is dispersed in the world at large. To open up places and sites of inquiry where "I don't know, and I'm not sure we have this figured out" is the theme of the gathering. To direct money toward projects of the commons that do not necessarily yield returns on investment.

And because blackness cannot stay in antagonistic wait for answers, that identity is also being challenged by a world too corrosive for steady boundaries. A different ethos of "transraciality" queers the oppressor-victim dichotomy. I employ transraciality as distinct from *transracialism*—or when someone of one race decides to represent himself or herself as a member of another. Transraciality would be a postcolonial, diffractive understanding of race as a partial emergence of bodies that already includes radical others in its genealogy of becoming, as well as a posthumanist notion of race as a queer material-discursive intra-activity of bodies beyond linear ancestry. Transraciality could inspire black collectives to seek to understand the positions of nontarget dominant groups, or even extend invitations and receive contributions from others groups made to their traditions that are still extant. Spaces of shared grieving can be co-enacted. And because words don't possess meanings or come preset with meanings of their own, I even imagine days of jubilee in which white allies are allowed to open that hydraulically sealed capsule, survey its vexed and contemptuous content—the slur "nigger" or its rehabilitated variation "nigga"—and compost it by saying it in a multiracial ritual that allows intergenerational trauma and ghosts to roam free, if only to redeem the word and reclaim it for less divisive connotations.

None of these are of course prescriptions for rekindling racial relations or without risk. None of these are solutions. Also none of these ideas are necessarily teleological or directed at an ultimate portrait of racial justice. They are provocations to "think otherwise, to become otherwise."[39] Different contexts contain their own enabling and disabling features, a point that reinforces the idea that responsivity is never unilateral or entirely human, but is the shared agency between. There is no correct response for all situations, or fixed racial singularity in the far distance to which we all must tether our aspirations and multiple yearnings. What *asé* as a new materialist, posthuman redescription of racial matterings and a different ethos of responsivity provokes are opportunities to be otherwise—opportunities to come in touch with times other than the one Future of neoliberal progress that has hijacked racial justice imaginaries. Opportunities to re-member.

Do I dare consider transracialities that invite us to live intersectionally? Do I dare dream of a decolonial politics that allows us to confront these troubling ties we have with the supposed Others? One that frames engagement not merely in terms of reconciliation or equality among races—since equal opportunity within a structure reinforces the structure—but in terms of seeking out crossroads, and pouring libations in the places our bodies intersect with the many others that are already and already yet to be part of us? Do I dare confront the present, and explore its depths for the many within?

✦

The day you were born was a Wednesday. You know that, dear. You've seen me make reference to that day over and over again, through these letters. You have perhaps also noticed that everything I have shared with you seems to happen on a Wednesday. That's because when you were born, the world stopped turning, and every day before that and every day that will come was/will be a Wednesday, so long as I breathe.

✦

Now let me end this letter by telling you about the hushes that occasioned these musings on race. And the "forbidden child" that brought them to me. I remember the moment she walked in—this forbidden child. I started to sweat. I hadn't expected her to be so beautiful, so enrapturing. I began shuffling my feet restlessly beneath the table. I stood as she came closer. I had on an "unnecessary suit" and a pair of shoes with soles that stuck out like a tongue from a diseased mouth. I shook her hand formally, came behind her chair, pulled it out, and allowed her to sit. Then I circled back to my chair.

I had noticed her before. From a shy distance. But the day before, I was overcome by a need to meet her. Something about her called to me. Now, here she was. Sitting before me, a sight for sore eyes: her face was a perfect geometry of form and delicacy, a study in psychedelic depth. I controlled myself from looking directly at her, but noticed my eyes drifting from eyeing her face to her slender fingers, which she rested gracefully on the table.

At that point in my life, I was caught up in my quest for bigness. Still many miles away from Bàbá. Still buried in my books. Still searching for my place in a scheme guaranteed to benefit the faithful. Still committed to modernity and its fixations with categories. When she came, she was like nothing I had ever seen—a shocking monstrosity of pagan virtue. For someone who had worked so hard to obey the rules, to stick to the map, I knew she was not a product of rules. Somewhere, some persons had transgressed the protocols inscribed into the heart of things. The totem smashed, the forbidden child—your mother-to-come—sat with me.

And we sat there together, in that Nigerian university canteen, with an unopened Coke between us, speaking of our lives, the names we had given to our cars, the fact that we even had names for our laptops, and the loss of our fathers when we were both young. She was an expatriate lecturer in the department of biology and natural sciences, and I, a lecturer in psychology. Between us, a fervid chemistry bubbled … a warping of timelines, a queer temporality, an involution of plot and linearity.

Many days later, she gave me a gift. Two gifts, actually: your mum loved collecting things she found on the way. She would collect snail shells and bugs, or identify a plant or tree with its Latin name—telling me why it bloomed the way it did or what medicinal properties they had if they were used or approached in a particular way. She had a gentle regard and respect for all life, a talent for noticing misfits, and an eye for the invisible—often arguing during her classes that, contrary to the doctrinal proposals about the human's centrality in the world that were pervasive in our Christian university setting, plants were in fact superior life forms: they didn't have to move in order to be nourished, and they hadn't built an outrageous world-canceling civilization. By that time, we already had one dachshund and two Lhasa apso puppies between us. We called them our children, all three of them—Hiccup, Sasha, and Mila. Hiccup lived with us in our apartment, even though pets were not allowed on campus, while Sasha and Mila were in India, in her mum's house, yet to join us in Nigeria.

We once found the dried but wonderfully preserved body of a scarily huge dragonfly in her backyard. She kept that thing for weeks, while my first impulse was to jump anytime I noticed it. So she knew I had a thing for creepy-crawly things—even though deep down I had a fond but wary brotherly regard for her creatures, for we all together had been rescued from the treacherous highway by the good missus.

Well, one day we went out, and she noticed something in the shrubbery while we waited outside to see someone important to us. She bent down and picked up two snail-like things. The tiny critters looked like pitch black nudibranchs with irregular hairy protrusions from the rear end of what looked like long flagella. "Hushes," she said with a smile. I was already five feet away, urging her to put them away.

"They won't bite! Just come here and feel them," she ordered. So I adjusted my collar, straightened my shoulder, and walked up to them.

"Are you sure these things are safe, dear? Don't they stink or something?" I stuttered, as I held out my index finger to touch the hushes, suspending that move as I observed the squirming bodies.

"The world isn't safe or meant to be," she replied. "And yes, they stink—but it is okay."

They are just different, that's all. And what's a world without differences?

As the hushes slithered across her palm, the one holding the other, she asked me to touch them.

The fear is in the moment just before you come in touch, she said.

So I did, at first closing my eyes, silently reminding myself that these hushes were considerably small.

She looked at me, holding back her need to blurt out laughing.

"You are so horrible at this, Bayo!" she said. I started to mumble something about being indifferent to them and all that and blah-blah, when she announced that we were taking them home, and that they were to be our fourth and fifth children. The fourth and fifth in a series that was yet to come.

We didn't take them home, and I quickly forgot about the hushes, but a plot thicker than linear time was afoot.

At night, we pray together. Your father usually does it reluctantly, rolling his eyes when we mention Jesus, or when you punctuate every sentence with "oh, Lord"—imitating the way I pray. When you ask him to pray, he usually does so begrudgingly, and then holds an annoying frown on his face.

This morning, after we share a prayerful moment together, he turns around, his face dejected and sunken. He has never been good at hiding his feelings. I ask him why he is this way, and he stutters to explain himself, saying that he has deep reservations about you growing up to be Christian, to be like he was—casting the world in terms of good and evil, getting worked up about sin.

I remind him that you are only three, and that he must trust you to find your own way. He counters by saying he does trust you, and that he wonders if he can count on me not to fix you in my faith.

I am now angry with him. And I let him know that I have questions too and that I am also exploring what my faith means. I tell him I do not want to "fix" you into it—that you are an analytic thinker with highly attuned ears. I also remind him that he is often locked away in his writing, and then shows up like a manager from behind his closed door to complain about the noise in the workers' room. I tell him he cannot expect to swoop in to save the day once in a while. I need him in the muck with me, not lingering above it.

I say to your father: "One can become fanatic about religion, and one can become fanatic about keeping away from it. Are you willing that we hold space for her even if she grows into something you disagree with?"

He lowers his head. He does that when he comes to see himself. He had once told me that "Just like plants need fertilizer to grow, we need to hold close our bullshit—and practice the slippery yet sacred art of self-deprecation." I remind him of this, and he nods his head gently.

From where I lie on the bed, I turn my attention to the hall, where you are playing with some Lego bricks. You are so blessed. How do I know? These struggles, these meetings with ourselves and negotiations of what it means to be there for you—often difficult and hypocritical and revelatory—are how I know. We are not perfect. We don't have this figured out. And that's okay.

No; that's perfect.

LETTER 5

TEARS DO NOT FALL IN SPACE

*If happiness knocks on your door, open your house,
but prepare room and board for two. For happiness
never travels without her lover, grief.*

Dear Alethea,

These saccharine waves relentlessly crash upon the shore—each mad arrival no less quizzical than the previous. The sun rises, then sets; the moon bleaches the undulating surfaces of an oblivious sea; a newborn roe fawn, graceful and ethereal, is eaten by lion. All this time, we ask, "What is this for?" What is its deeper meaning? Perhaps we are blinded by our addiction to reasons; we are done in by presupposing that things must have reasons behind them—guided by a sure hand, a resolute truth, a stern law, a cosmic debt, an abiding promise. Everything must be used up, taken in—nothing left to waste.

Each day, however, in my struggles for authenticity, I am reminded that the world is larger than my capacity to be purposeful or useful; I am reminded that "nature" is extravagant, awkward, irreverent—spawning species, only to ingest them again—and not in service of some larger plot, but in its own radical in/hospitality, sacred hypocrisy, and wanton spontaneity. "Why" becomes a chain that tethers me to the familiar, instead of a first unsure step into the thick.

Don't misunderstand me: I want to hold my reasons close; I want to hug them and nestle my face in theirs. But sometimes I want to lose them in the distance—and be part of a song that knows no lyric, no crescendo, no paradigm, no dramatic selah, no panting stop. I want to be lost in a bokeh of playful lights, with no sharp boundaries or specificity. I want to be unhinged from my slow circuitry around the gravitational pull of purpose. I want to dance to an incongruous stirring of noise and sunset, and know—if only for a moment—that what happened has no explanation. Or need not have one.

Love has a way of unraveling you, making you float above the imperatives of reason and logic, unchaining you from the gravity of teleology. Love doesn't make sense. Not everything has to.

When I met your mother, it felt like a homecoming. For a while, I didn't know my father's hauntings. Just the faint whisper of his blessings. Before your mum, I consoled myself with my books, doubled down on my repulsion with human company, and sought to figure everything out. Literally everything. I had a journal where I documented this romantic quest for final answers. I called it "Dear Josephus"—imagining Josephus to be a Palestinian Muslim cleric, who had more questions than any sacred text could provide answers to.

My correspondence with Josephus included reflections on creation, why I often felt so lonely or less than my peers, and what was the purpose of the incessant motion of things. "To what end do these things move, elder?" I would ask, sometimes in the dead of night. "Where is home?"

Sometimes he replied. Sometimes he spoke to me about love, about the nature of truth, about the deep pain that each ordinary passing second is pregnant with. The mere pain of being alive. The ache of breathing and the tension of other bodies.

Josephus often told me to be still, to be as perfectly still as I could manage, and when I thought I had achieved that, to notice that I was in fact moving … that my heart's rhythmic arguments sent a dialectic coursing through my body so eloquently that even my practiced stillness concurred with it—and thus moved.

We kept writing to each other—his reassuring voice comforting a young African man learning to find his way in the world. Now that I think of it, I suppose I was still reaching for my father when I wrote Josephus—naming him after Flavius Josephus, the Roman-Jewish scholar and historian who reportedly knew of Jesus, whose mysterious claims about heaven I so wanted to be true—because it meant I would never really lose anyone again. Including those I had already lost.

Maybe these letters to you, to this Alethea who now kneels by the seashore, by our side, is my way of wanting to learn from you too as much as it is a haunting of my father. My way of breaching the seemingly impassable gulf that lies between now and then—or the many nows that are produced by our (human and nonhuman) movements.

Anyway, Josephus and I eventually stopped speaking with one another. It happened when your mother became my every waking moment. When she said yes to me. To me.

I remember being curled up in bed next to her on most mornings. I would look at your mother's face, pinching myself to wake my pathetic head from the cruel dream imposed on me by a demon. How could it be that such a woman would lie next to me? It didn't seem possible. And yet there she was. She was real—her small head a treatise on proportion and subtlety, her hair a reverse waterfall—with the plunge pool of eddies of jet-black hair enveloping her head, and the river proceeding from the turbulence of currents, tapering off into a sigh at the nape of her neck.

One particular Wednesday, we should have been in our classes—me teaching about cross-cultural psychology and her taking something in microbiology. But as I watched the gentle blue outside yawn into the factory white of yet another busy morning, I knew I didn't want to be anywhere else but by her side. Curled into her without the interrupting bigness of things disturbing our serenity. That morning, we had a conversation that somehow led to Josephus—why didn't I write to him anymore, she asked. Because I don't need to, I answered.

In your mum—and I trust you know this already—I found a home. A beautiful stillness. She became my goddess just as the narrative of origins and bold destinies slowly lost their power over me. Truth wasn't out there, registered on invisible Books of Life and Death. It was right here, in this forbidden moment when I stared too much at her face as an eternal morning unfurled. In our temporal forever. It was here when I kissed her feet as my prayer—an act she didn't particularly subscribe to because of her own still-intact Christian beliefs, but which I sense she loved deep down, past the sedimented layers of her upbringing as a Christian child in an Anglo-Indian home.

Together we dreamed of you—how you'd look and whether you'd be stubborn and boring like we were. I used to tell her that you'd be a starry-eyed nerd like me, a prophecy she rejected by waving her right hand in a circle round her head and snapping her fingers—saying "God forbid!" as she did, and as most Nigerians do. Upon these many dreams, this excitement about the home we could build for you and the world we hoped you'd live in, we built our life.

Our eternal afternoons were often broken by a knock on the door, by someone inquiring about our whereabouts. There was this and that program to attend—this here and there to be at. Destiny awaited in classrooms or university assemblies: the greatness only the faithful knew.

But we wanted none of that. Even though I had been this fervent champion of arrivals, of becoming great, I suddenly longed for small spaces. When you are in love, no space is small enough.

We went about our daily chores. In the morning, your mum would wear her saree. I loved watching her do it by the mirror near the bathroom—the way she wrapped the fabric round her waist, tucking the edges into the undergarment she had on, and then delicately weaving the rest of it around her shoulder and over the tiny blouse that complemented the whole. The main part of her elaborate dressing ritual? Combing her hair. Sometimes her hair—in part Indian-straight/wavy, in part African-frizzy/proud, and other parts alien-sentient—behaved like the Big Bang, unwieldy, loud, and petulant, and because your mum's hair is so long, she often tired just trying to straighten it out. When she did, however, she'd let it loose like a black fountain or make it into a chignon bun. Then she'd ask me if she looked okay. I'm admittedly emotionally stunted—often shying away from situations that require me to display deep affections. How to tell her that *okay* was the most supercilious word ever contrived when associated with her was my own morning ritual. I found many ways to do it—some of which involved telling her she was the most beautiful woman in the world, or staring at her while she slept. When I came through, particularly when it mattered to her, she'd try to suppress a smile as she left for her classes, books held close to her chest "for protection."

At her young age she was already a widely published author and researcher—brilliant in ways I could never hope to be and confident in her stride. But she was often like a deer in the constant headlights of those that wanted her attention. I was told by some of her favorite students, who often came by to say hello, that when she was teaching, her classrooms were always full, with the boys seated—contrary to their "nature"—right in front, asking questions that didn't have any bearings on her animated explorations of the microbial world. The books she clutched to her chest gave her a sense of security, helping her sail through ogling crowds and back into the safety of our embrace.

Together, away from all things big, we met each other again and again, stitching an impossible dream to one day live a small good life. To a student who asked me what I wanted to do with my life, what I wanted to achieve, I responded in writing: "a shamanic affinity with my changing 'world'; a magical consciousness—which for me indicates some liberation from the shackles of patriarchal godhood stories; some freedom to subversively negotiate my origins and destiny; a small life of joyfully intense intimacy with those that I 'love and care for'; an ebullient sense of undying adventure and wonder; a restrainedly rapturous and liberating culture of insignificance—a life looking down on the wall clock, not up to it. Most of all, I long for a soft, poetic sense of serenity—a life mindfully improvised." Lali also wanted the same thing.

We got married in a vast garden, under the place where the branches of two tall trees intersected and met each other. We called our wedding "Enchanted Blossoms in Green June." It was so beautiful. I wish you were there. Though I kind of have a feeling you were, in the same way the world can no longer be thought of as a simple directionality from cause to effect. There were beautiful colors everywhere, in the majestic outfits of our many extended families that came to be with us—Indians and Nigerians together—and in the joy radiating from faces. I remember trembling as I tried to put the ring on your mother's slender finger. I was so nervous. Lali whispered to me in the calmest voice possible, "Take it easy, dear. Slow down. Breathe."

A year after you were born, we left the university. We packed our boxes into a truck and rolled out the gates. I had received an invitation to lead a project based in the United States, but one which didn't require me to be based there. We chose to come to India, after spending some time in Richmond, Virginia. We came to the land you were born in, this motherland of colors and promise and masala skies.

Here we are knitting a home for you. Things often get turbulent. Our stillness moves, our serenity breathes. But we are held together by cords stronger than our hands. And you are so much a part of that tapestry of love that enchants our days.

Are we always happy? No. Many times we are sad. I spend too much time writing and a surly distance brews between us. Or the strains of living in a new country—with some of its strange cultural assumptions and practices—test my ideas and patience. Your mum and I know how to argue well; we need to. Getting angry with each other is a testament to the strong intrapersonal bonds that make us part of the same fabric—and that fabric is no less subject to the waving elements than a falling leaf, splendorously waltzing with the air, is subject to gravity in autumn. And speaking of elements, you always come round, finger-wagging cross, asking that I say sorry to Lali and that Lali reciprocates. Just the sight of you waving your finger gravely, frowning and pouting to give off a stance of caricatured seriousness, often has the opposite effect. We would end up laughing, all of us together—while Lali stares me in the eyes and makes sure I carry through with an apology nonetheless.

This is why I write this particular letter to say thank you to you, my daughter. I once prayed to you while you slept; you were too small to know what I was talking about—just a few months old, I think. I asked you to keep your mum and I together—alive and in movement together, like starlings in a murmuration. Like the pollination song of bees clinging to the downdraft that sweeps the fields. And so far, you are doing a great job.

One day, you too will have grown and fallen in love with a guy or a girl or whatever. I hope you come to know that intense smallness I speak of, the rapture of a single moment that condenses the vast stretch of the universe and its galaxies, as well as the perverse experiments and pilgrimages in otherness that virtual particles perform, into a dense sigh. I hope you too know the freedom your own trickstery interventions help us experience. The stillness.

Keep in mind, though, that the stillness moves. There will be other times—times of darkness. It is darkness I have bumped into again and again since I began writing these letters to you, led off by the hushes in directions I couldn't anticipate. In noticing dust, the monstrous entanglement at the heart of things, the hidden story of matter as told by feminine reawakenings to Lilithian occlusions, and the porosity of race and identity.

It is obvious Bàbá—or the hush I whispered my question to—wanted me to learn about the agency of shadows. As such, I have followed a trail of enlivenment—not perfectly—and looked under the grimy folds of things. Being a clinical psychologist, I have had ringside seats to deep suffering, and struggled with the practices I was trained to perpetuate as a modern alchemist of happiness and well-being. So, once again, my pilgrimage takes me across space-time to a past that is not yet done and is still yet to come—with the fourth and fifth hushes leading the way into a consideration of "happiness" and its disenchantments.

✦

Enugu's green fluffy hills roll along, bursting out of the ground with a teen-age charm and a pagan abandon only to terminate abruptly in yet another residential block and industrial layout. Were you to view this old coal-mining colonial city from the sky, looking down below, you would undoubtedly be taken by its gentle lush landscape, spread out like thick curly hair on a good head, with just a few noxious ticks here and there interrupting its musicality.

Beneath the sky, however, different tensions are manifest. Like a few other West African cities, Enugu struggles with its legacy as the creation of old European merchants for European interests. After a series of skirmishes and a war between a confederacy of Igbo economic families and the Brit-ish Empire led to the collapse of the hinterland's last indigenous resistance in 1902, the British sought lasting control of the region. Seven years after the so-called Aro-Anglo War, British-Australian geologist Albert Kitson would discover economically important deposits of coal under the village of Enugwu Ngwo. A mercantilist administration would quickly engulf the emerging city, transporting coal on the Eastern Line leading two hundred–plus kilometers farther south of Nigeria to another coastal city created for British exports. Enugu would be so named to centralize the importance of its coal exports, leaving the banished ghosts of fighters and gods roaming without home. Without name.

The scars of these many interruptions still speak. There are no preserved battleground scenes or anything of that kind. On the contrary, the city is radically transformed after a hundred years under a new myth of progress. Enugu is snotty and anonymous like the big cities. The old Igbo traditional houses that were built with mud and the stems of raffia palm are now gone. They are replaced with modern brick buildings, shopping complexes, noisy bus parks and gilded neighborhoods where the rich are ensconced away in the obliging foliage of Enugu's hills.

But an unrest haunts the city in spite of its commercial buoyancy. And hell is emptied of its demons. I know this because I work at the Federal

Neuropsychiatric Hospital, where people are brought in daily, often dragged in screaming, or chained and gagged by hefty men. The men say these ones are sick, and that we must fix them. Others walk in on their own, stroll up to the receptionist and politely request a "wash-wash," the street term for a round of electroconvulsive therapy, otherwise known as brain shock therapy. Brandishing a wad of cash, they say that there's something eating away at their brains, clawing through their souls, and they need it out.

Outside the rusting red gates of my host's house in New Haven, where I am presently domiciled for the duration of my clinical internship, there are not many cars on the road. Traffic is sparse. A few *okada* bikes fleet across the wet glistening highway that separates me from the hospital's street. The air is sweet and delicate. Still sprinkled with the children of the overnight rain. Those among the Igbos that hold on to their traditions believe the *dibia ịhammiri* or rainmaker doctors can cause rain to fall using herbs, and the *dibia ịchụmmiri* or rain-dispellers can bring in the wind to drive away falling rain. Two mutually exclusive powers buried in particular relationships with soil and plant. Today, it is obvious that the rainmakers won the twilight battle.

I do not feel like walking today, so I hail a bike, offer him fifty naira, and point the way to the hospital. Even though I am a mere twenty-minute walk away, I am in haste. Today, I meet "Hope." This is not her real name, dear—hence the inverted commas.

Yesterday, I suggested to my supervisor that I would like to adopt a different intervention plan after his favored cognitive behavioral therapy modalities didn't seem to be yielding positive results with our in-patient. I wanted to try something that was more in line with gestalt therapy, something that was more honoring of the human being. He okayed my proposal without asking what I intended to do. I suppose this is a sign of trust.

As the bike pulls up by the gate, my heart beats a somber rhythm. I do this every morning: I arrive at the gate, and walk a few steps to the tiny office space that doubles as a consultation room. Just before I walk into the building, my eyes turn to greet some in-patients on my left. It's a familiar sight, one that is now seared into my eyes' eye: women and men walking around like zombies, disheveled hair and hunched backs, a vacant hollow gaze on their faces, their hands seemingly glued to their sides due to the numbing effects of Haldol. It is a vision of the human that is frightening and depressing. I often try to look away, but remind myself that I am here at this existential outpost to unravel the deepest secrets about human suffering.

Today, in the waiting area a few feet away from my office five male nurses and janitors are trying their very best to restrain a thick-jawed man with a neck that looks like the stump of a redwood tree. He is salivating, scream-ing at the top of his lungs with his eyes bulging out his head, insisting that he knows the Queen of England and needs to speak with her. I hear he was brought here by his family, and that his own mother made him mad when he walked through her door to visit her.

I will be meeting Hope in a few hours in our office—a makeshift room with paper-thin walls, a bare cement floor, and a working area no more than six feet wide and ten feet long. The office accommodates three persons: me, a colleague, and our supervisor. There are only four pieces of furniture in the room. A long table with drawers and three wooden upholstered chairs. And a calendar hung on the whitewashed wall. A large single window—span-ning the length of the room—opens out into the psychiatric wards that are regularly manned by the more prestigious, white-robed, drug-dispensing, title-toting psychiatrists. On her lighter days, Hope has often appeared out-side this window, her eyes ringed with a dark circles, pulling strange faces to make us three laugh. If tree rings track the annual growth of trees, the rings around Hope's eyes track stories and experiences too tragic to be told.

I am the first to arrive today. Standing, I look out the window. The wild grass grows unperturbed behind the perforated brick walls of the wards. A pied crow, its white feathered neck glistening with the righteousness of its cause, alights momentarily to wrestle a small lizard to the ground. The lizard struggles but is no match for the bird. I turn to look at Hope's open case file I left on the table the day before. I am no match for what is coming to me.

When Hope was eight, two of her uncles sexually molested her. They warned her not to speak of it to anyone, and threatened to kill her if she did.

She didn't tell anyone. Brought up in a dysfunctional family, she didn't have the luxury of a father. Her mother remarried. Soon, her stepdad was making sexual advances, mocking her to her face that her mother wouldn't believe her if she told her.

When she became a teenager, she was raped again by a trusted friend. She had almost gotten used to it by now, and began to think of herself as everyone's trash—until she met Emeka. This was while she was in the university. Emeka loved her, and she loved him back—at first hesitantly, but later without reservation. She felt herself ready to dream again. They began planning for a life together. In the meantime, Emeka had to travel someplace. He promised he'd be back. You probably know where this is headed.

Emeka never came back. Hope's sister came to her one day and told her Emeka had died "in December." I remember Hope telling me that she "died immediately."

But then she received a letter while she was serving as a cadet during the mandatory paramilitary service year for all Nigerian graduates. It was from Emeka. He had traveled abroad, and had married another woman, Hope's friend. He was sorry about not telling her, and hoped she would forgive him and his new wife. Hope blanked out, and fell to the ground. She was rushed to the camp hospital, where she was administered pentazocine injections—a narcotic for treating pain. But her pain was the bottomless sort—a black hole glinting in the rays of black sun. She needed more and more of the drug, and developed an addiction to it.

Back at home, and now working, she did everything she could to obtain more pentazocine. Spending her earnings, selling her belongings, borrowing from co-workers. She would later tell me during an interview I conducted with her: "I sold off all my jewelries, my gold—I sold off everything. I sold some of my sisters', and all of my mum's. My mum's own was worse off—I sold all her gold jewelries. They were worth five million naira. I'm not sure I sold them for up to about a million or five hundred thousand. Somehow it was—I felt like I was getting even with her." She felt deep resentment for her mother for not sticking up for her, for not celebrating her first period (while celebrating her sister's), and for turning the other way when her step-father mistreated her.

When she stole and sold her mother's jewelry, her mother, pained to her heart, fell ill, and became hospitalized. Hope didn't get a chance to tell her mum she was sorry before she passed away.

I wasn't there for her intake interview, after Hope checked herself in for rehab, but the first time I listened to Hope's story, I didn't quite believe it. How could one life be so consistently tragic? My colleagues actually felt there were factitious elements to her story, and toyed with the idea of making a diagnosis of Munchausen's syndrome after some of her family members— her sister, to be specific—told us her story was all made up, and that Hope had grown up with an excessive need to draw attention to herself. No one knew what to do with her. The psychiatrists might even have approved *"wash-wash"* for her, if Munchausen's had biological indicators. Healing by frying one's brains felt just as appropriate to me as trepanation, the ancient practice of drilling a hole in the head to let the headache and heartache spirits sail away.

Hope is now seated in front of me, smiling her endearing gap-toothed smile. My supervisor and my colleague in training are seated on the other creaky seats behind me. I lean forward and ask Hope how she is today. She is fine, she says. We talk about her stay at the facility, her family, and if she feels like she's making progress. She has some complaints about the male nurses. Other than that, she is fine and looking forward to going home.

I tell her I'd like her to speak with someone that is important to her. And that this is probably the last time she'd get to do that. As such, she has a chance to say everything she wants to say. I promise the person will listen. I stand up from my seat, dust it, open the door to the office and gesture as if letting someone in.

"Your mother is now with us, Hope—in that very chair," I say. Hope smiles. I wonder what my colleagues are thinking.

I had read in her file that she had a strong urge to duck or cover her head anytime she passed by her mum's home or anything that brought her to mind. So I figured that if her past conflicts with her mother triggered psychosomatic reactions, I could facilitate a gestalt role-playing scenario that might help her confront her deep-seated feelings. Her mother was the principal caregiver she looked up to for support and during the possible traumatic events of her childhood. She didn't get that support or the attention she needed. It was time for a meeting between the two.

The upholstered chair sits still before Hope. She just stares at it, smiling often, shifting her eyes to the unremarkable ceiling and then coming back to the object before her. I am leaning on the table. My colleagues are quiet.

Hope starts to speak. She greets her mum, calling by her pet name. She asks her how she is doing, wondering if she is well taken care of. Then she starts to talk about the events that led to her rehabilitation—the pentazocine addiction, the stolen jewelry, losing her. Before long, thick oleaginous trails of many tears wet Hope's face, like raindrops off the windshield of a moving car. I have never seen Hope cry before. Even when she narrated her previous ordeals, she always felt in control of her emotions. But as she falls apart before us, in libations of grief, I can't help but feel that Hope is coming home from exile in this moment of jubilee—and that the rickety chair in front of her has something to do with it.

Hope's crying is so fierce that it feels like she is possessed by Kali—or another member of the pantheon of shadows—and seeks to exorcise her otherworldly visitor through her mouth. She is leaking springs deeper than a single lifetime can allow. *Much more than several lifetimes, in fact.* Were it not for the professional oath of heady distance I have taken—the cross-legged, slow-blinking, fingers-interlocked, hmm-hmm-ing stance of therapeutic expertise that preaches empathy, not sympathy—I would be by her side, not trying to hold back my own tears.

I can understand the concerns of the early-twentieth-century psychologists who marshalled their literary prowess to invent the word to counteract the notion of sympathy as thinly veiled pity and patriarchal condescension. But in Africa, empathy is not calm and collected. She is not reasonable. She has flowing garbs, and her first instinct is to sweep the dusty floors with it when she meets you birthing pain. At my father's burial, there were people my father didn't know—and many who didn't know my father. But hearing of his death, and at the first sight of the convoy of cars slowly arriving his village, women in black ran to the car where his body rested. They hit their head and tore their clothes and yelled his name—and then some of them took the money they were paid for their service of mourning and went to their homes.

A professor of mine would later tell me a story of how a woman in his own village lost her only son in a motorbike accident and the ensuing intricate, bone-deep community wisdoms that came into play to break the news to her. It's a long story, but it is better told with his own words:

In July 1980, a very painful death occurred in a village in Igboland, an ethnic area in Nigeria, West Africa. A fifteen-year-old boy, Anayo, the only child of a widow, died in a motorcycle accident. Being a learner and yet speeding on the motorcycle, Anayo was unable to locate the brake. Unable to stop, he collided with a mosque, his head hitting the wall. He died on the spot. When the news got to Anayo's employer (until his death he was serving as an apprentice in timber merchandise), he sent word around to a network of his fellow male villagers in the city, informing them of the incident. Each, on hearing the news, reported to Anayo's master's house. When they all came they were sad, but quickly went into a crisis meeting aimed at deciding how to send the distressing news home. They divided themselves into two groups.

One group was to stay back and arrange for hospital preservation of the body until after everything had been set for taking it back home to his village and mother. The second group (composed of three villagers) was sent to take the news home in advance of the body. They did not go straight to Anayo's mother. Rather, they went to Anayo's uncle, who fortunately was at home when they arrived. They shared the news with him and then planned with him how to go about breaking the news to Anayo's mother, who was on the farm. They planned how to bring her home first, since the news could not be announced to her on the farm where she was working. They decided to send somebody she trusted to go and bring her

back. This person went with the message that Anayo had just reported home on
his way to Ibadan (western Nigeria) and would like to see her before leaving
again. Not suspecting anything in the message, she quickly left her work to follow
the messenger.

By the time they reached her home it was already late evening, a time consid-
ered conducive to the breaking of bad news or for holding serious discussions.
When Anayo's mother could not find him at home as she had expected, she began
to be disturbed. At that vital moment, Anayo's uncle and the three gentlemen
from the city poured into the compound, as if from nowhere. Anayo's mother had
scarcely finished welcoming them before they requested that she sit down for a
while. Anayo's uncle took up the task of breaking the news to her in the presence
of the others. She was told the true story: that Anayo had a motorcycle accident,
colliding with the mosque, hitting his head on the wall, and dying on the spot.
She was told that his body was already on its way home for the burial. Before
she could hear all these details she had broken down in uncontrollable wailing,
attracting the attention of neighbors and passers-by, who came and joined her,
crying in solidarity. And from that day, until some days after the burial, Anayo's
family home was understood to be a house of death and wailing.[1]

There was no fixing. It was an unctuous immersion into the necessary
alchemy of grief. A curdling so stern and gripping that the dark matrix that
led to it was never entered alone. A ritual of many hands and many feet and
dusty bodies.

Inspired by his studies in indigenous spaces of bereavement, I would later
investigate how cultures like the Yoruba understood, accommodated, and
treated "psychological disorders." Aize Obayan, a professor of counseling
with focus on multicultural issues (who was the "important person" and
mentor your mother and I would later visit when she found the two hushes),
would keep writing of "extensive" families, disturbing the dichotomized
categories of families as either "nuclear" or "extended"—the point being
that Africans live collectively, through many bodies, and that the atomiza-
tion of shared livelihoods into the Americanized industrial model of a father,

mother, and two blond (and freckled) children does not leave room for the many fluent means by which we fashion kinship with others and the planet.

Hope is now done. She is leaving the room after we have spoken about how she experienced the exercise. She says she feels like a heavy burden has been lifted off her chest. She feels free. Since she likes writing, I encourage her to write to her mum (an advice I find I can recommend to myself). My colleagues rub my back, and leave the office along with her. Am I coming, they ask. No, I'd like a few moments alone please, I reply. The office door clicks shut, and I turn around to face the large window that opens out to persistent suffering, the catatonic zombie-kind of suffering that makes sadness a sign of recovery. *The wild grass grows unperturbed behind the perforated brick walls of the wards.* The sky is turning gray. I lower my head and cry a little.

✦

There's a promise in the Book of Revelation—that when the Christ returns he will do so with an epic roar befitting his status as the long-awaited one, and then he will defeat Death itself. Anytime I walked past the inconsolable suffering of the inhabitants of that hospital, I would imagine that I—along with others—was moving slowly but surely to some utopian singularity, a day of reckoning, when suffering would be no more. I might have stopped imagining this day of recompense in terms of messianic arrivals by that time, but the activating questions pressed even closer: what do we do with pain? Why can't we just be happy? Was there some metaphysical protocol to be observed to bring a person closer to their "and they lived happily ever after"?

I decided to conduct a grounded-theory qualitative research into the suffering of some of my clients. I taped long interviews, allowing them to speak freely about the traumatic events that had brought them to us, the prevalent social conditions they were immersed in, the presence of social support, and the ways they made sense of their own experiences. By this time, a slow doubt started to fester in my mind: I was slowly losing my conviction that Western mental health care could rigorously address the lively issues the "patients" reported to us. I had been in one too many ward rounds and sat in psychiatric meetings where diagnoses were unilaterally assigned to "that patient," "oh, that woman?," and "yes, yes, that poor child." I had experienced the surge of vile power within me when a client begged me to tell her what was wrong with her, insisting that I was the expert and knew about her better than she knew about herself.

I had heard a fully grown Igbo man, with a big belly, a gruff physicality, and hustling quality to his face, tell of the time he refused to lie on a couch because it was a young female psychologist telling him to. He had told her, "Sorry. I have your 'type' at home," which was just his way of saying "others like you give me respect … I cannot do what you ask of me." Of course, even in conventional psychotherapy, many clients-to-be refuse to work with some therapists, and are eventually referred to someone they can be comfortable with. Yet, I suspected a deeper dynamic was at work, and longed to look past the colors of the capsule to the fine powdery substance enclosed within. Was it possible that one could think of mental health care, recovery, and well-being in radically different ways?

My grounded theory exposition allowed me to work with the narratives of my clients, generating a multiaxial story that suggested the avoidance of pain was at the heart of (my clients') suffering. This was the one theme that seemingly encompassed and paraphrased the tears, the stiffness, the dull vacant looks, and the occasional spark of life from within leathery eyes. My participants didn't think of healing and recovery as something that came as a result of pills and injections. Their limbs may have been cold, hanging loose from their torsos like rejected transplants, but their hopes for a better life reminded me of their humanity.

However, my grounded theory of pain avoidance felt half-spoken. It wasn't something I wanted to stand on a raised platform and share with everyone else—even though I eventually did share it before a committee of indifferent professors who were more concerned that I didn't employ statistical methods in a qualitative study—and also, to be fair to them, that I prefaced my work with a scathing polemic denouncing an entire generation of researchers who had used quantitative research.

Something was missing, and the clues of it became apparent when I walked the streets of Enugu, that anxious city like Babel where the ground is chastisement, and the sky, reward. You see, dear, one of the claims of modernity and those who advocate a developmental agenda for "primitive people" is that the modern world has made things easier for us. I cannot speak of your time, but in this time we are yet enveloped by the notion of distance, and protected by unwritten laws of anonymity. We—the consumers of modern tinkering—expect things to work for us, and become furious when they don't. We are like the poor shoemaker in the fable of the Brothers Grimm, who goes to bed and wakes up in the morning to find that the cut leather and nails of the night before have become shoes of great workmanship ready for the sale. We could care less if there were actual elves flying our planes, bearing signals with their mouths from computer to computer, or ensuring that trains arrive on time.

Divorced from the wilds, from the heart-racing immediacy of the world at large,[2] and cradled in the fantasy of our centrality, we have largely become a species of convenience—expecting things to work for us neat and tidy. Luxury seems to be the meta/physics of the least expended effort: technology brings things closer without us having to move so much. I have used the metaphor of adjusting focal length with the camera and thus "moving" while being immobile as a figure of the modern tendency to permanence: with a phone I can hurl my voice at great distances without ... well, doing that. And with a camera-phone, I have the benefit of hurling my voice and taking a picture. From all this, I suppose an idea gains a body over time, in trickling sedimentations, perhaps an unintended effect of fixating too much on the human figure: the idea that we are *meant* to be well. That *it* is our right, and we must have *it* now. That wellness can be produced unilaterally, and that even if we arrived at remedies and cures at great expense—or had a way to hold the sun in the sky indefinitely, that would be a good and useful thing.

The particular estrangements produced by modernity blind us from noticing that the dark we try to push away is not only part of life but necessary to it, and that nothing shows up except partially. To preclude suffering and pain, we turn inward. Modernity, in spite of its expansiveness and rhetoric of reaching for the stars, of endless covetousness and an eternally widening circle, is a collective turning inward. I might even say that curiosity as much as anxiety dwells at the tip of the shovel with which we open up more and more ground: we are hoping to cement our permanence deep enough so that nothing conceivable threatens our centrality.

We close up the orifices of our collective breathing, and stamp on the soft places where we once yielded to the loamy congress of becoming-things. Crowfoot, the nineteenth-century chief of the Siksika First Nation in what is now known as Canada, wrote: "What is life? It is the flash of a firefly in the night. It is the breath of a buffalo in the wintertime. It is the little shadow which runs across the grass and loses itself in the sunset." This attention to fleeting things, this utter temporariness and impermanence of things, this romance between wintertime and buffalo, shadow and grass and sunset, speaks of a world that is fragile—and is indifferent to our ambling quests and adolescent insistence on emotional gratification.

Walking the streets of Enugu, up and down Chime Avenue in New Haven, branching off into streets the names of which I need not remember nor burden you with if I could, brought me to wonder about the modern conditions that constitute us. The covering up, the asphalt, the rationalization of social being, the frenzy of catching up with time, the denial of competing agencies and their constitutive claims on human personhood, the metaphysics of completeness and wholly separate others, the myth of individuality, the circumcision of life's sensuousness, and the exclusivity of light and shadow. We often speak about getting lost in the dark, but it is also possible to get lost in the light. In fact, a consequence of high definition visuals is that it cuts away the generativity and creativity of an image; once things are so fixed, we become blind to their inexhaustibility. *Name the color, blind the eye.*

In Enugu, I imagined there might have been a time when women still gathered at the doorsteps, when women rolled in the dust and clutched their breasts and collective wombs, when practices of massaging the bodies with many hands mothered new mothers—a time perhaps before the Eastern

Line and newfound coal and colonial Nigeria. Now is a different time. We are sophisticated, and we no longer have many places to grieve.

·✦·

Since we are on about darkness, can I briefly revisit the playfulness of light, dear? I know I tend to sound like a broken record, what with all this talk about double slits and particles and complementarity and all that. But I keep returning here because the material world really does show that just because a thing is commonsensical doesn't mean it is "true." Well, I also keep returning here because—according to your jealous mum, who is now side-eyeing me—I also want you to see me as smart!

Consider this. In the shadow of a perfectly round object, you will find a rebellious glimmer of light—a bright spot in the middle. I'm not being metaphorical here. I really mean to queer the essential and disturb its eminence. What better way to do it in this case than to point to light at the heart of darkness, and vice versa.

Again, this phenomenon points to "diffraction," which literally means "breaking up." I like to think of it as porosity—that there is such a primal mutuality between "things" that nothing "becomes" unless it "becomes-with."

When the inventor of the word *diffraction*, seventeenth-century physicist and Jesuit priest Francesco Grimaldi, directed a focused ray of sunlight into a dark room, managing the ray so that it struck a thin rod and produced a shadow on a screen, he found that "the boundary of the shadow [was] not sharply defined and that a series of colored bands [lay] near the shadow of the rod." Up till then, the general views established that light waves interacted with surfaces by reflection and refraction. Reflection is when waves hit a surface and bounce back toward to source—which is how you are able to observe yourself in a mirror. Refraction works when waves penetrate a surface, displacing some angles away from the general direction of the waves. For instance, when you dip your hand into a pool or a bucket of water, your hand might seem cut off from the rest of your arm, or just plain funny. When Grimaldi performed his experiment, it showed light behaving in unexpected ways. It was as if the light bent around the edges of things to form fuzzy edges and colored bands:

> *Replacing the thin rod with a rectangular blade he observes diffraction fringes—bands of light inside the edge of the shadow. Bands of light appear inside the shadow region—the region of would-be total darkness; and bands of darkness appear outside the shadow region.*[3]

Grimaldi's work would later inspire Thomas Young in the nineteenth century to assemble his double-slit apparatus. However, Grimaldi's work was already showing that "there is no sharp boundary separating the light from the darkness: light appears within the darkness within the light within." In fact, "darkness is not mere absence.... [It] is not light's expelled other, for it haunts its own interior."[4]

This is true for everything physical. Nothing is complete; everything undergoes a "breaking up" in its co-emergence with "other things." Look closely at light, and it is haunted by shadows—then observe shadows, and you'll see traces of light. Light and dark are not opposites or estranged cosmic forces that one side must defeat—for there are no "sides."

Gloria Anzaldua writes:

> *There is darkness and there is darkness. Though darkness was "present" before the world and all things were created, it is equated with matter, the maternal, the germinal, the potential. The dualism of light/darkness did not arise as a symbolic formula for morality until primordial darkness had been split into light and dark. Now Darkness, my night, is identified with the negative, base, and evil forces—the masculine order casting its dual shadow—and all these are identified with dark skinned people.*[5]

Even though darkness is restated as evil or absence, this is not simply the case. Think about it, dear: don't things grow in dark places? Seeds tremble and crack open in the dark of the soil; babies grow in the darkness of the womb; photographs need darkrooms to properly develop; and, even though light is often centralized as the main "ingredient" in the production of biological vision, seeing would not be possible without the agency of darkness (if the occipital lobe's work, shrouded in shadow, is anything noteworthy). Little wonder Jung observed that darkness "has its own peculiar intellect and its own logic which should be taken very seriously."[6]

Darkness is not the absence of light as we've been so forced to believe. It is the very dance of light—it is light in rapturous contemplation of herself, in poetic adoration of her own contours and sensuous nuances. And we will never see this except we join her, unless we marvel at her rapid steps, unless we get caught up with her in her festive charade of realness, in her chaotic performance, in her heady spin, in full embrace of her extravagant sweaty waltz—for when we do, we will realize that shadows are merely the spaces she has tenderly left for us to place our feet.

What diffraction thus shows is that the world is continuously differentiating and entangling (simultaneously) in copious productions of phenomena. This reiterativity has no set pattern, and doesn't produce a final formula. As such, "there is no absolute boundary between here-now and there-then. There is nothing that is new; there is nothing that is not new."[7] Drawn out into its extensive nuances, Barad implies that even life and death, the animate and the inanimate, inside and outside, self and other, truth and falsehood are not estranged from each other. The things we call opposites are already diffractively implicated in each other.

However, we live largely in a world governed under a kingdom of Light, and this light implies a violent and forceful dichotomization of the world. It needs everything neatly arranged and easily categorized. It cannot afford that things spill into each other. It needs binaries—an inside and outside. The things that fall on the outside are thus thought to be evil, chaotic, and corrupt. As Stanton Marlan notes in his book *The Black Sun—the Alchemy and Art of Darkness,* this violence is endemic to modernity, which embodies this quest for totalizing light, and harbors the metaphysics of separation—a phallic, "male-dominated" rejection of anything that is "other," and demonization of the darkness. Modernity "sets the stage for a massive repression and devaluation of the "dark side" of psychic life. It creates a totality that rejects interruption and refuses the other from within its narcissistic enclosure."[8] Identifying this violent dichotomization of orgasmic life as the actions undertaken by the mythical/alchemical figure of a Sun King and his "heliopolitics," Marlan feels that we need to approach the Black Sun we often rule out in our hunger for fetish light.

If the work of feminist materialisms is to crack open the sealed places, to dispute the ontological imprisonment of things in Cartesian categories, and to show how the supposedly righteous and separate are already complicit in the "crime" of entanglement (to stretch the legal metaphors!), then we should pay attention to the interesting proposal that our psychic lives are richly embroidered with darkness. And living with the inescapability of darkness, meeting the dark on its own terms, acknowledging that darkness has its own prerogatives that are different from illumination, instead of attempting to fix it or look past it or make it a means to light, becomes our fierce focus. That is, opening closures—one of which is the closure of the dark psychic life—can help us understand how, in our modern comings and goings, happiness is so easily fetishized, so passionately pursued, and yet so defiantly in short supply.

A friend of mine, Charles Eisenstein—whose son Cary you once played with in New York when you were in your second year—told me a story of a woman he met who radiated a heart-warming and magnetic joy. He went on the prowl, trying to sniff out a story. He asked her: "Why are you so happy?" The woman replied: "Because I know how to cry."

If that seems at odds with what feels like common sense, then you are not the only one in this feeling. The feverish pursuit of happiness is so sacred to modern life and our understanding of human emotionality that it is literally enshrined in the constitution of a certain Western nation. We assume that happiness has Cartesian-Newtonian features—a given stability, determinate properties and weight—and that we can simply accumulate it. We can be happier than our neighbors on the other side of the fence if we gather more of the stuff to ourselves. It is easier to understand why—following the horrors of World War II and the rapid industrialization and proliferation of commercial products it engendered—global culture came to associate products and goods with happiness. With increasingly sophisticated advertisements, a dream was sold: buy more, get happier. An unfortunate culture of waste and planned obsolescence emerged with this helio-psychology.

I cannot help but imagine that this Fetish Happiness, this fixed "thing" frozen in modernity's violent light—to the exclusion of its darkness—is also agential, and subtly organizes modern society in this fantasy of arrival. In a race for a finish line. In other words, total happiness co-constitutes colonial elisions and their reductionisms, excavatory capitalism, and even the teleological pilgrimage for heaven and final rewards that characterizes the main religions. It is happiness stabilized as an eternal stretch—a "happily ever after"—without the corroding stain of sorrow that pulses mutely.

The Yoruba healer's words come to me again: "You have driven away the dark with your big development and your pills, and now you must find it. You must head into the forest to find the dark."

This generates quite a lot of feedstuff for our mutual consideration, dear. Let me see if I can parse them this way:

First, the invitation to "find the dark" or seek it on its own terms is shocking to modern contemplation. If darkness is granted any effects at all, it is as a means to an end. One is meant to undergo the purging of the means so as to attain the end. As such, a "light at the end of the tunnel" conception of psychic life relegates the dark to secondary status. The shamanic invitation to seek the dark places turns that conception on its head, and grants darkness "equal" status: the dark is just as much a means to the light, as the light is a means to the dark.

In fact, the shaman's tradition adheres to the archetype of the trickster. From the Yoruba Eshu (who is also described as the "first particle"—the one who brings balance) and Maui (the Polynesian deity whose tricks and deception gave us land) to Prometheus (the scamming Greek god who made mortals and gave them fire) and Pan (the horned guardian of the wilds), the trickster is the black sheep of the pantheon—not because his/her jokes are bad, but because he/she embodies the primeval generativity and diffractive ingenuity of things. The trickster is balance—not in mathematical terms of determining aggregates and averages, but in terms of entanglement. Psychic life is always poised in the middle of things, as the co-agentic mattering of "good" and "bad." There is no solution to the dark. We are never not broken; we are never not whole.

Secondly, *heading into the forest* to find the dark brings us into encounters with nonhumans, thereby stressing some kind of intra-subjective ethos or trans-affectivity. We are used to thinking of thoughts, feelings, knowledge, and choices as uniquely human attributes; those psychological events are supposedly happening in our heads or somewhere behind our skins. But in a world that leaks through and through, where nothing is granted the luxury of independence, we can no longer think in those terms. Personhood has changed address—no longer embodied in the human corporeal entity, but in diffractive enlistments spread out in the environment.

The idea that emotions are posthuman—part of the performativity of the world that recruits not just "humans" but nonhumans in its emergence—is not foreign to Western discourse. From the moment Freud deconstructed the myth of the pristine, rational self by introducing the wild unpredictable antics of the unconscious, the human figure has been composting ... like a seed acquainting itself with its own discombobulation. In other words, he brought the great outdoors into the great indoors, putting one more nail in the coffin of the idea that our inner lives are essentially private to us. I was startled to learn, quite late, that Freud's concerns about dream interpretation was a professional cover for his more scandalous interest in dream telepathy—or the transference of information via dreams.[9]

Carl Jung took it even further, stressing the irreducible collectiveness of the unconscious—painting a complicated picture of an ecosystem of mental life that accommodates (and is already constituted by) strange fellows. By diffractively rereading the ancient practice of alchemy (an example of why the "old" is still valid, and how the future can ontologically reconfigure and reconvene the past) as the journey of the soul in transformation, Jung drew entangling lines between "human minds" and base metals.

Because there's a whole lot of back history about the transcorporeal mind (or the inescapable entanglement between minds and bodies—not just "the" human body), there have been many experiments exploring ESP (or extra-sensory perceptual) abilities like clairvoyance, precognition and telepathy, the implications of which would mean that something far more radical than modernity (and its commitments to closure) can tolerate is afoot.

But I do not need to write to you about men who stare at goats, or the ability to know beforehand (queering temporality) to suggest that we are part of a flow of becoming—and our "inner lives," supposedly immured from the weather, is the direct effect of the weather. From the simple ways we communicate, as if *gesturing out* into the world, to the "simple" ways we are able to anticipate the direction someone is going with his words, and complete the sentences, we are beginning to rethink thinking, feeling, knowing, and communicating as the cascading performance of many others, reaching us in waves and heading on to wherever.

Thoughts don't come from "within"; neither do they come from "without." They emerge "between." It's the same with feelings. I like to think that the gentle dipping of a leaf under the weight of a dewdrop can set off a series of events that flow through us as (what we call) "depression"; and, that the molten formation of a rock, through the intra-activity of weather and technology and story, is experienced "joy" in a specific moment. I like to imagine that when a seed falls into the earth, it experiences grief, and its grief is met by the loamy femininity of the soil, and that is how trees sprout out with joy. Perhaps those moments of unspeakable silence, when depths churn and sides groan, when words escape you, when a pill or a diagnosis doesn't add up to much, when all you want to do is squeeze yourself into the tiniest place in the universe, it is because you—for all intents and purposes—are co-performing the disintegration of imaginal cells within a cocoon, and knowing the pain of becoming a moth.

Perhaps this is the next frontier: not outer space or inner space, but the spaces between. No more jumping to conclusions—no more leaping from already-formed "heres" to "theres" while avoiding the performance of the middle! The world is not composed of things, but flowing, half-uttered sayings, never congealing into an independent wholeness long enough to be considered separate, and always part of a traffic of intra-bodies.

Finally, heading into the dark is always a matter of collectives. In Yoruba shamanism, even if you were sent alone to the forest to retrieve something, there is still an irreducible collective implied in the effort. In the way a particular measurement can produce light as a particle to the exclusion of its complementary identity as wave, individuals are the productions of political-scientific-religious-economic measurements. What those measurements cut out are one's ancestors, tailing them in bacteria, dust, and memory. In this sense, we are all possessed; we are legion.

But while modernity fixes the frames, adjusts the lenses, and notices only the isolated person, many indigenous practices of healing draw in other bodies in the community as part of person-making. As such, healing in African indigenous systems is interactional (or intra-actional!), whereas Western paradigms,[10] as Nwoye notes in his study of African grief work, tend to place emphasis

> on the role of the *"totalitarian,"* or *"sovereign,"* or *"self-sufficient"* ego of the bereaved individual in resolving grief ... which has given rise to researchers' present tendency to medicalize the phenomenon of mourning, promoting the assumption that resolving grief can be achieved only in the clinic or through therapy.[11]

Therapy in these indigenous settings is not a fix as much as it is an immersion. It is a staying-with, a going-down-together. It happens in slow time, in soft yielding places where the logic of darkness is allowed to play out. There is no cure, no shortcut, and no detour. Just the long dusty road traveled with others. It might even be said that grief travels you, touches you, shakes you, beats you up, and scratches you. Because it is her own being, especially a force one must not look at with one's naked eyes, it is best to respect the spontaneity of grief and pain. The community's efforts are usually a negotiation and struggle with the provisionality of the dark side of psychic life. Of course, chronic negativity can be taxing on any community, and there is the possibility that even with communal support, a person may not find his or her way back. Nevertheless, the usual premise is that everyone must go through these moments—that people are born and die more generously and more frequently than a beginning and an end might presuppose.

"Mental ill-at-ease-ness" is debilitating, and there are of course times when a pill could work wonders. What is of course important to note is that nothing comes without its world. Pills and talk therapy might help in recovery, but they shut out other ways of listening to the others around us, other ways of giving darkness its day in the sun. And just like in Hope's case, when the burden of recovery is placed on reductionistic approaches, those tools can turn around to hold us in their grip.

✦

Someone once told me that civilization is the shared obliviousness to the fact that we haven't gotten rid of wild things, and that they dwell "within" us—somewhere beneath the threshold of normalcy. This wildness, this darkness, is not an "other." We are continually sourced, recreated, and reconfigured here.

Only under the regime of Light—the Apollonian politics of permanence—would death and darkness be treated as enemies. Perhaps this is why it is extremely difficult for moderns not to think that the world is here for us, for our own enjoyment, our own movements and definitions and terms. But the world is not "designed," put in place, or created for our well-being—at least not in the absolute sense that there is a universal harmony awaiting our awakening. The world dips in and out, retreats and proceeds, produces and eats up its own genius a mere gasp later.

Suffering needs a new onto-epistemology—not one that rules it out for eventual fixing, but one that recognizes its entanglement with well-being. Grieving must be part of the lives for happiness to become meaningful.

There aren't enough places to grieve around, since every place is adhering to the imperatives of development, but I do pray that your world will have "soft places to yield"—where the generativity of grief can be met with in its troubling presence, where darkness can be known as a menstrual wound, and failure, a portal to wild worlds beyond our ken.

It often takes Lali to remind me that you have to move and have your own way in the world. To tell you the truth, I cannot bear to see you in pain. Just the memory of your tears brings water to my own eyes, not to mention actually watching you cry. And yet, if I embrace you too long, then I lose you. I must learn the slow process of letting go, of allowing you the privilege of sorrow without seeking to console you to numbness.

Perhaps this is why I have written this particularly long letter, taking a break from my hunt for hushes ... to invite you to consider that your discomfort is a holy ally, a redeeming interruption. Where you are most confused, exhausted, distressed, and compromised is where the wild things grow. Where crazy colors, beguiling angels' trumpets, decadent air ferns, and wise old spruces sprout with festive abandon. Where the thrumming of frogs, the discourse of cricket limbs, the ambivalence of a nightly mist, and the audience of a delighted moon contrive an unheard score. It's where your primal self, where the unthought, calls to you softly—reminding you that you are not to be easily resolved, reminding you that you are larger than you could ever imagine.

You will encounter troubles of your own. You will be "traveled" by things words cannot encircle. Find the others who can hold space with you. Then, when in the alchemical dynamics of things, the sun emerges again, don't walk off rudely into his arms. Turn toward the smoldering darkness whence you came, and thank her for shaping you, for scaring you, for wounding you, and defeating you, and shaking you, because in her womb you were thoroughly purged, and made fresh for new glimpses of wonder. And as you walk farther into the domineering light, the dark will bless you with a gift to remind you that you are not as contained or as limited as you think, that there is more to you than what meets the educated eye, that whatever you do, the whole universe does the same along with you—imitating you with a childish keenness, and that you are never, ever alone.

That's why shadows were invented.

Are we making the right decision?

This question haunts me. One of my greatest fears and joys comes from world-schooling or unschooling you. Before the world gave you to us, your father and I had decided that we were not going to take the tried-and-true path of sending you off to school eventually. We had seen the effects on our own students and, even though we didn't think of school as evil, we felt that we wanted to raise someone freer and more alive to herself and to the world than our own education allowed us to be.

I didn't always have the words to say in defense of our countercultural approach. Everyone around us constantly tries to explain to us what a big mistake we are making. It is an ever-present battle, this struggle to make a different type of future with you.

We've had days when we were so sure we were on the right track and then days when we prayed that we were doing what was best for you. But one day, I met someone who helped me trust my instincts and, even more, your own power to learn, live, and meet the world on your own terms

We were out having dinner, the three of us ... you, your dad, and me ... happily chatting and joking.

You were enjoying your meal and making up silly jokes, trying to convince me that you were big enough to have a sip of my cold drink.

Suddenly, the mood changed: something had caught your attention. A little girl had walked in with her two elder sisters, and they seemed to be having an argument. The two elder girls left the little one in the booth to sit all by herself while they waited for the food they had ordered.

The little girl was bigger than you, but you stood up on the bench in the booth where we were seated and asked me if I could move a bit so you could pass. Surprised, I asked you where you were going, and you told me: "Can't you see that little baba is sad? She's lonely and she needs me to talk to her."

Astonished, I looked at your dad, who just smiled. I finally moved and you jumped down and went up to her and introduced yourself. While trying not to look so you didn't feel shy about it, I heard you say your name to this stranger, and then you just scooted next to her and sat there.

To me it was awkward. The two of you stayed silent. The little girl was clearly shy, and your bold entry seemed to astonish her too. Her sisters, on the other end, were watching, and soon they came over to the booth and said hi to you.

You smiled and left them, running straight into my arms, saying loudly, "You see? I told you she needed me. She was lonely, but now she's not."

That night your dad and I had a long conversation. I told him how people had been bombarding me, saying that unschooling was going to make you unsociable and incapable of spending time with those your age.

Their words had been bugging me for days before this happened. "I think the Universe set this up for me," I told him. I was looking forward to receiving some much needed wisdom from other moms who were unschooling their kids, or your godfather, Manish Jain, who is also unschooling his daughter. But the Universe finally opened my eyes to someone who calmed my fears better than they could have ever done: you.

Your actions that day helped me see that it was you doing the parenting. It was you unschooling me—an awkward turn of roles. The mother becomes the one who learns trust from her daughter.

Thank you for being my greatest teacher, love. My guru.

LETTER 6

AWKWARD

From a politics of the mainstream to a politics of many streams.
—MANISH JAIN

Dear Alethea,

I have lately enjoyed thinking that the whole world, and not just me, is in speculation—and that this basket-weave of bodies and breath is conducting an inquiry into what it means to be alive, what it means to be at home, and why that matters. Imagine that for a second: I am not searching for hushes *in* the world; the entire world is flailing and bending and seeking with me, because I am not in the world, I *am* the world in its specific self-inquiry. I am accompanied in this fabled pilgrimage for good fatherhood, and the world at this very moment is also in search of hushes to enact this ritual with me. Therefore, as I stretch to reach you, to embrace you, in this diffracted moment, I am tugging at the sleeves of distant galaxies; I am disrupting the astronomical and the atomic, leaving tremors and rumors in the wake of these efforts.

It's a stunning idea, isn't it? But you know what makes me gasp even more, dear? When I consider one of the more mesmeric implications of this idea that we are in this together for all the questions we pose to the world, and all the claims we make about what feels fair and just, I realize that the asking itself—the mereness of a question—might be inexhaustible in its own right and may not require the redemptive intervention of an answer for it to be valuable or profound in its way.

Questions have a complete partialness. Another way to say this might be to say that the way to think about or think through our problems—how to ask this question of home, how to navigate dislocation, how to reconcile ourselves with the matterings of the world at large, and how to understand pain as the larger project of a community of others—may not be available yet. Let me elaborate.

It is often taken for granted that the opposite of a question is an answer; there is a cosmic, platonic double-step logic about it. Black is to white, as night is to day, as cats are to dogs, and questions are to answers. But what if questions are not free-floating formations that are summarily resolved with answers? What if questions are not made only of words? What if questions are material things, speciated and tactile, with body parts, particular histories of their own, affective accompaniments, genealogical ties, and burial grounds? What if questions are like guests to a home—to be welcomed, catered to, dusted up, considered affectionately, spoken with, and put to bed? And what if giving an answer is sometimes the ethical equivalent of slamming a door on the face of a guest as soon as you've said hello?

Could this be the reason why we need tricksters? To slow us down from the treachery of a swift resolution and the quest for a binding reconciliation of contradiction? To keep the world fresh? To help us consider the many ways questions trigger, exert themselves upon, and shape us? Could there be value in the yet unanswered question? What if questions have colors, sometimes spritely and gay, other times dour and withdrawn? What about textures? Can we think of textured questions? Glossy, smooth, and finely finished? Or rough to the touch? Ungainly and threatening? Lustful questions? Desiring questions?

Think about it. A question doesn't just appear out of the blue like most things Cartesian. It sizzles and pops and snarls and hisses at the frothing edge and moving face of a material process that might have touched exploding nebula and congealing planet and noble rock and riverbed and trellised sky and falling leaf and unrequited skin touch and curdled moon in its becoming. So that an "answer"—equally diffracted and grand—is not always the way to respond to a question. Not even the right way.

A friend of mine, Lori Kane, wrote these words to me when I shared my sentiments with her, and I thought to include them in this letter:

A question feels like a river to me and an answer feels more like a stepping stone placed within it. Useful in slightly shifting the river. Useful to human feet just trying to get across sometimes. Useful as a record that humans come this way often. That you're not alone. And often most useful when so thoughtfully honed and placed that others are stopped for a moment, can look around, and maybe be swept up into the beauty of the place herself. Or maybe leap from the stone to swim for the fun of it. But an answer wouldn't have to be a stone. It could be a tree branch too. Something that fell there more clearly of its own accord. This makes me wonder: is an answer more knowable than a question? And this is reminding me that a stone, like an answer, is really under no obligation to be useful at all. The beauty of its presence is plenty.

As I lay on this gritty shore, on the unspoiled and secluded beach of the Great Mattiscombe Sand here in Devon, the sweeping nuance of blue up above, and a crowd of sandy witnesses covering everything in its warm blanket, I think of you. The thick "you." The little girl I have left five thousand miles away, back home in Chennai, who is now running a slight temperature according to her mum's urgent yet reassuring message. The screaming tot this pale blue dot belched out that frantic Wednesday evening at 6:33 p.m.—the one I promised, quite "chapless and knocked about the mazard," to find a home for. And the "little girl" I haven't met yet, who holds this letter, who crouches on the sands of a different shore, next to me and your mother. In writing these letters to you—a vocation I at first didn't feel good enough to respond to—I am secreting the has-been, the might-have-been, the might-yet-have-been, and the yet-to-come.

I have many questions. They don't need answers. Just the asking is good enough.

First, are you in love? Did you just say, "Yes, Dada, I am!" or did you look into the eddying gray-blue ahead of you, recalling a recent heartbreak situation?

Perhaps you have children of your own? Or are content without them?

Does your hair flow like the naive wind, or is it resolute and grounded like my short hair?

Do you cook as wonderfully as your mum? Do you eat meat as I do?

Do you swim? Remember that time your Dada almost drowned—on his birthday swimming in the Yuba River in California? I'm still the only one in the family who is witless in water.

Where do you live? And do you live with others?

What do you do for money? Are there still nation-states and fiat currencies and giant factories?

Are there still dolphins and whales? Spiny crag lizards and Asian elephants?

Are you well?

Are you home?

By the way, I am not here on these sands alone. There are many others here, citizens of these borderlands, who have questions too. In a sense they have been on their own rough trails of enlivenment, gathering metaphorical hushes, wondering what to do with them, taking one unsure step after the other into the not-known. I am here in Devon, teaching a short course at Schumacher College about my quest to find a home for/with you. I am five hushes away from completing the ritual.

There are students here that could be my grandparents, others just as young as my littlest sister. We are all here—veteran activists, poets, one psychologist, one pianist, many storytellers, alternative education practitioners, policymakers, and at least one Irish politician who is running for election and detests establishment politics. We are passionate about justice; angry with industrial activities and their harmful effects on the environment; and learning to reacquaint ourselves with the meat of the earth—with the shit we flush away. A permaculturist is learning to plant her own food; one young man has recently become Christian as an act of rebellion against oppression—recovering the life of Jesus as a young insurgent who challenged the Romans. Together, we are seeking to occupy other places of power, learning to see our naturalization within systems of oppression, and are doing our best to be responsive to futures forgotten.

What have we come to the sea to do? We have come to the sea to honor our many questions, and to surrender them to the waters. We have come because we are bleeding, our skins are rupturing. A deep crisis disturbs us.

Among us, there is a sense of smallness—a not-too-distant and humbling awareness that the planet that seems to stretch out to infinity before our very eyes is but a speck's mite in the unfathomable expanse of the universe. We know the world doesn't spin around us. That we are not the center of the universe. We are not even the center of our own selves.

This feels like a humiliation of the bluntest sort. And yet, we have not shrunk away; we are not embarrassed that we've never had clothes on even though all this time we have insisted that other earthlings notice the rich embroidery of our ornaments. Instead we are here at this edge—because even though we are very small and blissfully inconsequential, we understand that the same molecules that cooked in the heart of ancient stars, exploding into space, and birthing other planets gave birth to us and the many others around us. In this way, we are here partly because of the continuity of processes around us. We are recognizing that we are not autonomous—so that concepts of size and worth collapse in the face of this web of bodies. If anything, this is a spiritual awakening of some sort.

We are not merely admitting that the world doesn't spin around us—because owning up to this still preserves, in small doses, the idea that we are *apart from* the world, instead of *what the world is doing*.

Our humility lies in recognizing that we are the world's spin, the dizziness of things. As such, aloofness, independence, or aloneness—whether it takes on the varieties of religious piety, scientific perspicuity, genetic purity, political in/correctness, or militant activism (or resistance by any other name)—is impossible. We are not alone. Everything is compromised. And though we might like to think it so, fixing the world is more complex than getting our act together. We are a troubling congealment of an ongoing-ness without a name—and we are spread out in a boundaryless play of co-becoming. In this way, our shared humiliation is a coming to our (many) senses and a calling to be witnesses to the strange voices that respond when we call out, "Is there anybody home?"

I cannot believe that I—an African boy who once had to sell chicken barbecue on a street in Lagos to help his fatherless family get by—is now conspiring with these strange yet familiar others. But this is the measure of our times and the strangeness of the moment. Those that are wise have to unlearn their wiseness with the stupid.

When I was younger, the world seemed a simpler place. A lot less complicated. There were undeniable doctrines that were true for me: life was about "making it" or, if one wanted to beat around the bush, "following your passion." In any case, to do this, one needed to go to school, to speak one-tongue, to travel abroad and see other places, to develop entrepreneurial skills, identify problems, and cash in on providing a solution to those problems. I was "Nigerian"—a citizen of a nation-state, whose good leaders were the ones that made it look like the televised pictures we saw from Europe and America. The purpose of human collectives was to use the natural resources God had given us to make bridges, build factories, make rocket ships that went to the moon, and invent technologies that could save lives. Just as important, perhaps even more so, the meaning of life was to be holy and exclusively devoted to a single faith. All other faiths and their adherents were either stupid, ignorant, or wicked.

But all of this started to change. Slowly but surely, my naive wallpaper started to peel away, exposing other colors I never thought possible. First, in giving myself so completely to my faith, I began noticing its limitations. I had taken deep baths in its philosophical waters, and they didn't wash the sticky stains my everyday movements in the world gave me. In short, many things didn't add up: the notion of sin, the exclusivity of religious compliance in a world too culturally complex for single opinions, the very idea of beginnings, and the narratives of destiny. And don't get me started on the church's "prosperity gospel" practices that seemed at odds with the conditions of the poor and, worse, totally clueless about the colonial-neoliberal conditions that generated inequality in the first place. It wasn't that these beliefs became less true or untrue; it is that truth itself became provisional and performative—no longer an act of correctly representing the world as it was behind the scenes, no longer an act of reaching out, since I noticed I was already in touch and complicit in enacting this vicarious barrier between me and the sacred.

It took the implosion of that lone sun in my psychic and intellectual life—Truth with a capital T—for me to notice, in little drops of insight, that "making it" was more often than not an empty phrase for clinging to the rules of life-denying pyramids of social ascendancy. And because there was some hidden dialectic in the concept of "making it"—a "me against the world" or "me in competition with others" thing—I also came to distrust the magical highway that led to one's place in the sun. And school? In most parts the colonial heritage of a particular way of seeing the world. English? One-tongue. Development? The anthropocentric denial of our more humble place in the world and a quest for transcendence. Being "good"? Yet another flight of Icarus to escape the sensuous, unwieldiness, and ethical extravagance of the material world.

In short, dear Alee, I lost my faith. One day it was … just not there anymore. Swallowed up by the once microscopic traces of doubt that had obviously grown too big. This might sound tragic enough—this loosening of the threads that hold us together. This losing of one's faith. But, you see, faith might be the lack of resistance to what we hope is possible and true. But doubt is the awareness of those possibilities. I was suddenly "empty" enough to be filled anew, and lost enough to notice that there were other interesting paths, through the nonchalant roadside shrubbery, that led to delightfully magical places the highway could never take you to.

This is why we are here. On Great Mattiscombe Sand. This is why we linger at this place where no further steps can be taken. An ancient people like us, called out from captivity, also roamed the shores of the so-called Red Sea for a while. Just when it seemed their strivings for freedom were to be dashed by the heavy approach of their slave masters and former owners, the impossible happened. The sea parted down the middle, splitting into great watery walls on either side, leaving dry ground for escape.

Whereas those people were called out to separate themselves as "holy" (the Hebraic word for "holy" is *qadosh*, I think—which means "set apart"), we are called into an immersion. Here, we are not expecting pillars of fire and angry clouds of gathering dread. The Atlantic Ocean will not be torn into two before our eyes. That is because our dead end is of a different sort: for a "species" that has lived as if everything were possible, as if we are unlimited and without threshold or edge, we need this dead end to stay resolute. We are not here to get around it; we are here to meet our limitations, to sit with the trouble of discontinuity, to know what it feels like to stop, to know the privilege of being refused further access, to feel the pull of gravity on our feet, to know we are claimed and we are not our own.

We are also not here in some kind of ritual to relinquish the human; surrender is not antihuman. Someone asked me recently, "How do I get rid of the ego?" My response? "Good grief, why would you want to undergo such a terrible procedure?!" (I really should have begun my reply with something more profound, like "Jumping Jehoshaphats!" or "Blistering Barnacles!") Surrender is not a state of being egoless. In fact, I might argue that the quest for egolessness is the ego's last defense mechanism—its most patronizing trick that underscores an inability to recognize that it is not at all separate from the rest of the material equation we hesitantly (and often rudely) call "nature." The ego is not the problem; the problem is maybe the paradigm that amputates it, treats it as diseased and alien, cut off from the rest of the world, out of touch. The "solution" is not to empty ourselves of it, but to notice the umbilical cords that still tether us to a festival of vitality.

As such, we are here as part of an always-unfolding politics of surprise. We are here because the smarting, tingling sensation of our phantom limbs calls us to lean closer and pay attention to a troubled world.

We are hoping for a different kind of miracle. These lives here are a testament to the fact that we are weary of the familiar. We have tried everything we know to do. We've explored the possible. Now we must try the impossible. We must wait here, with questions that may not have answers, as the universe turns to meet us halfway.

Why are we here, dear? We are here for you and all our children that will live after us.

✦

We close the windows, and bolt them shut. A few minutes ago, your grandmother had called to say a massive cyclone was about to hit, and that she hopes we've stocked up our apartment with food and supplies. You are three years old, oblivious to nature's motions of fury. Already, we can hear the whistling sound of rapid, passing winds squeezing through the tightly packed buildings in our neighborhood in Chennai, India. Merely the spinning tassels of Cyclone Vardah's ceremonial dress. The news stations and their reporters are saying Vardah will make landfall any moment. At 3 p.m., she does, snaking her way to land from the Bay of Bengal, grinning and spinning like a maddened Kali, lifting cars and uprooting trees, tearing through buildings and ecosystems, making palm trees bend and look away as she purges everything.

The next day, the fury is done, but Vardah—a name given by Pakistani observers that appropriately means "red rose"—has left death and destruction in her wake. In spite of the fact that the Tamil Nadu government has evacuated tens of thousands of people away from coastal regions, the cyclone uproots twelve thousand trees in Chennai, destroys electric poles and transformers, drowns seventy-seven cows in Kanchipuram, and blocks 224 roads—2.1 billion dollars in public infrastructure and private property is estimated to have been lost. That estimation has nothing to do with the lives lost—up to forty people, including a three-year-old child.

Not quite "Chennai's Hurricane Katrina," which had eleven years before claimed 1,800 lives and caused destruction to property that exceeded a hundred billion dollars, Vardah's gust speeds of more than seventy-five miles per hour (the most severe in more than twenty years of cyclonic storms) still rekindles memories of the 2004 Indian Ocean earthquake and tsunami— which your mother barely escaped coming home from school, but which resulted in the unfortunate loss of up to three hundred thousand people.

Apart from calls by concerned citizens for the Tamil Nadu government to protect its coastal cities with better infrastructure, old questions rage: was Vardah punishment for our sins? Was this climate change?

In the evening of the next day, we are picked up by Peer, a family friend, who takes you and me in his tiny car to purchase some items at a nearby store. As we navigate past felled trees, bits of billboards and shrapnel of wood strewn across the street, mangled electric cables hanging precariously over the street, the extent of Vardah's wrath is made manifest to me. My jaw hangs open as I gaze at empty spaces where familiar landmarks should be. For the first time since we moved to Egmore, I am able to see the insides of PT School because its fence has been breached by the falling of a massive oak tree, its thick trunk making the road inaccessible. I cannot help but feel we are in a war zone.

As Peer parks the vehicle, I carry you out of the car gently and hold you tight as we walk into the store—still open even now. "Dada! Let me walk," you snarl. But I am not about to let go. Not now.

One month later, in the opening weeks of 2017, scientists would move the Doomsday Clock thirty seconds closer to midnight, positioning the globe at two and a half minutes to annihilation. The Bulletin of the Atomic Scientists, established in 1945 by the University of Chicago scientists who helped build nuclear weapons in the Manhattan Project, designed the Doomsday Clock to draw critical attention to threats to humanity, and inspire world leaders to take action about events, trends, and issues that significantly diminished the odds for human survivability. With the rise of "strident nationalism" and the rushing populist-antiglobalist wave of identitarian politics—embodied by the startling and disturbing emergence of Donald Trump first as candidate, then as Republican nominee, and then as forty-fifth President of the United States, as well as the Brexit referendum vote by Britons to leave the European Union—the scientists would feel there was an increased likelihood that international cooperation to control carbon emissions, especially among leading industrial states, could suffer. Carbon emissions would therefore not drop fast enough to avert danger, even after the much vaunted successes of the Paris Climate Accords in late 2015.

Moreover, after several U.S. intelligence agencies publicly announce that Russia had in fact done all they could to manipulate the 2016 presidential election in favor of the outsider Trump, the political tensions between the two superpower states (as well as the riotous brinkmanship of Trump and North Korean leader Kim Jong-un) would give grounds for the clock-keepers to worry about thermonuclear war. Not since 1947, when the clock was first designed against the backdrop of nuclear threats, has the hand of the clock leaned so close to midnight—the point of no return, which the scientific community warned might be a global catastrophe of permanent repercussions.

In the eyes of these scientists, the fact that Donald Trump, who had expressed dismissive opinions about climate change and promised to withdraw the United Sates (the world's biggest contributor to carbon emissions) from the "bad deal" in Paris, cast climate discourse and action back several decades. Apocalypse could come like a thief in the night. According to old yet relevant reports, India could be two degrees warmer by 2030, at which time you'd be turning eighteen. Sea levels will rise due to thermal expansion—warmer water takes up more space than cold water—and threaten India's four thousand miles of coastline. By these calculations, inhabitants of coastal megacities like Chennai, meaning us, already experiencing the brunt of heavy floods and unprecedented cyclonic storms, will suffer the most damage to their farmlands and public support systems.

In the store, we try to pay for the items we've picked, including biscuits and apple juice for you. The cashier takes Peer's card, inserts it into the credit card reader, pulls it out and tries again ... and again. "I'm sorry," she says in Tamil. "It seems the internet is down." We have no cash to offer, no thanks to the prime minister's demonetization scheme that, much to the annoyance of the general populace, had rendered large-currency rupee notes obsolete. The ATMs are not dispensing cash either. We drop the items, and leave the store. As I descend the steps into a street with felled trees and debris, trying to create some excuse for not picking up the biscuits that you can understand, I remember Kutti and his family and the precarity of their living conditions, and I realize just how fragile everything is—so that one bolt out of place could dismantle the feverish contraption that is our modern lives. It feels like the end of days.

It's 1993. Wednesday. Night falls in Kinshasa as a violet-blue sky weaves a deceptive tapestry of coziness across the tense landscape. Tito is lying on the leather settee, her eyes closing to sleep. Wendy, about a year plus, is sleeping in mummy's lap. Lou Dobbs is on television with his haughty macho media voice, reading the news moments after James Earl Jones's voice had announced: "This is CNN!" Dad and mum, both dressed in their pajamas, are sitting down eating from a small bowl of peanuts, facing the TV. They are, however, not watching it. They are speaking rapidly in Yoruba. I am lingering behind them, near the inside wall aquarium, simultaneously watching the monstrous fish chase away the colorful spritely small ones, and trying to listen for clues about what they are saying to each other.

I am not totally oblivious: earlier this week, there had been reports about disgruntled soldiers leaving their barracks and ransacking the homes of diplomats in the country to exert their fury for unpaid salaries. Zaire's stylish president, Mobutu Sese Seko, wears leopard print hats and ornate skin suits lined with bulletproof protection, flies in a Lebanese barber every Wednesday on his personal Concorde to maintain his hair (according to Eric, my father's own Rwandan barber), and walks around with an elaborately carved wooden stick that our butler, Uncle Bernard—who, in spite of his violent epileptic seizures, has served several Nigerian high-ranking diplomats before my father—whispers is the source of his enduring power and longevity. Tito and I had talked cavalierly about soldiers invading our home, and hatched a plan to take them down. First, I'd hide behind the gates, and scare them. Seeing nothing but shadow, they'd run toward our swimming pool, where Sumbu, our sentinel, would trip them up with an outstretched leg, and Tito would Chuck-Norris them to their watery demise. And then we would call Bimbo—who is in the Nigerian Navy's secondary school back home—with dad's briefcase mobile set, and tell her how "*gen-gen!*" we are.

Tonight, however, with Tito now fast asleep, and my father in his striped pajamas, we do not exactly cut the picture of a disciplined fighting unit. There is consternation in my mother's voice. She is saying she is worried. My father looks irritated, and assures her no harm can come to us. Why should she worry so much? What could possibly happen with Sumbu outside, our heavily fortified doors and all that? Watching him speak, with the delicate gold chain encircling his slender neck—as if to ennoble every word from his manly throat—I feel safe, and carry out conversations with mum in my head: "Yeah, mum. What could happen?"

And then, as if in response, she tenses up and says "Yomi!" under her breath, gripping my father's arm. She points outside, to the colonnaded wall. The violet-blue sky is now an impenetrable midnight hue, but I can still discern them: a pair of fingers, and now four pairs of fingers, and now camo-sleeved arms, scaling our impenetrable fortress.

Could this actually be happening?

My dad rushes to switch off the lights, and whisks us—in a single move—to the master bedroom, through the corridor where our family portraits hang on white walls. We lock ourselves in the toilet, just as the electricity goes out. We are all here, Dad, Mum, Tito, Wendy, Uncle Bernard, and me, in the same place we've dyed my father's hair jet black, preserving his youth in alchemical scoops of magic. This place where we laughed at my mother's cluelessness about action films. This place my father first called us "the golden family."

A dead silence falls. We are still wondering what just happened, our hearts still racing. The dark is threaded through with soft murmurings of my mum weeping and praying. Otherwise there is n—

A crackling sound smashes the eternity of our horrid wait, like unexpected thunder. *Kprak! Kprak!* And then, it rains. Bullets. From up above. The sound of guns crackling and of feet stomping on our flat roof and shouted orders in Lingala leave us all a whimpering huddle of dread. Something breaks in the bathroom.

Moments later, we hear male voices barking even more orders outside the toilet door. They've found us. Uncle Bernard is speaking with surprising calm in his native tongue, pleading with the soldiers to leave us be. But the angry retort, officious and French, does not yield: *"Ouvre la porte! Ouvre la porte!"* They threaten to bring the door down if we do not open it. My father, in fluid French, joins the heated cacophony of barked orders and firm entreaties. My French is no good too, but from the tiny space between the toilet and the wall where I have squeezed myself, I hear numbers. A countdown. *Dix! Neuf! Huit! Sept! Six! Cinq! Quatre! Trois! Deux!*

A foot crashes through the bathroom door and withdraws immediately, and the tip of a machine gun peeps into our sanctuary. Dad and Uncle Bernard have already backed away from behind the door by the time it caves in.

The whole place erupts into an explosion of voices. I can hear my mother—she is praying louder now. My father is speaking; Uncle Bernard is pleading; and the men—big, armed with bullet belts, oily skin glistening in the faint glow of restored electricity, red eyes, worn-out leather boots, and berets the color of blood. They hold a pistol to my father's head, dragging him out. Mum is screaming in Yoruba now, saying she will not let him go, and that if they want to kill him they should take her too. Tito and I are sobbing. Wendy is blasé, not even crying as she is used to doing when strangers show up. She is quiet, in mum's one hand. A soldier comes to her, tries to pull her away from my mum, but she spits fire in his face. He holds her ear, surveying Wendy's earring, and orders my mum to take it off. Both of them. Now.

Meanwhile I can hear commotion in the hall, the sounds of husky voices and glass breaking. I even see women, whom I will later learn are the accompanying wives of the renegade soldiers.

It all comes down to this moment: the big boss in the group quietly tells my father he has to die, and asks him if he owns the Peugeot 505 parked outside. My father says yes—their conversation held against a backdrop of escalating chaos in the rest of our house. The boss calmly says my father should come outside with him. My mum says take me too. Her jaw is trembling, her eyes a primal white of animal rage. But her body knows with certainty that she is not going to live one moment longer than my father if he is to die today. Something about her matter-of-fact way of saying "take us both" makes the boss delegate the dirty task to a boy soldier in his flanks and leave the room. He tells the boy to kill us all, as he walks out with Uncle Bernard following, still pleading for our lives. We are pushed back into the bathroom, the doorway guarded by the un-bereted boy, who withdraws his gun. Tito and I are crying. My mother is praying furiously, at the top of her lungs. I close my eyes. I can hear a loud gun cock. My father steps back, his arms out, covering us behind him.

✦

If my father lived to see Trump's nativism and Le Pen's angry anti-immigrant rhetoric in France today, he might have been concerned, but just as uncannily calm and collected as he was that night in 1993. Unlike me. I inherited my mother's drama and tendency for elaborate displays of emotionality. I inherited her worry. Thankfully, your own mother, otherworldly in her composure in the face of chaos, is a better parent than I'll ever be.

But what does one do in these times? Pressed into a corner by the intimidating gun cock sounds of possible thermonuclear war, corporate malfeasance, and excavatory capitalism? I have written about race, about painful colonial elisions, about the ongoing efforts to convert our common wealth into wealth for the few—under the banner of neoliberal development and progress. I explored these issues on my trail for home, on this hajj to become the father I promised to be to you. Surely, answering the question about how we respond to these crises is vital to my quest, is it not? I think so. It is.

So what do we *do*? How do we respond to the fact of our Normal—this consistently grinding premise of social ascendancy, this numbing to the effects of the material climate on our bodies, this suggestion that our very breath—the things we take for granted like the techno-consumeristic paraphernalia we employ to be "more effective" human beings and to enjoy ourselves—is built on the backs of generational occlusion? How do we "rise" to meet a world that well and truly seems skewed in the favor of the rich? A world where people like Kutti and his family, even though they are reconfiguring their lives at the edges, are also produced by a giant machine that takes away people from their lands and gives them to large corporations? How do I respond to these dispossessions, to the horror of residential areas carved out for the nations of Canada, to the snaking infiltrations of big oil into the solemn waters of the Sioux people at Standing Rock? How can I come to terms with the fact that due to rising sea temperatures, you will grow up in a world without the Great Barrier Reef, or that the tall trees in Munnar, Kerala, which you enjoyed visiting when you were only two years old, might be extinct in a few years because of mining activities in the state? Should I care that what lubricates our easy movement from here to there in the modern world might be the blood of whales, the blood of the sea, and the blood of people we cannot see? What happens when we connect the dots?

Only yesterday, I read an account of a purchase made in an Arizona Walmart store with a story at its heart. The item purchased, a purse, had in its zip compartment a tiny note from a Chinese slave who worked fourteen hours a day producing goods for U.S. consumers, and didn't have a lot to eat. The note read: "Inmates in the Yingshan Prison in Guangxi, China, are working fourteen hours daily with no break/rest at noon, continue working overtime until 12 midnight, and whoever doesn't finish his work will be beaten. Their meals are without oil and salt. Every month, the boss pays the inmate 2000 yuan, any additional dishes will be finished by the police. If the inmates are sick and need medicine, the cost will be deducted from the salary.

Being a prisoner in China is even worse than being a horse, cow, sheep, pig, or dog in the U.S."[1]

Were it not for the letter, it would never have crossed the buyer's mind that her purse was so diffracted that it is composed not merely of the threads and leather with which it was sewn, but the criminal justice apparatus in China. The fashion label on the purse didn't tell the whole story; in fact, the brand was an agent of reduction, hiding away the fascinating (and tragic) entanglements of the purse. To stop and consider that momentarily might give us the occasion to see that we do not—nothing ever does, in fact— emerge fully formed, independently realized. There are certain conditions we are framed in that make *us* possible—the terroir for our being/becoming.

In Ursula Le Guin's short story "The Ones Who Walk Away from Omelas," she imagines an idyllic city, "bright-towered by the sea"—a place so happy that it feels too good to be true. It is a city of noble architecture and profound science and deep wisdom. A truly responsible happiness irradiates Omelas. Why this utter and wholesome joy? The narrator doesn't tell or doesn't know, but enlists the reader of the story to fill in the details on their own. The details of what makes them so happy "doesn't matter," the narrator just knows that they are happy—and not the insipid, vacuous, "goody-goody," "puritanical," derivative, stupid, or plain-minded kind of happiness, but a real, embodied, intellectual, and affective liberation.

While the narrator does not know all the details about this city's happiness, she is quite certain that it is made possible by the utter misery of a small child placed in a grimy, unsanitary windowless basement:

> In a basement under one of the beautiful public buildings of Omelas, or perhaps in the cellar of one of its spacious private homes, there is a room. It has one locked door, and no window. A little light seeps in dustily between cracks in the boards, secondhand from a cobwebbed window somewhere across the cellar. In one corner of the little room a couple of mops, with stiff, clotted, foul-smelling heads, stand near a rusty bucket. The floor is dirt, a little damp to the touch, as cellar dirt usually is. The room is about three paces long and two wide: a mere broom closet

or disused tool room. In the room a child is sitting. It could be a boy or a girl. It looks about six, but actually is nearly ten.[2]

To tell you this story properly, my dear, I have quoted the author extensively, because she writes so evocatively about this one in Omelas. This child knows no daylight, no love, no sunrise or wind in face. It "is so thin there are no calves to its legs; its belly protrudes; it lives on a half-bowl of corn meal and grease a day. It is naked. Its buttocks and thighs are a mass of festered sores, as it sits in its own excrement continually." It is not pretending to be wretched; it *is* wretched, and the narrator takes pains to disabuse the mind of the reader that this child is proto-human or some kind of machine devoid of feelings and yearning:

> *It is afraid of the mops. It finds them horrible. It shuts its eyes, but it knows the mops are still standing there; and the door is locked; and nobody will come. The door is always locked; and nobody ever comes, except that sometimes—the child has no understanding of time or interval—sometimes the door rattles terribly and opens, and a person, or several people, are there. One of them may come and kick the child to make it stand up. The others never come close, but peer in at it with frightened, disgusted eyes. The food bowl and the water jug are hastily filled, the door is locked, the eyes disappear. The people at the door never say anything, but the child, who has not always lived in the tool room, and can remember sunlight and its mother's voice, sometimes speaks. "I will be good," it says. "Please let me out. I will be good!" They never answer.*[3]

Do the people of Omelas not know that the child is there? "They all know it is there; all the people of Omelas." The narrator explains that they sometimes come to visit, not to console or offer a kind word or bring blankets, but to watch it for a time and then turn away. They know it has to be there. "They all understand that their happiness, the beauty of their city, the tenderness of their friendships, the health of their children, the wisdom of their scholars, the skill of their makers, even the abundance of their harvest and the kindly weathers of their skies, depend wholly on this child's abominable misery." Parents explain this to their children—but no matter how well they do, everyone that visits her is shocked. Some understand, but others want to do something about it—except that the moment they offer even so much as a smile, "in that day and hour all the prosperity and beauty and delight of Omelas would wither and be destroyed. Those are the terms. To exchange all the goodness and grace of every life in Omelas for that single, small improvement: to throw away the happiness of thousands for the chance of the happiness of one." These are the absolute terms. The very poignancy and potency and vitality of Omelas' culture—their gallant walls, their genuine knowledge of many arts, their enthusiastic benevolence toward one another and hospitality to all—derives from knowing the child is there. The people of Omelas know "they are not free"; it is because the child is there that they can show compassion and be kind to others.

Eventually, many learn to let go of their guilt after harboring a "rage" about the precarity of the child.

> *They may brood over it for weeks or years. But as time goes on they begin to realize that even if the child could be released, it would not get much good of its freedom: a little vague pleasure of warmth and food, no doubt, but little more … their tears at the bitter injustice dry when they begin to perceive the terrible justice of reality, and to accept it.*[4]

The narrator then finds most incredible the fact that some who go to observe the child never return home in their tears; they go past the farmlands, past the noble courts and good roads of Omelas, and leave the city for good. The narrator cannot tell whether they do know where they are going, but they leave—wandering away.

In retrospect, Le Guin's story would have been an excellent exemplification of the themes I explored in my previous letter to you—you know, the one about the part of psychic life that is irredeemably dark and our need to come to some way to hold that. That darkness cannot be solved. But back to this: if you feel a certain anger just contemplating the child's misfortunes, and vow you'll be one of those that rise up in arms to do something about it, I will sympathize with you, dear. I felt the same way reading the story.

Le Guin's masterful stroke, however, is in holding back from imposing moral judgments about the situation. She doesn't conclude that the people are evil; she doesn't paint them in unflattering light. A creeping soundtrack of something sinister lurking behind the apparent joy of the city dwellers does not play in your ear while reading it. And so it is—that one of the motifs made clear in Omelas is that nothing shows up "completely" ... that, like the oblivious Walmart customer's purse, things appear diffractively—enabling and disabling, upholding and eliding, simultaneously. It is not possible to find a position or stance that is without these tension of worlds and possibilities forgone. Our very real material economic-political-ethical realities are forged as an ongoing Faustian pact; even the concepts of good and bad are haunted by a child in a windowless room, locked away from view.

In relation to the question of how to respond to crisis, Le Guin's story teaches a subtler lesson—one that speaks about entanglements and diffractions and intra-actions: she teaches that this particular question of "how to respond to crisis" has its own agency that often occludes us from seeing that we are *already in response*. Another way to put that might be to say we are asking the wrong question when we ask what to do, how to get home, how to leave a beautiful world for our kids—but that would be too heavy a brush to paint with. What's calling for attention here is that ethics is not a thing that comes "afterward." We don't observe the facts and then decide to do something about it. Ethics is not external to the material doings and undoings of the world, but emerges with it—so that our bodies themselves are ethical responses of the world to its own complexity.[5] To ask "how do we respond to crisis?" can give the idea that *doings* are human affairs, and that there is a place to stand *outside* the world to contemplate the best, most appropriate ways to respond to it. But there isn't. We can't respond *to* the world if we are the world.

Chinua Achebe therefore looks askance at Archimedes' declaration: "Give me a lever and a place to stand and I will move the earth." To that he replies by saying, "The impatient idealist says: 'Give me a place to stand and I shall move the earth.' But such a place does not exist. We all have to stand on the earth itself and go with her at her pace."[6] There is no place to stand. There is no lever. There is no outside. If you are flowing downstream in a rapidly rushing stream of mud, there is no time to be clean. Just thinking about the world or understanding it in specific ways is performatively infectious; it is action ... a performance that does not even originate in us as it diffracts through/with us.[7] To think is to think-with. Trying to understand the world without changing it in the selfsame moment is just as feasible as trying to startle your own mirrored reflection.

As I think of the world's problems and what *to do* about them, I am learning to offer different questions—more generative questions ... bubbly, hospitable, and humbling questions: how are we *already* collectively responding or in response to our specific crises? How are we mattering ... or how are we *showing up* vis-à-vis the specific challenges we are encountering? How do we account for these emergent realities in terms of what is missing, what we find unintelligible, or what is being excluded?

What these questions bring us to contemplate is the ways we are already complicit in the production of certain realities at the cost of complimentary others. They open up the possibility of redescribing our many activisms not in terms of solutions or final arrangements, but in terms of an ongoing accounting for the ways we are part of a universe touching itself ... already in response and being responded with. Indeed, what happens when we say we have solved a problem, say, climate change or poverty, is that particular political-economic-ethical-technological forces have enacted a "cut" or drawn a convenient line in the sand ... we are caught up in practices of looking away from the world's ongoing-ness. But we—the thick "we" comprising a porous posthuman string of many bodies in flow—are not to be resolved.

✦

They say that when one is about to die, your life flashes before you. You see those you love, those moments you cherish, in spontaneous psychic edits of final longing. Perhaps that is only true in specific situations where one is distant from your loved ones. For me, right here, I need no private cinematic bursts of my life and my loved ones; it is all here. They are all here. In the flesh. In this bathroom. I can see them already. And they are about to be murdered by the gun of a Zairean child soldier—who, with gun in hand, stands at the doorway, watching us.

Everything is fading into a psychedelic, muffled alchemy of sound and image. I think I'm clinging on to Tito and everyone else, but I can't be sure. Now I sink to the floor, crouching at the feet of my family. I can hear Mummy's voice—even through this mist I'm enveloped in, her voice is still distinct and even stentorian in her assertion of our survival. I cannot hear my father's voice.

And then silence. The mist clouds out all sound and voice.

I do not know how long I've shut my eyes, or how long this silence took me—but I can hear a conversation. In Lingala. My ears seem to clear open, much in the same way stuffy ears are unclogged after one alights from a plane. I open my eyes. Uncle Bernard is here, and he seems to be translating the soldier's comments to my mum and dad. Uncle Bernard tells them that the soldier boy pities us. He saw my mother pray, and since he is Christian too, he will not take our lives. But that he doesn't know what his boss will do to him, and that they will all be going soon—when they have taken all they want from our home.

So long as I live I will never forget her face—this wave of relief that washes over my mother's splintered face as she collapses to the ground, saying "Thank you! Thank you! Ah, thank you!" I cannot see my father's face, just his back. But he is speaking to the soldier in French now. I turn to Tito. And Wendy. We are all here. Still in one piece. There is no greater feeling than coming to the edge, and knowing that is not the absolute end after all.

But the danger is not yet past.

Moments after the soldier had spared our lives, he escorted us to my own room, where he hoped we'd be safe. There was a wild orgy of deconstruction happening around us. Our home was being dismantled over our heads, beneath our feet, and before our very eyes. I wondered if this was what it was like to be dead: to see things unraveling, peeling back, dropping their skins, and spraying away into the oblivious as ash into sky. We stayed in one corner of my bedroom, near a large office table pushed close to the wall. Scattered around us were bullet canisters, the traces of their fury marking the walls with angry holes.

Suddenly, another member of the raiding party came to us, and then dragged the boy soldier outside by his ear. Uncle Bernard said that they might kill him for defying orders.

I wake up from a dreamless sleep, and survey my surroundings. I am still in a fetal position under the table in my room. There seems to be some calm now. At least that's what my body desperately wants to believe. Before long, I drift back to sleep.

"Bayo, wake up! Wake up, *jo!*" Tito is leaning over me, stirring me awake. I get up. A glistening white streams in through the window on my right. It is a princely morning in Kinshasa, the morning after mutinied soldiers ransacked our home and almost killed us. "They've taken everything," Tito is telling me.

"And do you know even more soldiers came?" she continues.

"More soldiers? Where's Daddy and Mummy?" I ask.

We go through the bullet-riddled corridor, watching our steps as we try to walk past broken glass and toppled ceramic vases. There are droplets of blood on the floor and blood splatter on the wall opposite the entrance to the living room. In the living room, nothing is recognizable anymore. The wall aquarium wasn't broken; it was totally pulled out. Where blue water and playful fish should be, there is a large rectangular hole through which one can see the large foyer that goes to the kitchen. Dad's super loud music system is gone. Some of his CDs are on the floor, shattered. Bob Marley's smiling visage and dreadlocks are still recognizable from a tiny disc fragment. There's the 1993 Peter Justesen catalog in the shelf, largely untouched. The TV is still there too, broken on the floor a few inches from its former resting place. Its electric cord, taut, is still plugged into the wall. The settees are gone. The curtains. Even the water closet toilets. I'm left wondering how they were able to uproot so much in one night. And how they were able to bear them away! Did they come with a truck or something?

I would later learn that no room in the house was spared. In the kitchen, two deep refrigerators and their contents of frozen chicken are all gone too. Apparently, a major fight had ensued between smaller factions within the troops that stormed our house. Some of their wives had struggled for the same items; their husbands had brought out their guns and shot at each other. This is what Uncle Bernard says. The bloody drag marks on the tiles show where bodies had been, Mummy in one of the rooms is praising God and saying it is a miracle that we survived—and not just that, but the soldiers started to kill one another! I am beginning to get a sense of how improbable our survival was, and indeed how much a miracle it is that we are all here—in one piece.

Well, all of us except Sumbu. During the pillaging, he had locked himself in one of the wardrobes in the house, hoping to escape notice. I do not know all the details, but he was shot at, and barely escaped a gruesome death: the bullet whizzed past the right side of his face, burning its livid trail into his skin. He is pressing an icepack on the wound, his right eye unable to stop tearing up.

Sitting on a tiny stool in the middle of this pandemonium is my dad. I go straight to hug him. "Good morning, Daddy," I say, wrapping my small frame around his warm body. Were it not for the softness and innocence implied in the greeting, the irony of those words would have been too great for any of us to bear without laughing. Or perhaps crying. Or both at the same time. He holds me tight, with one arm, and tells me to find a pair of slippers. It's too dangerous walking around without one, he says, against a backdrop of men picking up bullets into bags and making notes of damaged items for the report I trust my father would soon begin to prepare for the Nigerian Embassy.

Mummy comes out into the hall, and I hug her too. She is more in a hurry, but no less strong-willed and grateful that we survived the ordeal. She is carrying a bag with what is left of Wendy's things. I look into it to see if I can make her bottled hot milk for her. There's hardly anything in the bag, except a few feeding bottles. "Where's the Nan, mummy?" I ask, referring to the baby formula milk. My mum then tells me that she had the last one packed up inside the bag, and had set the bag in the middle of the hall and gone back into the room to retrieve any salvageable items for the trip we are about to make. When she returned to the hall, a strange kid, scantily clad, was already in the house, surveying the contents of the bag. Alarmed, Mum started to shoo the boy away and was going to chase him off—when the boy pulled out a gun and just pointed it to her with a dead stare that was maybe more chilling than the prospects of an unusual death. Raising her hands and backing away gently, she asked him to take anything he wanted and just please go. The boy took the Nan and scuttled out of the ruins of our home, leaving my mother calling frantically for my dad.

We have no food, no water, and no clothes. Embassy files, Dad's off-white Peugeot 505 with the musical horn he installed to make us laugh anytime he came home, shoes, clothes, suits, slippers … all gone. I remember our dogs, Sasha and Maiden, with a crushing feeling of vertigo: I had not considered them during our ordeal. I wonder if they are anywhere to be found. A man in a red cap comes through the black gate, and my father goes out to meet him, and then comes back after a while to find Mummy. "It's time to go," he says. He is still in his pajamas—the only item he can claim as property. My mother nods her okay and takes us all into the room to change into some clothes that had escaped the soldiers' gaze.

In a moment, we are out under the foreboding sun, gathered in the compound by our black gate. Mummy, Tito, Wendy, Uncle Bernard, Sumbu, and some men—including the man with the red cap, who is now telling my dad that we are lucky, because the French ambassador was killed in his home.

I turn around to look at the house that had held us all this time. The first home we had moved into when, three years ago, back in Nigeria, my father received an official letter from the Ministry of Foreign Affairs informing him that he had been posted to China. We were excited. China was Bruce Lee and cool martial arts. But then our excitement was short-lived because he came back with a new letter: the Ministry had changed its mind and posted us to some country in Central Africa I hadn't heard of: Zaire. We made the journey to Kinshasa via Air Zaire. I remember the no-smoking lights were permanently lit, to no effect, as cigarette smoke swirled in the space above our heads. It was the most turbulent flight ever—but we made it. First to the beautiful and extravagant Nigerian Embassy at 141, Boulevard du 30 Juin, next to the more conservative Israeli Embassy, where my dad played table tennis with other members of the diplomatic corps every Wednesday night. And then to this house—this place where I got my first robot toy—the blue one with eyes that glowed red as it screamed inaudible sounds and crashed into the wall; where I learned to climb the palm kernel tree in the backyard; where Ms. Ruth Montacute, our headmistress at the Zaire British Association School, had told my dad about my naughty note to Bhavna, an Indian girl in my class I had a crush on, while I trembled in the room; where I learned to toss food from my plate under the dining table when mummy wasn't watching; and, where Bimbo, Tito, Wendy, and I would wash daddy's hair in his bathroom … to preserve his youth.

Now we had to say good-bye to it, because it could no longer sustain us.

I turn away from the house and toward everyone else. Dad is barefoot. Mum has Dunlop slippers on, as do Tito and I. Mum whispers to us that we have to find a way to the embassy, where she promises we will be safe. Our bodies are shifting restlessly. The sky is crackling with the energy of apocalyptic endings. If we weren't in it, what we just experienced the night before could make a great adventure movie. We are scared, but we cannot stay here. Outside these black gates, beyond this poor facsimile of a barrier, on the streets littered with corpses, thick columns of black smoke and yelling, are men with guns, who would take our lives given the chance. How do we make our way through the lot? What lies beyond this fence?

✦

As incredibly pressing as it may sound, the story of humans going out to fix the world that they are destroying still feeds a politics of binaries and tells a story of nature being the vassal of culture, of mind preceding matter, of "thought" being an alien brooding over the deep, and of man rearranging the whole world with language. This isn't to deny what we feel in our bones to be urgent: the need to address poverty, to create governments that truly exist for people (and not for big corporations), or enact radically different political imaginaries that sidestep the biased distribution of suffering made possible in nation-states.

The "problem" is that thinking in terms of agential loneliness, or thinking of the human as a homogeneous block of agency, has powerful material effects, and—in my reading—often leads to more sameness and disenchantment. Until we see activism as a politics of encountering the unsaid, of meeting the abject "other," of sticking with trouble, of noticing how entangled we are with a world which the language of fixture and solutionism presumes is external to us—until we see difference-making as a becoming-with, instead of a coming-through, the violence and rudeness of the familiar will hinder us from the bold and risky "newness" that lingers on the edges of awareness.

In short, "saving the world" is sweet tongue for sidestepping not only the troubling discernment that the world is more complex than language or thought or story (and therefore, "solutions"), but the confounding realization that the world is not a dormant palette for our most austere dreams or best intentions. Atlas shrugs, and the world shrugs back.

Perhaps, dear, nowhere is the world's wayward shrugging more apparent than in most institutionalized attempts at resolving our many troubles. From SDGs to carbon emissions trading and microfinance as a way of tackling poverty, our globalizing crisis-response imaginary has at its core the sticky idea that we can—if we put our backs into it—rise above the fray and create the world *we* want. Again, I hesitate to wield the easy brush of generic statements that lend themselves to sloganization: I cannot rule out that there are situated practices that call for institutional action; neither do I presume to have arrived at some new onto-epistemology of activism that supersedes and makes irrelevant our best efforts at creating "a better world." If I am learning anything critical through this ongoing journey that an old shaman back in

Nigeria inspired, it is that the world is too preposterous to be decided in one neat framework.[8]

And yet, while admitting that there is no "successor regime" dynamic at work here, the case could be made that when one pays attention to the material-cultural practices that create modernity's understandings of time, history, and our place in the world, we meet a deeply anthropocentric-mechanical notion of change and causality.

The figure of the tinkering human, cleanly abstracted from his environment, with power of foresight and the agency to marshal the world to his beckoning, still casts its shadow across our landscapes. It is the archetype of the one who must find his way—who must brave strong winds to find sanctuary. The prospects of arriving, of coming to definite solutions, are central to this myth of the sole human agent.

This "human" has consciousness *inside* with which he can change the world *outside*. Like Le Guin's wretched child, what is excluded in this framework is not only the idea that the world outside is *doing something* and is not "outside" at all, but that what we do on our own is actually what the rest of the material world is doing. If our assumption of a "reality of continuously intermingling, flowing strands of unfolding, agential activity"[9] is correct, then journeys are not dead things you travel. They shape you just as much as you shape them.

Journeys are not the tame servants that bear you from one point to another. Journeys are how things become different. How things, like wispy trails of fairy dust, touch themselves in ecstatic delight and explode into unsayable colors. Every mooring spot, every banal point, is a thought experiment, replete with monsters and tricksters and halos and sphinxes and riddles and puzzles and strange dalliances. Every truth is a dare. To travel is therefore not merely to move through space and time, it is to be reconfigured, it is to bend space-time, it is to revoke the past and remember the future. It is to be changed. No one arrives intact.

We have our life and derive our being from a flow of activity. The continuity between the human and the nonhuman asserts our more humble place in a never-ending tide of entanglement. To "sever ourselves" from this flow (which is to deny its significance) is to lose our porosity and thus adopt "one-size-fits-all conventional meanings" that reinforce the same realities we try to escape. In this sense, how we are already responding to crisis is part of the crisis. It is not a case of something *yet* to be done (as contemporary narratives about the benefits of constant innovation indicate).

So let me tell you a story as best I could. Keener people than I have told it, but you can trust your dad to try.

Climate change is believed to be the single most threatening phenomenon facing humankind today. All around us, the ineffaceable marks left by how much we've fundamentally altered the planet's climate and environmental systems have inspired scientists to contribute a new word to our lexicon of dread: the "Anthropocene." It was coined as a label to signify a new geological epoch sedimented from human activity—and as an ethical imperative, to rally attention around the destruction brought upon the planet by our seemingly ravenous species.

The elementary argument of climate change theorists is that the planet is getting warmer—and this warming phenomenon is causing adverse weather conditions that have multiplier effects on the ways we organize our lives and on the places we call home.

From melting glaciers in the Arctic regions and the pronounced risk of flooding, to rising sea levels as a result of warmer waters, and fragile ecosystems due to imbalances brought about by the loss of biodiversity, the untoward effects of climate change are well known and widely published. As a result of these observations, scientific leaders have raised their ram horns over the cliffs, urging a concerted political effort to counteract a global phenomenon that doesn't respect national boundaries. In response, a new climate politics—a dramatic sequence of global actors and data accumulation set against the ticktock soundtrack of eventual apocalypse in a sure future—gained ground.

A year before you were born, in 2012, a volcano in Iceland—with a name I can only write out but couldn't possibly pronounce even on pain of death—called Eyjafjallajökull, spewed 9.5 billion cubic feet of ash six miles into the air over the course of a few months. Larger volcanic eruptions have taken place, and scientists believed Eyjafjallajökull's tantrums were a small event. However, that eruption disrupted flights across Europe, and affected the entire world. The effects weren't just limited to travel disruption: with no air freight heading for Europe, perishable consignments like flowers and fish exports from African economies rotted at airports. Asian car makers canceled production of units due to delayed parts. Sports events were canceled, and movie premieres had to be relocated. One might say the geological bled into the economical, the political, and the cultural.

The volcano's eruption, like Cyclone Vardah's mutinied ransacking of our home city, Chennai, underlined just how susceptible civilization is to natural hazards. Long before Eyjafjallajökull, many scientists had long held a consensus view that—barring an extinction-level event by nuclear warfare—the world as we know it will end as sea levels rise up to two hundred feet higher than today, submerging cities underwater. Noah's flood repeated—unless we did something about it.

Today's conversation about climate change insists that the only way to stop our certain demise under towering pillars of water—the foretaste of which has visited Chennai in recent years—is by adopting policies that discipline the otherwise unregulated market production effects on the environment, and by investing in developing cheaper green technologies that remove dependence on extracted fossil fuels—the black oil that poisons the skies in millions of internal combustion cars across the planet.

A new transnational imaginary grips the planet—spilling out in talking points, haunting conscientious travelers worried about overdrawing from their carbon wallets. Like the hand of God on the wall announcing the end of an era, this new myth inscribes new parameters of responsivity in the sky, infecting everything with its logic, and folding itself around the new enemy: carbon emission. Everyone is in on it. The new ethical imperatives that have seeped into mass culture enlists celebrities, funds research (and therefore determines research imperatives), inspires new initiatives and nongovernmental organizations that desire to tackle climate change, and even spawns disaster movies that capitalize on fears about climate catastrophe. New terms have come into the rapidly developing field dedicated to advocating for and spreading awareness about climate change—terms such as *climate justice, climate ethics, carbon literacy,* and *ecocide.*

In 1997, the Kyoto Protocol emerged from this social milieu as an instrument of the United Nations Framework Convention on Climate Change (UNFCCC), engaging states to adopt standards and practices designed to reduce the effects of anthropogenic activity on the environment. As a way of enforcing pollution control, policy makers convened around an idea for a carbon tax or emissions tax, the seed of which initially blossomed in twentieth-century English economist Arthur Cecil Pigou's proposal to levy a tax on market activities that had negative externalities.

Basically, carbon trade "assigns monetary value to the earth's shared atmosphere," forcing businesses—especially those in participating nations where carbon emissions are high—to pay attributed fines that are proportionate to the damage done. With the recent ratification of the complementary Paris Agreement (in 2015), additional measures—such as capping carbon dioxide emissions so that they eventually fall to preindustrial levels—are now in force to fight the scourge of carbon. The new watch-term is "negative emissions," which conceptualizes the next logical step from merely planting our feet in the ground: pushing back against the enemy and reclaiming lost ground by removing the excess of carbon in the atmosphere with new sequestration technologies.

All these timelines collide at a single nexus of measurement practices: carbon metrics. It is what allows us to measure how well we are doing; it sits at the heart of the big puzzle set of popular climate discourse.

So, are these practices any good? Are the innovative varieties of offsetting strategies drawing attention to a planet in peril? Are they "working" at mitigating climate change? Is the earth getting warmer, or have we successfully turned the tide on carbon? Are we winning the war? Global climate reports say the year 2016 was not as warm as its predecessor, but that isn't necessarily good news. We are in a tense gridlock that shows no signs of easing up in our favor. Cars are still produced. There is no cheap ecologically sensitive energy alternative on the horizons. And, with the rise of radical identitarianism blowing across the United States and Europe (I write this as France is about to go through its own electoral baptism of fire—choosing between a nativist politics that would build walls to chase out foreigners, and a globalist politics that trusts in neoliberal determinism), what with its distrust for climate change science, stringent environment policies are likely to be repealed. The prognosis isn't looking good. The voracious hordes of orcs—if orcs are escalating numbers in carbon emission data—still press hard against the gates and, without the provision of even stricter measures to slow down carbon emissions and the philanthropy of deep-pocket billionaires like Elon Musk, our house of cards will eventually fall.

But this story of my time's most captivating civilizational myth—this great and powerful parliament of world forces—wouldn't be complete without its own inflections and plot twists. Today's politics of climate change hinges on the confidence that carbon emissions are the main drivers of global warming, that the science is largely accurate, and that one mustn't allow fools to slow down our hurried pace to shore up our walls against the *outside*.

The problem with accuracy, however, is that it comes with costs. Scientific accuracy isn't about how well the world "out there" is represented, it is about how well other possibilities and accounts about the world are excluded from mattering or hardwired out of view. Remember waves and particles? Don't fret, I won't go there. Just keep them in mind! Especially the idea that the world is an ongoing series of co-becomings that matter in terms of what is cut out simultaneously.

Climate change politics is not so much the practice of depicting the truth about climate dynamics as it is the multiagential co-production and maintenance of an abstraction—carbon metrics—with which a particular worldview sustains itself to the exclusion of other complementary accounts of the ways climates matter. In the same obstructing way that economic measures like gross domestic product force us to privilege monetary transactions, income, and corporate/industrial activity by discounting the nonmonetary practices of caring that happens in small places or the contributions of trees to weathering the planet and our well-being, carbon metrics reduces climate change to the amount of carbon in the atmosphere and the ability of emissions markets to meet sustainability goals. As part of a climate imaginary that is produced by a neoliberal agenda of progress, linear time, anthropocentric control, separation from nature, and technological optimism, today's carbon discourse and activism obfuscate other ways of thinking/acting with weather.

First, "the myth that human bodies are discrete in time and space, somehow outside of the natural milieu that sustains them and indeed transits through them"[10] denies the ways bodies are already entangled with weather—in other words, weather is what "we" are collectively doing with each other. Astrida Neimanis and Rachel Loewen Walker say that what we are called to respond to in climate is not something "outside" or faraway, but something as immediate as the operations of our between-bodies. We do not observe climate or weather as if it were happening outside of us; instead bodies are constantly *betweening* with the elements: the sun leaks its rays on plants, which furnishes the atmosphere with oxygenic depth that fills our lungs. This is not a sequence of independent objects mechanically influencing other independent objects in domino-like fashion. It isn't a mere interaction when the effects of the sun only arise and derive their agency in the context of other effects—that is, the orifices of my body, the bacterial contributions to cloud formation,[11] atmospheric effects, and even the discourse on the sun are the condition of its materiality. The climate is not an externality, because we intra-act with it. We are weathering bodies.

Even "natural disasters" are specific intra-acting arrangements and collaborations between bodies that a molecular attribution of cause does not appreciate. If we think of the world as a container for discrete, autonomous bits of things that have effects on each other, then we end up with a notion of causality that is blind to the "viscous porosity," animation and betweening of bodies. This is why Barad speaks of queer causalities, echoed by Neimanis and Loewen:

> *Although our traditional mechanisms of understanding retroactively search for causes and effects (seed plants cause hay fever), in a world of intra-activity the hay-feverish body cannot be traced back. It was not once an autonomous body whose borders have been breached, but rather an expression of transcorporeal collaboration as plant and human orifices together weather a season's change. The body (a human body, a gust of wind, striations of rock) can no longer be understood as an autonomous entity, unaffected by (and ineffectual in) its environment. Instead, the very conditions of its possibility rely on its entanglement with a dynamic system of forces and flows.*[12]

This is a sensuous reframing of causality and time and climate: tracing back to find an active cause for, let's say, the chicken pox that swarmed over your little body recently might imply that bodies move *in* time, or that time is static ... a container for things rubbing against one another. But that would be another instance of essentializing or absolutizing "time" and bodies. New materialisms challenge the constancy of time, showing it to be out of whack, queering befores and afters, sprouting more tentacles than thin linear progression allows—hence its "thickness." Time and bodies and poxes do not have any independent reality of their own; it is only within the porous relationships they are already part of that their materiality/meaning becomes evident. Our conventions of speaking find it difficult to express the idea that the operations of pox on your body were not *in* time; instead, your body intra-actively produces time with the pox. A firmer collaboration is made—there is no "before" to return to, since an entirely new history is produced in the collaborative intra-mingling of pox and body, or pox-body. As such, the pox did not *cause* the rash on your body, the rash-itchy-body is a co-emergent phenomenon, a "new" ontology altogether that seemingly makes it seem that has always been the state of affairs.

Likewise, with "transcorporeal weather"—the material ways in which specific bodily practices, both human and nonhuman, are co-constitutive of weather, we come to see how the contemporary patterning of responsivity to climate change (within the frame of sustainability) seeks to assert our control over the elements and invests in scale, repeatability, standardization, and climate apocalypse narratives to the exclusion of a different ethos of responsivity. Because we see climate as something outside, something foreign, we have mounted this luxurious and exhausting framework—the elaborate maintenance of which calls on an ethics of big funds, lone interacting actors, money shots, and political promises. Not that there is a "better" way, a deeper layer of action that can resolve this crisis.[13] What we are in effect attempting to do is to control temporality, which is a monumentally tasking project of maintaining our autonomy in the world. In time. In weather.

The whole apparatus is thus framed from a Newtonian metaphysics that caters to the concept of human exceptionalism and the inexorability of a single timeline and future along the lines of human activities. I say Newtonian because it was Newton who conceived time as an absolute linearity, a straight line dotted with moments. The consequence of this spatialization of time is that we see ourselves as within time, or time as exterior to us. We have to be *in time* much in the same way we have to catch a train. However, what this throws out is that there are multiple temporalities, that bodies secrete and reconfigure time in every gesture, movement, and act. The temporalities created by lava condensing into rock are different from those that are summoned in the blooming gesture of yawning garden phlox.

I might use one of the West African stories I used to tell you to elaborate further: Who is faster, Rabbit or Tortoise? In the story, they have to race to a finish line. Tortoise wins, of course—not because he is faster, but because the rabbit gets cocky and overconfident in his skills, and actually sleeps at the tip of the finish line. The tortoise crawls along all this while, and crosses the line long before the rabbit jumps awake to meet his folly. Slow and steady wins the race, we then say. And yet, there is a sense in which the temporalities secreted by Tortoise's and Rabbit's bodily intra-actions with environment are incommensurable with each other. Tortoise isn't slow, he is Tortoise-in-collaboration-with-context. In the same way, houseflies avoid being swatted because their metabolic rates are different from ours. Scientists say they are able to do this because they perceive time in slow motion. Time perception, however, is not the issue—since time is not something out there. Instead flies inhabit/co-weave different temporalities; their bodies intra-actively produce slow-moving others.

We—all bodies in their specificities—are time-making and time-diffracting.

Because we imagine ourselves autonomous, we act in ontological tension with massive time, and because we see the world as a linear series of cause spilling into effect ad infinitum, we want to time-travel to a human future by time-freezing ourselves in the present (hence, the paradigm of "*sustainability*") and removing the extraneous variables of competing causes crowding our performances of permanence. It's an expensive endeavor.

The unit of climate change is thus not carbon emission measured by supposedly neutral metrics. Carbon emission is an abstraction with universalizing effects; it is too narrow, too linear, and too stunted an explanation for climate change.[14] Moreover, it serves a single Future. It is the colonizing race track that imposes a teleology on the world, and tacks on the politics of sustainability to this furniture. Greater carbon emission equals bleak future equals no humans. It is in lockstep with colonial time—and this not because the climate isn't changing (it always is!), and not because humans aren't contributing to these changes (we are weathering bodies, after all), but because colonial time imposes a single dimensionality and directionality, makes room for a single class of actors, and invests in a solutionism that alienates a more sensuous "politics of possibilities" … a politics of many streams. This politics is yet to come, and still it is not something yet to be articulated or awaiting complete theorization. Indeed a relational ontology of thick time compels us to notice the small—and not just in terms of isolated moments of complying with our learnings in carbon literacy: "A climate change imaginary of 'thick time' pushes us to hold together the phenomena of a weather pattern, a heat-absorbent ocean, the pleasure of a late-fall swim, and the turn of a key in the ignition as the interconnected temporalities we call 'climate change.'"[15]

The traditional climate imaginary in fact loses sight of climate change and the extent to which weather is transcorporeally manifested and iterated between bodies when it emphasizes a "stop climate change" approach. Hijacked by the linear time, by human exceptionalism, by the metaphysics of an agentially ineffectual nonhuman world, and by the intergenerational (and perhaps inter-traumatic) politics of development, climate change becomes menacing. We cannot stop climate change, or control it according to predetermined plans. Does this mean we shouldn't care about global warming? I would argue that moving outside the framework of progress expands the space of caring and being accountable, and opens up a space where new patterns are possible for being responsive to the myriad ways weathering bodies are co-enacting the ground beneath, the sky around, and the spaces between us.

The gluey metaphysics of progress—the suggestion that we are here to stay and that the world owes this to us—spins the clay pot so exclusively that those of us immured with modernity find it difficult imagining other ways to live. What if our human civilization and our experiences were structured by and oriented toward the delightful exploration of the finer details of ecstasy? What if carbon reductionism was not the only way of understanding climate change? What if, when we met, we exchanged singing seeds, shared stories of psychedelic expeditions through the portals of normal wakeful states, and swapped wisdoms and rituals on navigating the ambivalence of life? What if we weren't so addicted to growth, progress, consumption, and independence? What if we befriended dying? What would life look like?

I have often asked these questions in company of colleagues, who look at me quizzically, wondering if I'd gone mad. Why would anyone question progress or sustainable development?

Progress is the name we give to the curious idea that it is more important to compete in an abstracted space with faceless disembodied avatars, to sit at a cubicle-contained desk punching numbers into a computer in return for figures, to climb up an imagined ladder where real worth awaits, and to run a race whose winner is its ultimate victim—than it is to attend to the riddling yelps of a young child, to acquaint oneself with the shape-shifting mysteries of play, and to lose oneself over and over again in the swirling eddies of love. In a culture that largely defines worthiness, sanity, and success in terms of how distant we are from our feelings, how far and fast we run away from our roots, how numb we are to the fluency of our bodies, daring to slow down … daring to be still is the most damning act of rebellion.

Sustainable development is not our way of embracing our entanglement in the web of life; it has nothing to do with revitalizing our inescapable tethering with "nature" or recognizing that we are materially constituted by agencies and actions outside our control. It is our way of sustaining the primacy of economic advancement and cultural homogenization. If you are in any doubt about how skewed the paradigm of sustainable development really is, look at its indicators. They are all entirely economic. In other words, the way we know we are in a healthy relationship with nature is by looking through the lenses of economic development; in other words, our alliance with nature is directly proportional to how estranged we are from her. Nature in this conception is the network of raw materials awaiting redemption in our Calvinistic universes, and awaiting meaning and direction in our Cartesian coordinates. Making "nature" an "other" is the singular motif that keeps emerging in every new approach to addressing our crises today.

The issue of responsivity still remains. Saying we are entangled and already alive in a stream of transcorporeal imbrications can often come across as deterministic—as if we were in fact saying that there is nothing we can do about what we already do. Or that we are the same with everything else. But as Neimanis and Loewen note, entanglement is also a "space of difference," not enforced homogeneity. This means the world is constantly challenging itself, and that very specific intra-actions produce differences (which do not imply separation). This is not a picture of determinism nor the theocentric ideal of "free will." In both conceptions, the mind-body duality problem is well and alive: nature is fixed and machinelike, while mind is free.

Some theorists fall on the side of determinism, pointing to the ways social, psychological, and biological principles shape behavior. Those who advocate the notion of free will place the mind totally outside of these machinelike circumstances, but find it difficult to say "where" this freely disembodied quality resides and how it interacts with matter. A "third" addition to the classic debate is compatibilism, which posits that determinism and free will are not mutually exclusive—but even that doesn't address the strict dichotomy between matter and discourse.

New materialisms like agential realism ease the tensions by rethinking nature as fluid, open, and generative. Again, nature cannot be conceived apart from mental stuff, or discourse, or mind. They are already entangled. As such, our rigid formulation of matter as dead stuff gives in to a different conception of matter-mind as ontologically indeterminate. Barad's contributions in quantum philosophy point exactly to such an indeterminacy. Humans are neither predetermined nor free disembodied creatures: we are betweening-bodies in an ongoing reconfiguration of "space-timethics." This does not mean we cannot act or be creative or be directional or organize; but it does mean that we never act unilaterally. We act in murmuration.

I think that certain topological openings and potentials, occasioned by new materialisms like Barad's and interest in what indigenous cosmologies can teach us about the world, are now making room for new kinds of politics. These concepts are co-producing new directionalities, and creating "the provocation to think otherwise, to become otherwise."[16] I do not know how to characterize the possibilities opening up—since the feminist materialist spaces opening up do not enforce or rigidly recommend types of action. The "new" possibilities invite performance artistry, rekindling or improvising indigeneity, writing and speaking about "deepening" our responsibilities to climate matterings, and learning to take care with the nonhuman populations around us.

Maybe a different otherwise, a home, lies in another ethos that reframes the questions about survival. Maybe other places of power[17] open up when we relinquish our convenient narratives of human exceptionalism and triumphalism—those stories that centralize human agency and enthrone human interests as supremely paramount in the multiverse. These new materialist concepts enjoin us to decenter ourselves not simply because we are now regaining some awareness about the nobility of other species and life forms—and not entirely because we are ourselves now humbled by our less than spectacular origins—but mainly because these times of upheaval call on us to revisit what is implied in being human. Do we continue to insist that we are lords over all, masters of the universe—uniquely distanced from the fleshy, dirty discourses of "nature" or from weather—ravaging plagues burning soil and earth into asphalted forms of our own making? Or do we recognize our relatedness to all things, our real dependence on the land we supposedly transcend, and that to be human is not a magisterial decree of isolation, but a chorus ... a syncretic process of shared ecological participation?

Upon leaving the university, I allied myself with a specific "new world" type of activism and with practitioners who had spent many years working with marginalized groups, calling out the damaging effects of neoliberal capitalism on local well-being, researching into alternatives to mainstream approaches to climate action, exploring other ways of conceiving education, and so much more. I suppose it was the "natural" next step to take when we left: I had always wanted to "do some good" in the world, and not sit behind a desk. Your birth situated my intellectual exertions for social justice, this quest for home in a world that often feels increasingly hostile to homecomings.

I was offered a platform to speak quite early, even before your mother and I decided to leave to create a life for you. I traveled quite frequently, speaking in places as far-flung as Byron Bay in Australia, as animated and evocative as Istanbul, and as enrapturing as Penang, Malaysia. In the past few years since we left active academic work, I have clocked in more travel time than most people I know. Your Yoruba grandmother has a nickname for me—"Àjàlá Travels." Don't bother figuring it out; the reference is also quite lost on me! I hear it in her voice anytime she calls—a bafflement that often borders on worry. "You travel too much," she'll say, noting that even my dad, who was a diplomat, never traveled quite as frequently. The irony is not lost on me: I leave you behind, I leave my dear Lali, and travel far away to talk to strangers about finding home. And then when I return, I'm too busy to play with you, because the next invitation has only just arrived. You are missing a father in my quest to become a good father.

And therein lies the Omelas-like tragedy in my quest. This urge to run. To fight something. To prove something. To be vindicated. Fretful slivering things that live in the shadows that haunt the roads we take.

Justice is awkward. *Awk*-ward. Not forward. "Forwards" speak of gold-plated futures in wait. "Awkwards" take note of something else. A Middle English word for "clumsy," "backward," or "perverse" was *awk*. The word itself evokes the idea of things lacking a certain grace about them, being of many minds as opposed to walking resolutely in one direction. In spite of the many negative connotations attached to the idea of being awkward, awkwardness is a profusion of grace, and not the absence of it. When we don't know what to say or what to do or where to go, it is often because many paths are open to us, many possibilities are known, and many agencies are making themselves heard. The tip of the tongue is a diving board into finer waters.

This is how things move. *Awkly.* This is what we have to consider: that the straight and narrow road that begins where we are—in the doldrums of modern life that denies us community, on the wrong side of colonial history, in the pit of dark places—and purportedly terminates at the place we want to be—a better world, an economically just arrangement, a race-celebratory society—is not always the road to take. Indeed, there is no such road. The world is thick. Bent out of shape. Out of whack. The square-jawed causalities Enlightenment sustained, this vocation to unhook ourselves from the umbilical connections to our bodies and their queernesses, promise us a justice it cannot deliver.

A poetics of the real insists we come down to earth in her bashful awkwardness, in her stuttering eloquence, and meet her in that place—ourselves shorn of our heavenly glow and tasseled garments. Down here, in our bodies, in torn cuticles and unruly hair, in not knowing half the words we say, in first birdsong and last gleam of light, in these bodily negotiations with chicken pox, in sacred hypocrisies, in catching a cold, in making New Year resolutions and failing each of them, in the promiscuities of a longing eye, in the provisionality of a zealous believing, in snoring, in breathing, in laughing and dying, lies justices-to-come. That enlightened quest for the long arc of justice, spanning the sky like a leprechaun's rainbow, shimmering in the distance, above everything, must now be abandoned for a keen noticing of the life worlds and doings of the things around us. I would say that the slime trail of a hush is the transient mark of justice.

That the world resists convenient causality and stable natures is a concept that can open us up to other places of power, other ways of acting or partnering with the world. When Karen Barad writes that "there are no solutions; there is only the ongoing practice of being open and alive to each meeting, each intra-action, so that we might use our ability to respond, our responsibility, to help awaken, to breathe life into ever new possibilities for living justly,"[18] it might seem like the most blasphemous thing to utter—especially to people in precarious situations who do not have the luxury of philosophical musings.

What about cars, penicillin, and Facebook? What about more money? That would seem like a pretty nifty solution to many, wouldn't it? But the point, if I can stress this, is not that these things aren't there, but that they are threadbare and tentacular, and they tug on the fabric of the world and pull in agentic effects we often do not or cannot account for in our neat models of change. Summarily, you can only expect solutions in a world where humans are truly separate from everything else, where we can disclose the elegance of things from a vantage point. Not only is such a standpoint not possible, but it has dangerous imperialistic consequences.

Does that mean we shouldn't do all that we can, and work harder in the particular ways we can? Of course not. A neomaterialist offering like Barad's doesn't pretend to teach the "correct way to act/think"; it doesn't offer a model or platform that guarantees the results we might want to see. It doesn't postulate a "background reality" that we are ontologically distanced from, and to which we must tie our actions if we want "true" or lasting solutions. It doesn't dismiss the "previous" or think of itself as truer than other explanations we give for the world. Instead, it can serve as a strategy for examining the material-discursive frameworks of assumptions, of place, of time, and human and nonhuman populations that produce specific realities—to the exclusion of others, and the ethical implications of those we have taken for granted and those that are occluded. In other words, agential realism can help us examine how differences are co-enacted—how we draw lines between old and new, good and evil, correct and incorrect, fact and fiction, and so on.

If we were to take seriously the idea that we are entangled with the world, that the way is awkward (not forward), then we must also take for granted the idea that we are always acting, that this acting might congeal into what we now call "solutions," but these in turn raise new questions and trouble the fields they are already aspects of, and that even the things we rule as "evil" or problems are not still or stagnant. This is not the same as the ethos of "anything goes" that is closely associated with social constructivism. Saying "anything goes" rejects the materiality of limitations. The "real" that is described by new materialists has limitations aplenty. We must make do in a world where particular ways of thinking or acting or being may remain unavailable to us. However, these limitations and exclusions and obstacles are not abstractions of independence—they are subject to the elements, or to Siva's discipline, as well.

The concept of entanglement can move us to reexamine the discountenanced. It can train our senses to be alive to the ways we are implicated in the co-production of reality. We are ourselves products of language, culture, milieu, and environment, as Mowles notes:

A moment's reflection on our own circumstances will bring to mind how our habits and categories of thought, our ways of being in the world, are framed and guided by the particular society and time we are born into, the language that we learn and the cultural habits, the habitus, we accept as natural. At the same time by reenacting this culture, by reflecting on what we are doing and thinking about how we are thinking and acting, we recreate it in slightly different ways. We take up general themes in particular circumstances creating the potential both for repetition and renewal both at the same time.[19]

To make a new world, to move it, to wipe the slate clean, to start again, to retell these stories of injustices and exclusions and untimely death and soiled seas—what a heady and ravishing proposal(!), albeit one haunted by a troubling prospect: the fonts of a "new story" are not ours to wield. Our maps—no matter how detailed and punctilious—will always be sabotaged by the territory; the world has her own genius, her own dips and curves and whispered nothings and chuckled blasphemies. The world is bigger than plot, lengthier than conclusions, keener than comeuppances, nobler than anthropocentric thought, more curious than solutions, and more abundant than arrivals. In short, we don't make the world alone, the world makes us too. Maybe the world also wants to make us a better place. To know this is not to finally be at peace, or to be enlightened, or to be at home ... it is to continue to experiment, to theorize, to touch the always-fresh blister that is our tale of becoming. It is to see how we are seeing.

The awkward thus softly beckons us into a playground so animate and dense with cross-cutting trajectories and unbelievably intricate activity that drawing a straight incontrovertible line from here to there is impossible. It's not that "there" is even there to begin with, and that new materialism is saying our work is now more difficult to accomplish. We—remember, a thick "we" that comprises humans and nonhumans—make "there" by moving, closing, and opening new channels by the smallest gestures.

Perhaps this is why Karen Barad speaks of justice-to-come, why Achebe resists the figure of the Archimedean hero who moves the world from outside of it, and why many attempts to "save the world" only end up reinstating the status quo: quantum queerness undoes identity, and undoes the spatial-temporal project of arriving home intact. Even straight lines are haunted by the points displaced in their unfolding.

If you have a knot on a long piece of thread, the bumpiness of the knot might give the impression that it is *on* the rope—instead of *what* the rope is doing. The rope proceeds, wraps itself into a knot, and then carries on from there. Perhaps this is a metaphor useful for a new sense of "a-count-ability, a new arithmetic, a new calculus of responsibility."[20] One that situates us firmly in messy places that reconfigure the geometry of solutionism and deepens our responsibility to other possible worlds.

The highway is not open. We no longer walk into the future, we limp. We move *awk*-ward into the thick now.

✦

The road is empty. There's no one in sight as our company quickly walks past the stone-walled homes of our neighbors. It seems some homes were touched, and others were not. Stray dogs bark at us from behind. We quicken our pace, gently urging each other on, watching out for the dangerous items on the avenue leading to our street. Some of the electricity wires connecting two poles that skirt the sides of our street hang loosely, dipping in the middle, as if a giant toddler had mistakenly stepped on them. There is a smoldering car tire in the middle of the road, potentially blocking the way for motorists. In the visible distance, just beyond the red rooftops across the valleyed landscape, several columns of smoke rise into the air like dark screams ... clotting the sky with a gray warning. We are not out of danger yet.

I look around me. Mummy has a head tie, plain clothes, and prayers on her lips. She has tied Wendy to her back. Dad is in his striped pajamas. He walks briskly, all six feet of him, with Tito's hands wrapped around his neck, and her skinny legs dangling down his sides. The man in the red cap is jogging ahead of us, urging us in French to keep up our pace, his own exhausted voice shaking with the momentum of his pace. I keep looking up to my father, just to make sure he is okay—and back to Mummy, to know that she is fine. Up ahead, the street breaks out into the main road. But the red cap in front bounces on, missing the turn, leading us through the shrubbery at the end of the avenue. We had been chauffeured in embassy cars to school, every day, through this street. Not once did it occur to me that there was another world leaning so close.

A path breathes open, snaking into the congress of bowing tallgrass. We are quiet, the whole world is quiet. It is just the sound of our labored breathing and, sometimes, the sound of my father's Yoruba and my mother's Yoruba, both reweaving threads of encouragement and hope. After what feels like hours, we come to a clearing of scattered homes and small shacks. The red cap tells us to slow down our pace. We come to a gutter built with slabs of concrete bordering its walls. A flimsy plank of wood has been laid across the gutter for easy passage. Dad helps mummy walk across, and then he guides me halfway but I lose my balance as I step off the plank, falling to the ground and scratching my right foot on a stone. I can see the white of my flesh under my black skin, peeled back like a potato under a knife. My dad rubs his hand in my hair, saying sorry, and urging me to keep moving.

We go through curious neighborhoods, past cartons of fluffy bread my family calls *"moko quarante,"* which is what the roadside bread sellers yelled as they pressed their fresh smelling wares through the window—often times throwing it into the car and then requesting money for it. Tito and I had thought *moko* was Lingala for bread, but we learned it was just Lingala for "one." How disappointing. "One for forty zaire" was what they said. And then my mum, irritated by all the bread in her face, would quickly pay the closest, most persistent seller with one hundred zaire, asking for her change as she did.

I am hungry; I feel the urge to ask for a small loaf, but that might be dangerous. And we can't wait. The embassy is expecting us.

We get to a clearing I recognize. We've made it. We must look quite a sight to some car owners—a few of whom stare at us as they drive past. There aren't many cars on the road, and those brave enough to drive are driving with one foot pressed down hard on the throttle. Down the road, across a few sidewalks, past an avenue of trees, the white-tiled green-roofed building sits in wait, seemingly undisturbed by the commotion of the last hours. A buff security man swings the door open upon seeing my father, and we skip into the clean premises—out of breath, our feet sore from running. The green-white-green Nigerian flag flutters in the wind, as if welcoming us to our new home. For now.

Today, my body is cut up into many tearful pieces—with each piece now at war with the other. My legs do not feel my own. Your brother in my belly is rolling and restless. You gave me just as much trouble when you were big enough to run around inside me.

I remember the day you were born. We were waiting to hold you because we were sure that when we held you we would know … we would know if the name Alethea was for you or not. It was.

As soon as we were sure about your name, we asked all our family members and friends what they would like you to call them. Some said aunty, some uncle, some said mama, some papa, and some said you should call them by their name. It's the right thing to do here. To seek out your many other parents.

All of these persons have played a significant role in your life; they are always present and invested in raising you. Your community, your village.

As you grow bigger, you continue to have someone there to offer their wisdom and support for you. Amazingly, even with all these individuals smothering you with gifts, reproving you when you were too stubborn and impossible to deal with, you are blossoming into an interdependent rather than a dependent girl.

"Do you know how lucky I am?" you asked me one day, your eyes twinkling. "I have so-o-o many mothers. Everybody shows me so much love, and I need to love them too."

I am about to become a mother again. And even though I sometimes feel I am not doing a great job mothering you, I am learning that I will not be enough. You are too big to be completely embraced by a pair of arms. You are born of a village. Remember this is your real wealth.

Not just the village of people, but the village of mysterious beings and objects around you. You are a village girl.

When, in a few weeks, I roll into that same clinic you were born in, and when your brother Kyah pierces through—making your father (and I can predict this) cry again—I will look to you and to him for strength. I will know that I am not alone, and that this womb will always bless you for making me your mother. Even if I am just one of them.

THE CALL OF COMPOST

Requited or unrequited, to love is to move between homecoming and exile.

—DAVID WHYTE[1]

Dear Alethea,

You sit up rubbing the sleep out of your eyes, then you leap off the bed and run out of the room in search of your mama, screaming "Mama!" at the top of your lungs. I smile at your little-limbed enthusiasm, the happy spring in your steps, the way the strong golden light of Chennai's sun conspires with that moment to paint a portrait of joy. Though I still need to snuggle into the sheets a bit longer, I can no longer close my eyes. Your life is infectious.

You've been looking forward to this for some time now. Lali is tending to our small garden in the balcony, and you want to help. Lali says you can help. You jump on the bed where I am still laid out in a lazy heap of yawns and half-smiles, and you scream into my ears: "Dada! Wake up, Dada!" Ten more minutes, I plead—recalling my all-night writing vigil, but my soft protests fall on ears too bewitched by the playful melodies of the morning to register an adult's excuse. Your mother appears through the balcony door, tall and gracious, with strands of midnight curled around her head, and beads of sweat anointing her forehead. She asks me to help fetch a bucket of water from the bathroom. "I'll do it! I'll do it myself," you scream, racing ahead of me to turn on the tap of water into the green bucket. I climb out of bed sulking and get to the bathroom door just as the water pours. The thin stream beats hollow rhythms as it impacts the plastic. You turn to me, standing by the door of the bathroom. We lock eyes. And we smile.

Your helping often comes at a cost, though: it has to be total and exclusive. As the water fills two-thirds of the bucket, I turn off the tap and lift the bucket. Your immediate outburst of muffled cry-speaking tells me I've crossed a line again. It takes a little while before I figure out you want to lift the bucket yourself. So I make you an offer: let's do it together, shall we? You nod your head gently. I lift the bucket by its handle, and ask you to help by resting your hand on mine. And so we gently bear the precious cargo a few feet to the barricaded balcony, where your mum kneels by several earthen pots out of which proceed aloe vera, *tulasi*, mint, cactus, and tomato plants. She is plucking away brown leaves, pruning and watching for little caterpillars that leave holes in the leaves.

"Have you said good morning to the plants, dear?" I ask. I have taught you in the past that these plants feed you, nourish you, and mother you—and that our love wouldn't be complete without their material participation.

So you place your palms together, close to your chest, and then you do a soft, gentle bow. "Good mo-o-orning, plants!" you say to each one, letting your fingers touch a leaf here, a tender sinewy stalk there, or the rich brown soil we've cradled them in. With a small plastic cup, you and mama water the plants, giggling as bits of soil fly everywhere. Unlike the sound water makes when it streams into a plastic bucket, the deep thrumming bass of watered soil betrays a nobler partnership. The hum of very old friends. A beautiful entanglement.

This almost-daily ritual has turned our balcony into a small Eden. A miniature version of the hanging gardens of Nebuchadnezzar gracing this little city of little bodies and little gestures.

These moments are home. For now.

Our apartment is like most new apartments in Chennai—a cell in a bee-hive. Or rather a hole—one of many—in a slice of Swiss cheese. It isn't "small"; it's "necessary." Our street is narrow and crammed with necessary homes piled on top of homes, most of which share the same walls. There are no rooftops, just flat terraces and clotheslines as far as the eyes can see.

Down the street, there's very often a large cow, seemingly at guard at the very entrance of our small avenue. She doesn't begrudge the strange visitor; she just sits there, her horns painted blue and red, her forehead touched with a finger dipped in turmeric paste. Slowly munching the food some passers-by often leave her with gentle bows and palms gently pressed to their foreheads, she welcomes barking stray dog, African immigrant, and buzzing auto-rickshaw. And when the time is right, when blue gods seated on lithic thrones lean closer to gaze, when the stars align, and her bowels nod their fleshy consent, she spills on the concrete-slab street, her urine gushing like a burst government pipe, anointing the hard road. This is a blessing to all those that know that the things that most repel and disgust us are our sacred life-keepers—if we learn to meet them anew. A few feet away from her massive frame lies a dried-out chunk of shit, pressed down in the middle where motorcycle tire tracks mark it. Those brown tread marks will continue for a while until fading, often leading into the street Viji-ma comes from, every morning, to clean our apartment. She will often come with gifts—some Samba rice and pepper water or neem leaves. Or a strong rebuke for Lali for not giving me food. We couldn't possibly pay her for what she does.

It's not just Viji-ma. It's Peer-papa, Allen-uncle, Rachel, Peter-uncle, Zeru-ma, and the entire congregation of people that come to your grandma's house every Wednesday, to pray and clap and share many meals. It's those you call your mothers, Sanju, Keziah, and Nancy. These people know you, they've carried you down the street, taken you on bike rides, given you baths, brushed your teeth, fed you rice with their fingers, held you aloft during your birthdays, and chastised your mum and me when our love became a stifling doctrine of obedience.

It is the peculiar lilt of their accents that you know and imitate—their head wobble, the way they structure their sentences. You are rich because their palm prints are tattooed on your skin, in palimpsests of body-warping affection.

And at night, when I take you for a walk, swinging your arm as we sneak past the majestic cow, the moon asserts her own parentage and her often unappreciated contributions to your well-being. She shines through like a haunted orb traveling through a mist, surveying the village we call home. Walking under the moon, both of us stretch out our hands wanting to reach her. For me, I know this wandering stranger has lit the paths of those before us and those who will come after us. She will be there churning the seas that border your own homes-to-come; she will call forth the seeds you've buried in ghostly raptures, their nightly trajectories of ascent marked by green leaning stalks in daylight. She is part of your village. So I pray to the moon. Your mother teaches you to pray to Jesus; I teach you to pray to rocks and cows and nodding moons—as I myself have learned to pray to your mother. There is a sense in which the faraway and the near, the still and the dancing, the sacred and the mundane, the light of the day and the dark of sleep, and all the worlds between ... all the others in the middle ... make you.

This morning, like most other mornings, you erupt from sleep as if bangers had suddenly gone off under the bedsheets. You run out to help your mother with watering the plants. This time you let me sleep a bit—only to come afterward to shake me awake, screaming "Dada! Come and see! I've found something!" What is it, I intone grudgingly—not so much asking a question as I'm desperately trying to return to sleep. Then your mum's voice, coming from the balcony, joins the siren song disturbing my precious sleep. "You are going to want to see this, Bayo," she says. As I come away from bed, I make a mental note to hide in the wardrobe to sleep from now on. Slouching and grouchy, I walk with you pushing me from behind toward the balcony, where Lali is standing waiting. She smiles mysteriously, and then points to the earthen pot that hosts an aloe vera plant and its thick, fleshy leaves. "What am I looking at, dear?" I ask. She pulls back the leaves a little—and there, almost invisible under the shadows of the leaves, are four little furry balls, pitch black, moving along the inner circumference of the pot. I know what they are. Nine out of ten.

I turn to face both of you. You have your mouth flung open in mock surprise. I look at Lali and she has her head cocked sideways with an "I told you to get out of bed" expression on her face. She rests her clean hand on her protruding belly and rubs it. We recently found out you are going to have a little sibling. A little brother. It will be four of us—you, Lali, me, and your brother, Kyah Jayden.

I know what to do: that moment speaks to me. I ask both of you to touch my shoulder. You both do—even as you ask, "Dada, what are you doing?" and Mama encourages you to do what I say. I touch the hushes one by one, each of them, stringed to each other by infinitesimally delicate strands of their hairs. They stop moving. I close my eyes, and whisper some words of gratitude for the journey now coming to an end, praying that the last hush will meet all four of us well. Bàbá said when the tenth hush is found, I will know how to pray, and what I should ask for—suggesting that my understanding of home might change along the way with the questions I would learn to ask.

Moments later, our bell rings. You run out to open the door, while your mum follows after you to stop you from opening it without seeking to know who comes. I stand up from the pot. The hushes are still immobile, perhaps frozen in fear from my touch. "Thank you for being a part of our village … you are us and we are you," I whisper, then return inside as I hear Viji-ma's distinct voice fill the house.

※

Stephen Hawking, a well-respected theoretical physicist and cosmologist, predicted that mankind would have to find a home in the stars within one hundred years if we are to survive.[2] A new place to live. His prophecy was based on the observation that we have collectively destabilized the earth, making it potentially inhospitable in a few years. Last year, he had given us a thousand years to rethink our ways. To work out the puzzle of climate change and address overpopulation. But with asteroid strikes, the threat of thermonuclear war and raging epidemics, Hawking's hope for some longevity had diminished drastically. Now with less than a mere hundred years, we would all have to come together, find another planet home, and—most importantly—find out how to get there.

If he had made these prophecies twenty years ago, he might not have found an audience willing to give him an ear. Today, however, is different. The race to space that pit the United States against Russia fifty years ago has been superseded by a race to colonize Mars. NASA (the National Aeronautics and Space Administration of the United States) hopes to pull it off in sixteen years (2033—when you'll be twenty years old), while Mars One, a private initiative with a vision to establish the first permanent human settlement on Mars, has already selected one hundred potential colonist hopefuls to make the 225-million-kilometer crewed journey in 2024, nine years before NASA's hoped-for departure for the red planet. Elon Musk's SpaceX project, probably the most lauded, is planning for liftoff a mere five years from now—though timelines are continuously revised. Musk argues that we won't live on earth forever, and that the only way to survive might be to become a spacefaring multiplanet species. Some are calling this the next great leap for mankind—recalling the moments Neil Armstrong set foot on earth's moon, stamping its alien surface with our collective aspirations for place and new boundaries in a universe whose outer reaches seem to defy measurement.

Of course, there are cynical questions around these projected adventures into outer space. Who gets to go? Do we even have the technologies to sustain those who successfully make the trip? And if we do, why not apply those technologies to our current planet? Why rush off into the unknown blackness, the seemingly uncharted regions of myth and imagination, with the same exploitative technologies that are making our own planet uninhabitable?

All of these seem like valid questions to ask. They make the assumption, however, that this is a choice between staying and leaving.

I have to admit I have often imagined you reading these letters by an alien shore, kneeling before an ocean thicker and denser than any ocean on earth, underneath a sky lined with the secreted trails of giant whale-like creatures floating and humming beneath multiple moons. This might seem outlandish, but outer space is not as external or as distant as billions of dollars and millions of miles might suggest. We are entangled with those radical extraterrestrial others, with those endless miles, each mediating morsel of which is itself a destination of intersecting stardust, meeting in a trellised orchestra of music that plays unendingly in the formation and destruction of homes. Indeed, we are already a part of a cosmo-poietic unfurling of skin and form—our lives intra-acting with orbiting bodies, our individual destinies often tracked by the measured astrological positions of worlds we do not know, our telluric surfaces riddled with invading rocks small enough to never be noticed and large enough to make the headlines. In a sense, outer space is here, deep undercover, on the inside of things. And we are already where no man has gone before.

The space-faring imaginary also thrives on a single timeline—the same timeline that accommodates constructed memories of an innocent past and apprehension about an apocalyptic future, with mankind, well defined and distinct, moving along that line. We want to go to other worlds to survive, to thrive. We want to remain intact, to pick ourselves up and move from "here" to "there." But that is not possible. To arrive at a new destination is to change the destination as well as ourselves. Arrival always changes the parameters, creating new ontologies of the journey that supposedly preceded it. The traveler doesn't reach home eventually; home is not a place we inhabit, a fishbowl that can be emptied of its contents and refilled. To suppose so is to see new homes as voidal and empty, until we arrive. Home intra-acts with us. Stakes its claims on our skins, on our lungs, taxing our bodies, altering our conventions, challenging our breathing. Home is homey because of particular sympoietic practices that are not entirely within our control.[3]

In light of this touching of the outer and the inner, this dissolution of distance, this recognition of indeterminacy, this embrace of home and exile, perhaps the vital questions we might ask today do not simply concern just the math of how we get from here to there, but questions about the thick politics of what we are co-becoming. Questions about boundaries, and differences, and how we are already imprinted with the lives of many others. Calculations of an astonishingly different pedigree. Where love is not a bridge to be traversed in neat space modules, but a hyphen—projects of meeting and touching the other again and again, and thus meeting ourselves for the first time. In short, the sacred is here. The far is nearby. Space stations are everywhere around us, within us.

In the precarious other like Kutti, we meet a life at the middling edges of our city, and encounter questions about our space-making and sky-penetrating projects of home-building—along with our fears for property and what will be enough in an overpopulated world. In dust, and in the bated breaths of those made invisible by the colonial imperatives of sky-bound economies; and in Hope, whose dark and wild places are ruled out by petri dish cultures of sanity, we may be finding that new homes are produced by new ways of coming in touch. New geometries of touch.

I am a with-ness to these underground excursions to places where no one has gone before. To the shimmering, star-studded, milky boundaries of the other. You might not find any of these projects in the news, but they are there all right. With little or no funding, in humble and modest earth practices of partial recuperation, a subculture of adventurers is meeting the universe halfway, building space stations to travel to the spaces between. They are not "good" or "awakened" people; they are not holy or special. And I do not want to write about "them" for fear I might help create a separate class of people. But it is important to note that a particular kind of work is being done—one which might be understood as a response to the call of compost. The call to take seriously the generative implications of living with a *world*, instead of on it or in it.

Once, your mum and I took you to visit the Luray Caverns in Virginia in the United States—a rolling, geologic orchestra of drip-dropping water, fluid limestone, perverse shapes, eroding layers, haunting pillars, frozen draperies, patient deposits, and magical sonorous chambers. I recall thinking to myself when we arrived inside: this is what it means to be inside a stone's story. Lali said to me: "This is how nature ridicules art." It was a very poignant thing to say, especially since we—a day earlier—had begun touching upon the ways life transcends story, and the way our overarching themes and plots divest the material world of its "telling-ness."

The guides, shouting instructions at a teeming crowd of selfie-taking families, heedless youngsters, and screaming toddlers, kept reminding us that the caverns were discovered in 1878 by five local men, including Andrew J. Campbell (a local tinsmith) and his thirteen-year-old nephew Quint. They told us about the Washington Column, the wishing well (which was now filled prominently with dollar bills, rupees, and coins from indeterminable countries) that had raised over a million dollars for charities in Virginia, and the famous Stalacpipe Organ. The floors of the cavern had been tamed with tiles, and some of the naturally occurring pillars were fitted with soft yellow lights encased in concrete cups, making it easier for families to embark on the thirty-minute walk through the cavern—gaping at its ghostly stalactites and stalagmites, aahing and hah-ing and taking pictures with the formations.

It was a bit too touristy and modern for me. Somewhere within, I felt something crucial was missing. It was like walking through a museum where something alive had been put up for display; it was like walking into a community without seeking approval. A certain kind of awe was missing, a wordlessness that was hushed by stories of discovery. And time. And achievements. And charity. The creeping figures and lithic curtains and petrifying deposits were vibrant in ways that mocked ideas of origins and shape and form. When the ethereal sounds sifted through the formations, enveloping the "great cathedral" in music that could not be heard by ears alone, I felt the stone—this one stone that was the cavern—had its own yearnings that could not be honored by multiplying its age by millions of years, or giving one of its "parts" the name of a former president. I came to the edge of tongues. I gasped.

I feel, however, I learned a thing or two from the cavern, whose name cannot possibly be Luray. Each of the individual stalactites that were being generated, piercing toward the cave floor like a billion needles, might have looked "individual" to me—but they were anything but. In a sense, each formation, each proud pillar (and one particular formation that looked like a giant candle melting into a puddle of wax and adoration—I called it the "goddess of the cave") was what the "cavern" was doing. A telluric involution.

I took this recognition as a gift, and placed my head under a falling drop of water to be "baptized" and blessed (something that everyone in our company later did) by the cavern, to be touched by a parliament of things. I appreciated how our claims to authorship, to ownership, to control, to moral coherence, to structure and instrumentality often get in the way of wilder wordlessness, a lithic silence more fluent than prose. The guides and their managers tried to make sense of a dead cavern by putting it in boxes that were understandable to them, hoping to electrify it with lightning bolts of discovery stories—but the stones were alive long before this. They didn't "need" those labels as such—they were already enfolded with meaning and yearning and wonder and shadow.

I read the "writings" of the cavern and felt in a resounding way how meeting trouble, encountering irony, and noticing intra-ruptions are "invitations" to languages deeper than jots and tittles. Maybe when we gasp, and do not know what to do or say or write, it's "because" we are silently aware that not all sentences are made of words. Maybe becoming imperceptible is learning to be still—for by being still, we might notice the grandeur that stillness and words are stitched into. Maybe my in/sincere attempts at self-effacing scrutiny, and my occasional theo-clinical quest for moral supremacy and professional exactitude, are what the "cavern is doing," a queering of beingness too precious to last, too transient to not be forever. Maybe being in exile is part of what it means to come home, and being at home is a preparation for exile.

This dance of exile and home, outer and inner, future and past—this resituating of human bodies in a web of eco-political matterings we do not control gives birth to different notions of hope. When we speak of hope, the picture that comes to mind is that of a sparkling future—one with endless possibilities. Hope, however, is not all light and bliss. There are aspects to hope that are haunted, dark, and shadowy. In a sense, to entertain hope is not merely to give in to a linear unfolding of events; it is to allow oneself to be touched. It is to recognize that there are other possibilities—wild possibilities—and that these possibilities will not leave us intact. To meet hope open-faced is to surrender to a logic that is beyond our ken. It is to come to an arcana of many agencies. We never begin at the beginning. We always begin at a place already massaged by footfalls aplenty, by sighs embedded in loamy layers of earth, by nightly negotiations and strange rituals and spilled blood and muffled sounds and startling textures and painful interpellations and the budding promise of continuity. We begin at the edges in the middle. Hope is an affair of material middles.

Radical possibilities for transformation dwell in the unsure path ... in the obstructed path—not the one cleared solely by human hands, bound to repeat the same oppressive timeline heading for the same apocalyptic Future, but the one where we acknowledge that we are not alone and never were, and attempt to meet the thing that stands in the way as an agent of change, not a mere dead object to be destroyed. I reckon that if we imagined that the between-space is just as charged with possibility as outer space, we might be more inclined to turn our attention to the fecund depths of our co-becoming with earthbound critters. What could turning our attention look like?

On a recent adventure to Brazil, I met with an exploratory group of people from around the world who were, just like me, asking questions about what it means to live with the planet and how taking seriously the idea of co-becoming allows for other practices of economy. I remember eating with others I hadn't met. Eating slowly in community, sometimes raising my head to meet the eyes of another fellow explorer, and washing our dishes together. Then holding hands in a circle as we responded to playful chants issued by a local. I remember distinctly thinking there were other ways to be human my body had not yet known as I moved in sync with many others.

In Devon, where I had gone to teach a short course with your Manish-uncle—who co-founded an alternative university called Swaraj University in Rajasthan, where there are no fixed curricula, grades, or certificates, and where you're likely to find *khojis* (or seekers who co-design their own learning journeys) sitting in circles dealing with grief, learning in intergenerational groups how to make a short film that highlights ecological issues, or embarking on a "bicycle *yatra*" trust adventure across the country with no money, phones, or food—we opened the "Shop of the Open Heart" on the last day of the course.

This "Shop of the Open Heart" ... sounds elaborate, doesn't it? Then you'll be surprised to know it involved a single table, a decorating table cloth, and items we had invited our cohorts to bring to the "shop"—items that meant something to them, not things they wanted to give away. We had told them that if they felt a tug of pain as their hands slid over an option, then it was probably a good selection for the shop. We eventually arranged items we had gathered: books, boots, trinkets, pictures, and even the dried-out remains of a shark's egg capsule (which had an uncanny resemblance to the first hush I ever touched). We then invited each cohort to walk round the table, simply surveying the items, without taking any away—listening to those that called out to them. Instead of positioning themselves as owners by identifying who had dropped what, we allowed the objects to "be themselves"—their own stories written by their own bodies. After a short space of time, we invited the cohorts back to the table. Each of them could now pick items—and afterward, the previous custodians of the items could tell a story about how the items came to be with them. This simple apparatus of gift-giving and sharing might seem innocent enough, but were you to witness it as I have done several times, you might know its true power: not only have people broken down in tears in sharing intimate stories or in receiving an item (which one could mindlessly purchase off a shelf in many instances), they have gone on to share those items received, passing it on to others as this practice of nonownership opened up other geometries of touch.

What feelings we have not felt, what concepts we have not conceived, what possibilities we do not account for are tied to radical new places where we practice being middling agents of a home that is wilder than our fences.

Apart from learning to grow our own food, your mum and I have also begun practicing our "Rainbow Wednesdays" with the Shop of the Open Heart. We are taking seriously the redescription of the world as an entangled and entangling place. A year ago, we co-initiated The Emergence Network, a curator collective and a commonwealth of earth-wide curated projects designed to examine the ways particular activisms and their frameworks of thinking reiterate the status quo, and to explore/experiment with the between-spaces of justice-to-come. I think of it as a way of remaking indigeneity after the "Fall." And in a few weeks, your mum will be embarking on new unschooling adventures with the "Broken Compass," which—like Swaraj University—is frontier work, at the borderlands of a system that brands kids as failures, and pretends to be "life itself." None of these are "solutions" or meant to be universalized. They are our own efforts at re/turning to the dynamics of the local (as Helena Norberg-Hodge has often urged in her explorations of the eliding dynamics of the global corporate industry), of learning to see with new eyes, of working with our immediate contexts to reconfigure and decentralize our place in the world—which is why I say to you, my dear, wherever you are, on Earth or off it, where you are at the moment is the most sacred place you can be in. Life is not a ladder, whose topmost rung is more valuable than the ones before it; life is not a race to see who crosses the finish line first; life is not a circle with a discernible center or a proscribed circumference. The language of deficit drops you on a linear path, where you are never enough, where what you do doesn't count in the larger scheme of things, where you feel guilt for not doing enough to save the planet, or where you do not always rise to your cherished shibboleths and values. Your job in this framework is to rack up achievements, faster than others, sooner than most. But what if life is a fractal with interlocking images, with parts reflecting the whole? What if life is a web, where past and present and future melt into a rapturous immediacy, glimpses of which we perceive in heightened moments? What if you don't have to beat yourself into shape? What if there is no outside force to which you must measure yourself? What if your questions, your imbroglios, and tooth-chips are just as sacred as "having it all together"? What if you are in the most interesting place you can be in now? This home that is a dance with exile?

This realization that there is no permanent home, no permanent ground, just rupturing places and condensing fields of welcome—only for a while—drives us to find new kin in plants and mountains and human others. As your mum and I are deepening our accountability to you, we meet the many others who are your parents as well—the cow down the street, the wet anointing she spills on everything, the moon that nods as we stroll by.

We are learning to see that *we* are in this together—and nobler words could not be spoken at this time of vexed exclusions, legitimized exterminations, and weaponized boundaries. This is a time to linger at the edges, to lean into the troubling intersection points where the differences between me and you, us and them, queer and straight, nature and culture, living and nonliving, man and world, are not given and done, but still in the making. This is a time to stay with the trouble of knowing that there is no becoming that is not a becoming-together.

The things that stand in the way are "aspects" of our ongoing reconfiguration. Enemies, bottlenecks, seething memories, gnarling fetishes, haunting creeds, howling specters, grumbling boogeymen, careening splinters, frowning clouds, green giants, gaping holes, chuckling forests. The challenge is not to go "through" them and come out unscathed on the other side. The invitation is to know them, to stop for a drink, to resist unsheathing a sword, to be grateful for a wound, and to share a joke with shadows. The challenge is to gasp—as microbiologists do when they see that the bacteria that inhabit our bodies exceed the cells of our own bodies—as we realize how strange we are also.

In small ways, we are coming to see that the things we name as obstacles are invitations to shapeshift—to reconsider the genealogy of the forms that we have assumed, and to work with others to see what we might become. If you are looking for the path that's most promising, look for the one with the dead end. The unmapped one haunted by swirling ambiguities and moaning ghosts and Sphinxian riddles and yellow slit-eyed peering shadows. A good journey is about dismemberment, not arrival.

Encircled by crumbling fences and by an encroaching wildness, without maps and without answers, we will have to improvise if the sun is to shine on us tomorrow. The world needs you to fly, to rush into virgin fields and, with hands outstretched, pollinate the flowers; to walk out on that career path that everyone feels is so important to have and spend time listening to the throbbing melodies of your own heart; to witness the sun rising as if for the first time; to experience unbridled fear at the precipice of life and realize you've been anointed; to hug a confused stranger whose brisk steps on the concrete pavements of our civilization are his only claim to meaning; to wait for guidance from a tree; to protest carbon markets and the extinction of our earth-siblings by standing still in the rain; to do something preposterous; and to tell us why one and one could equal sixteen. These are the days of ritual, of changing parameters, of paradox, and of humble courage. These are the days of realizing our best answers and questions are always provisional. These are the days we must fall apart to become larger. These are the times of many voices. When those haunting have to be met ... because the future is not fixed, and the past is yet to come.

✦

Dear Dad,

Packing our bags of new clothes that Wednesday morning at the embassy was the most difficult thing I had ever done. Mummy had told us the week before we set sail that you might not come back with us to Nigeria because the government needed you there. There in the raging wars of Kinshasa, in 1993. She wanted to palliate the effects of the inevitable. But we knew. I remember feeling this heavy gravity that pulled down everything within, as if I had swallowed a wrecking ball. The thought that I might not see you again, and know you as the hero you were, frightened me.

We drove in the embassy's Pajero SUV to the busy docks. You were smart as usual, eternal in your manly haircut, rich mustache, and impeccable command of the French language, which you spoke with when you passed instructions to your officers along the way. There was a lot of commotion when we arrived. There were blue helmets with sturdy guns in their hands—the UN soldiers on peacekeeping missions. The world was angry that the French Ambassador was killed. But they almost killed you too—and I was grateful that I had a father who could never die. Who was the suited equivalent of a superhero. Who would live forever without a strand of gray on his head.

The airports were inaccessible, so you and your colleagues had determined that we would take the ferry across the Congo River, and sail to Congo Brazzaville, where we would be received by the Nigerian Ambassador there. There was shoving and pushing, and you occasionally had to wade in to make sure we were not harassed by those who wanted to be paid for carrying our bags.

We got on the ferry, and I remember you kissing mum good-bye, leaning over to us with stinging tears in your eyes. You promised you'd return, that you'd come back soon. We hugged you tight and didn't want to let go. But we had to. I had to.

And when the boat started to drift away from the quay, you stood there on the platform, your legs an actionable distance apart—a long cool figure cut out from the pestilence of the background, silhouetted against the din of the ordinary.

You did come home many times after that, until the day you came home in a box. But that final posture you assumed on the quay, as our ferry drifted farther and farther away from the concrete shore, will always remain for me your final stance. Your good-bye tears.

I have a daughter now. I'm sure you know that because you haunt me. Even now as I write this, in a room flooded by the light of the golden California sun, and with an empty chair in front of me, my tears remember the hands that once wiped them. Alethea is my daughter's name. She is beautiful and strong and carefree and deliberate in one lump of embodied goodness. Her mother, whom I call Lali, but also goes by "Ej" and "Ijeoma," is your daughter; you'd have been proud of her and cared for her just as I do.

I write you to remember you, dad. To let you know I see you standing on the quay even now, when leaves rustle with passing wind, when your wife and my mum calls us on the phone, when your granddaughter asks about you and calls you "Yummy grandpa"—that's the way she sounds when she calls your name, "Yòmí." Most of all, I see you when I remember the promise I made to Alethea, to be a good father for her, to worship her mum, to think with her, to listen to the ghosts that wander the streets as they whisper about worlds forgone, and to live in small places where I never forget that to be Alethea's father is the deepest honor the universe bestows on me.

I love you. Don't leave me alone.

Epilogue

Re/turn

That night, the door came down. The men brought it down, kicking it in. I held you through the latticed window, my hands wet from your tears. When the door came down, your mum ran into the room and picked you up, spinning you around. "Mama!" you cried. And for a moment, the whole world was still—all of Chennai silenced, even the petulant ladder that had been croaking its disagreements a little earlier—as things came together, as the wooden notions of our separation came apart. I watched you in your mother's hands, through the window, tired but grateful.

I remember you smiling as you held Lali when I got back into the house. Everyone shed silent tears—your Indian grandmother, always loath to show emotional fragility, pretended she had something in her eyes.

From that day forward, we never let you wander behind closed doors again.

Even now we won't allow you the old luxuries of thinking you are alone, for you are not. You remember this and remember this good: you never have and never will be alone.

I never did find that last hush. After the four you and your mother found, the last one never came by. I saw plenty of hushes after that, but they didn't call out to me. I called on Bàbá to know his feelings about this. He didn't pick up the phone. I even made a trip to Nigeria, to his town, to seek him, but on getting to his home, I met a woman who told me he had moved away somewhere else. By this time I had been seeking hushes for years, finding only nine out of ten. The tenth hush must have sailed long before I could reach it.

And yet, I think there is wisdom hidden in not arriving, in not reaching the destination, in not figuring out the answer. This is why I wrote these letters to you. Something tells me that if the eyes that fall on these letters were to look around them, they might alight on that tenth hush, and meet themselves in a new way.

Home is such a slippery concept. She misbehaves. She shrinks and then vanishes in the tightening grip of your efforts to own her. Maybe there are no words to finally rope her in. In the stead of words, a gasp: home is then that moment when you, in a fit of sovereignty, would have given names to the glory-weary sun, and to the council of mountains that hum gently in his praise, and to the sea that yearns to be reunited with her lunar lover in the sky, and to the splendid assortment of color and texture and bulbous shapes that hang from trees—names for all—and then turn away satisfied, only to hear behind your ears the whisper of the world, "You! We shall give you a name too!" It is not enough to find one's way home. Arriving will not suffice where naught is still, where everything moves.

So do not pray to arrive safely. There is room for that, of course. Do not yearn too much to win the trophy. To break through the line. To win the seat. To find the mountain peak. Surrender to the journey—in the ways only you know how to. Let the loamy fingers of this dark soil envelope you, unmake you, fiddle with you, disturb you, unsettle you, conspire with you, and birth you.

For me, this feeling of home ... it looks like my own father, *your grand-father*, standing tall at the quay, saying good-bye. I can still see him there: silhouetted against a background of camo-wearing soldiers, walkie-talkie-toting suits, and white open-air jeeps with the letters *UN* painted in light blue on their sides. Tears stream down his face as he rushes us aboard the ferry that will carry his family, his wife, and three of his four children away from the *pillage* and the murmurings of a full-scale war that is afoot in Kinshasa, Zaire, and across to the neighboring country of Congo-Brazzaville. I feel his prickly mustache as he presses his face into mine, explaining what I already know at that point—that Daddy isn't coming with us back to Nigeria, that the Nigerian government has requested all families of its diplomats to return to the country on account of the civil unrest provoked by insurgent Zairian soldiers protesting their flamboyant dictator-president, Mobutu Sese Seko. I feel the unspoken promise of reconciliation in his smile, as the anchoring ropes come undone, and the ferry drifts out, dancing on the currents in the wake of other departing vessels. This, all of this, is how home feels.

Home is your mother, in whose entrails and dust I will be entangled with—long after memories are congealed into new stars.

Where you are going, we cannot come.

So take these letters, pack them in a neat heap, and burn them in a fire. Put the ashes in with us, where we now lie, in the single pot you've kept by your side throughout these readings.

Release us into the ocean wind, let her carry us away so we will always be close to you.

Run through the fields, my darling. Run to your new kin. To your new fathers and mothers. To the ones who hold you close as our dust churns a new night. Gather your children close—if you have any—and tell them of us, your mother and me. Especially your mother. Tell them of your mother.

And when you dance through the wisps of Thursday's bright morning, know you will not dance alone. For we will haunt you. We are cool like that.

Notes

PROLOGUE

1. Hello, Alethea! Right, so I thought to include these endnotes to further explain or clarify aspects of the letters, and to pay homage to the many voices that speak through these pages. You should visit here often, if my writing does not already make you weary.

2. James Odunbaku, "Importance of Cowrie Shells in Pre-Colonial Yoruba Land South Western Nigeria: Orile-Keesi as a Case Study," *International Journal of Humanities and Social Science* 2:18 (2012), 234–41.

3. This divinatory method is still practiced in syncretic religious ordinances by descendants of slaves shipped to the New World from the seventeenth century.

4. Okonkwo is the tragic character in Chinua Achebe's *Things Fall Apart* (London: William Heinemann, 1968), whose exposure to colonial powers leaves him estranged from the community he had always called home, and—in the crisp telling of Achebe's deft words—leads to his tragic suicide. I read *Things Fall Apart* for the first time when I visited the small library within the compound of the Nigerian Embassy in Kinshasa, Zaire. His story took on more urgent tones when I learned to see myself as a subject of colonial regimes, and sought a path of decolonization.

LETTER 1

1. In the Christian text, in John 14:2, Jesus, speaking to his disciples, promises them homes in heavenly places. Of course, there are some, including Wave Nunnally ("What Did Jesus Mean by 'Many Mansions'?," PE News, March 7, 2016, http://tinyurl.com/yatym9db) that dispute whether he

was talking about palatial estates for each disciple, and suggest that there is a deeper subtlety at work in Jesus' description of home.

2. H. P. Lovecraft, "The Call of Cthulhu," *Weird Tales* February 1928.

3. Markus Gabriel, in his book *Why the World Does Not Exist* (Cambridge, UK: Polity, 2015, 90), notes that we can only know sections of infinity and that there is no sensible way to speak about the real because "the world" is not neatly singular. It's a sentiment I agree with because like other neorealists, Gabriel acknowledges that one cannot explain everything in a single metatheory. In fact, I would say with him that the true merit of any theory is not how much it tells us about things or facts, but how much it holds close and refuses to lose sight of its hubris.

4. Matthew 5:14.

5. Saint Augustine, Sermon 103, 1–2:6, quoted in Philip Schaff, ed., *A Select Library of the Nicene and Post-Nicene Fathers of the Christian Church* (Edinburgh: T. & T. Clark, 1896–1900).

6. Saint Augustine, *The Confessions*, trans. Henry Chadwick (Oxford, UK: Oxford University Press, 2009), 56.

7. "Brick Like Me," *The Simpsons*, season 25, episode 20, May 4, 2014.

8. Genesis 3:9–10. My theology might need some dusting, but I often wondered why anyone could escape the all-seeing gaze of a supreme being. There are some commentaries that suggest God's "Where are you?" was an inquiry about Adam's existential condition, not his physical location. The distance was one of the heart, not of feet. Because Adam had sinned, God's question was designed to force the culprit to examine his circumstances. So God asks not because he is ignorant, but because he seeks to allow Adam's own agency to show itself, to give account for his recent behavior. And yet, my reading of the Fall—as a dissolution of the eternal or the notion of sin—generates a perverse plot twist that need not be factual (any more than any myth is factual) for it to be instructive, if only for literary purposes: God's love shines through by his own coming undone. He is not left unaffected. Michael Marder writes in *Dust* (New York: Bloomsbury Academic, 2016, 36) that "God addresses his own

regret of being dustless by creating the world and, specifically Adam and Eve, through whom he became dust vicariously, well in advance of Jesus' incarnation."

9. Marder, *Dust*, 44.

10. Ibid., 38.

11. Ibid., 49.

12. Ibid., 36.

13. Susan Hekman, *The Material of Knowledge* (Bloomington, Indiana: Indiana University Press, 2010).

14. Frédérique Apffel-Marglin, *Subversive Spiritualities: How Rituals Enact the World* (New York: Oxford University Press, 2011), 5.

15. Modernity seems to me to be the set of practices that hope to expand the autopoietic (self-preserving dynamics) to the exclusion of the sympoietic (co-constitutive becoming). But, as is the thesis of this letter, there is no ideal explanation of the concept of modernity.

16. I don't mean to suggest that there is a uniform entity called "science." There isn't. But that's the risk you get with naming things, or even speaking at all: you push out controversies, contradictions, inner tensions, particularities, and more. The alternative is not to speak at all. And even that—not speaking—is populated with nuance and texture.

17. Marder, *Dust*, 34.

LETTER 2

1. Avery Gordon, *Ghostly Matters: Haunting and the Sociological Imagination* (Minneapolis: University of Minnesota Press, 2004), 4.

2. Brunella Casalini, "The Materialist Bent in Contemporary Feminist Theory," *Periódico do Núcleo de Estudos e Pesquisas sobre Gênero e Direito Centro de Ciências Jurídicas, Universidade Federal da Paraíba* 2 (2015), 140, https://goo.gl/5SROkl.

3. Rebekah Sheldon, "Form/Matter/Chora: Object Oriented Ontology and Feminist New Materialism," in Richard Grusin, *The Nonhuman Turn* (Minneapolis: University of Minnesota Press, 2015), 195.

LETTER 3

1. Anuradha Mascarenhas, "Sex Determination: An Old Law, a New Debate," *The Indian Express,* February 4, 2016, http://tinyurl.com/y8ph7hg5.

2. Susan Hekman, *The Material of Knowledge: Feminist Disclosures* (Bloomington, IN: Indiana University Press, 2010).

3. Casalini, "Materialist Bent," 137–38.

4. Ibid., 142.

5. Samantha Frost, "The Implications of the New Materialisms for Feminist Epistemology," in Heidi E. Grasswick, *Feminist Epistemology and Philosophy of Science: Power in Knowledge* (New York: Springer, 2011), 69–84.

6. Ibid.

7. Fien Adriaens, "Post Feminism in Popular Culture: A Potential for Critical Resistance?" *Politics and Culture* 4 (2009), http://tinyurl.com/y947tgr3.

8. Perhaps the fluidity of parkour—the free-running discipline that conditions the human agent to be able to skirt and traverse boundaries and obstacles—could serve as a figure for postmodernism in its rejection of rejection.

9. Adriaens, "Post Feminism."

10. Jodi Dean writes of communicative capitalism in her essay "Communicative Capitalism: Circulation and the Foreclosure of Politics" (*Cultural Politics* 1:1 [2005], 51), describing our postmodern conditions of fetishized rapidity and the expense of political groundings: "The fantasy of abundance leads to a shift in the basic unit of communication from the message to the contribution. The fantasy of activity or participation is materialized through technology fetishism. The fantasy of wholeness relies on and produces a global both imaginary and Real."

11. Hekman, *Material of Knowledge,* 3.

12. Iris van der Tuin, "New Feminist Materialisms," *Women's Studies International Forum* 34 (2011), 273.

13. *Naturecultures* is Donna Haraway's neologism to show that nature is not a thing apart from culture, but already impacted by and impactful on culture.

14. Once someone asked me if I believed in God and if I had proof—unshakable proof—that could refute His existence. I told him that I didn't believe in "belief," or rather "belief as arrival," and that I wasn't sure how to characterize my relationship with the notion or concept of God anymore ... or if there was even the possibility of naming that relationship. I told him that I do not have a watertight argument to back up my "status," but that whatever "I" was, was inexhaustible. Like Graham Harman notes, it's not the case that conceptual shifts occur because a profound argument has been provided; people move on because the problem or the question ceases to be interesting any longer. The question—"Does God exist?" or even "Which God exists?"—is in that sense uninteresting to me. It just doesn't have that much of a hold on me any longer, any more than the notion of origins still grips a quantum physicist who understands that time isn't linear ... stretching from some distant beginning to an unheralded future. On the other hand, embodiment frightens me. Seeing how things assume different shapes, seeing how things differ from other things—that's very interesting to me. The old "pagans" who loved chemistry and dabbled in mixtures and perverse things—that's a form of spirituality that seems more at home with my explorations. Having said that, I do not presume that focusing on emergence or materialism represents some evolutionary turn—and that we must leave the question of deities behind. They are not suddenly fossils left in the wake of our theoretical sophistications. The question of god or God or goddesses is part of our emergence, and will always—I suspect—play some role or the other in what our species strives to grasp. Our beliefs will, however, always be provisional; we will never arrive. And that's maybe a good thing. Likewise, new materialisms are not accusatory successors of the previous.

15. Frost, "Implications," 74.

16. Karen Barad, "Posthumanist Performativity: Toward an Understanding of How Matter Comes to Matter," *Signs: Journal of Women in Culture and Society* 28:3 (2003), 801.

17. Casalini, "Materialist Bent," 138–39.

18. Ibid., 138.

19. Stacy Alaimo and Susan Hekman, eds., *Material Feminisms* (Bloomington, IN: Indiana University Press, 2007), 4–5.

20. I like this word *transpose,* meaning "to switch places," "to shift location." To exchange, but in a sense that is secretory and orgasmic and boundary-corroding. Those fearful that the idea of a "material turn" might reaffirm the dualism and representationalism inherent in "successor epistemologies" could perhaps think of a material transposition, where the implication is not of succession and tyranny over the "previous" but of dynamic movement and hyphenated encounters.

21. Karen Barad, "Quantum Entanglements and Hauntological Relations of Inheritance: Dis/continuities, SpaceTime Enfoldings, and Justice-to-Come," *Derrida Today* 3:2 (2010), 255. doi:10.3366/E1754850010000813.

22. Ibid., 256–57.

23. X. Y. Zou, Lei J. Wang, and Leonard Mandel, "Induced Coherence and Indistinguishability in Optical Interference," *Physical Review Letters* 67:3 (1991), 318–21.

24. Mike May, "The Reality of Watching," *American Scientist* 86:4 (July–August 1998).

25. Barad, *Meeting the Universe Halfway.*

26. There's a good story about Craig Lewis by Carrie Feibel, "Heart with No Beat Offers Hope of New Lease on Life," NPR, June 13, 2011, http://tinyurl.com/6hyjrox.

27. Frost, "Implications," 70.

28. Donna Haraway, "Tentacular Thinking: Anthropocene, Capitalocene, Chthulucene," *E-flux* 75 (September 2016), http://tinyurl.com/ycrw63wf.

29. Brian Onishi, "Terror and Terroir: Porous Bodies and Environmental Dangers," *Trespassing Journal* 6 (Winter 2017), http://trespassingjournal.com/?page_id=1022.

30. Barad, *Meeting the Universe Halfway.*

31. Susan Stryker, "My Words to Victor Frankenstein above the Village of Chamounix," in Renée R. Curry and Terry L. Allison, eds., *States of Rage: Emotional Eruption, Violence, and Social Change* (New York: New York University Press, 1996), 199.

LETTER 4

1. Andrew Walker, "The White Priestess of 'Black Magic,'" BBC News, September 10, 2008, http://tinyurl.com/58bhg8.

2. Ankita Dwivedi Johri, "Africans attacked in Delhi: Tracing the Faultlines of Open Racism and Distrust," *The Indian Express,* June 14, 2016, http://tinyurl.com/htxlq42.

3. Ayi Kwei Armah, *The Beautyful Ones Are Not Yet Born* (Boston: Houghton Mifflin, 1968).

4. Leo Igwe, "The Osu Caste System," Mukto-mona, http://tinyurl.com/k3kq7a9.

5. Chinua Achebe, *No Longer at Ease* (Portsmouth, NH: Heinemann, 1987), 121.

6. Igwe Alupuoaku, "Osu Caste System in Alaigbo," *Osondu Newsletter* 4, http://tinyurl.com/l3c8vaa.

7. Ibid.

8. James W. Perkinson, *Shamanism, Racism, and Hip Hop Culture: Essays on White Supremacy and Black Subversion* (New York: Palgrave Macmillan, 2005), 3.

9. By the way, if you ask me right now what purposes these hushes serve, I still cannot tell you with any confidence. I suspect, however, that I have perhaps been thinking of the hushes as "individuals" with cosmic secrets about my own questions, the answers to which they can unilaterally whisper in my ear if only I lean closer. In short, I reckon I have been thinking about them in the wrong way. I remember taking the hush that Karen Barad gave me—you remember, the one that looked like a fossil or stone—sitting with it for days, holding it close to my ears, putting it under my pillow (with the hope that it might visit me in my dreams), and even

trying to pry it open. In that way, I depended on the kind of reductionisms that would make one open up a bird to discover what makes it sing sweetly. Perhaps, in the same way the song of a tree is the wind passing through it—sonifying its thick bough, the birds that inhabit its branches in specific configurations, and the raindrops that tap-tap-tap on its leaves, the hush's wisdom is not an essence but a community, an assemblage of moments that brings me to the edge of what I know. An invitation to the troubling queerness that is (at work in) the universe. I had been looking at the hush alone—wondering about it—instead of considering the place itself, the dance of the wind around it, the curiosity of a stranger observing my approach to the hush, or the tears in the eyes of the one giving it.

10. Ben Mathis-Lilley, "The Short but Intriguing History of White Americans pretending to be Black," The Slatest, June 12, 2015, http://tinyurl.com/pvuhrxs.

11. Ijeoma Oluo, "The Heart of Whiteness: Ijeoma Oluo Interviews Rachel Dolezal, the White Woman Who Identifies as Black," *The Stranger*, April 19, 2017, http://tinyurl.com/kfslals.

12. Ibid.

13. Jerry Rosiek, "Critical Race Theory, Agential Realism, and the Evidence of Experience: A Methodological and Theoretical Preface," in Jerry Rosiek and Kathy Kinslow, *Resegregation as Curriculum: The Meaning of the New Segregation in U.S. Public Schools* (New York: Routledge, 2016).

14. There's a video of the talk here: Bayo Akomolafe, "How I Am Unlearning My Whiteness," Santa Rosa, CA, May 11, 2017, https://www.youtube.com/watch?v=vvqrI6MhI_Q. I have not watched it. I cannot stand the nasality of my own voice.

15. Madison Gray, "Philip Emeagwali: A Calculating Move," *Time,* January 12, 2007, http://tinyurl.com/y8uerurn.

16. NWA, "Fuck tha Police," *Straight Outta Compton,* 1988.

17. Perkinson, *Shamanism,* 4–5.

18. A. Roulin, "Melanin-Based Colour Polymorphism Responding to Climate Change," *Global Change Biology* 20:11 (November 2014), 3344–50. doi:10.1111/gcb.12594.

19. Which is not to say that we can change the past, go back in time and correct it, or simply come up with new interpretations of happenings, as if the world were simply a product of our meaning-making ventures. Immersed in a world that is constantly becoming, the past is always yet to come, differentially sedimented via intra-actions. Does this do away with trauma? Does this efface the marks on our bodies? We cannot turn back the hands of time simply because time is not even an external parameter that is universally apportioned in terms of a past, present, and future. Instead the past is constantly "resynchronized" within ongoing practices. The marks don't disappear, but "new" ones can be formed in discontinuous entangling loops that challenge the smooth flow of a history without breaks.

20. Many thanks to Isoke Femi, an African American woman I met while visiting Sonoma County in 2017. Isoke brought up the question of call-response patterns in African dialogic encounters, inspiring me to come to terms with an idea that had lingered at the tip of my tongue for so long, hardly ever finding expression—which all gives honor to the idea that we often meet ourselves for the first time in the eyes of strangers.

21. This probably explains why I have almost always left a speaking engagement, where the audience was largely Indian, feeling like I didn't communicate at all. There is something of a relative muteness, perhaps a deferential silence or blankness, that clouds the face of the crowd … which is suddenly lifted as soon as I finish speaking.

22. *Aló* is a Yoruba word for "story" and is often used in a call-response fashion in storytelling encounters to begin the story to be told.

23. Asar Imhotep, "Understanding *Asé* and Its Relation with Èsù among the Yoruba and the *Ase.t* in Ancient Egypt," January 4, 2012, http://tinyurl .com/ybruv33m.

24. Imhotep, "Understanding *Asé*."

25. Funso Aiyejina, "Èsù Elegbara: A Source of an Alter/Native Theory of African Literature and Criticism," lecture at the Centre for Black Art and African Cultures, Lagos, 2010, http://tinyurl.com/y95ajurr.

26. Ibid.

27. Imhotep, "Understanding *Asé.*"

28. Karen Barad, "Diffracting Diffraction: Cutting Together-Apart," *Parallax* 20:3 (2014), 168. doi:10.1080/13534645.2014.927623.

29. Trinh T. Minh-ha, "Not You/Like You: Post-Colonial Women and the Interlocking Questions of Identity and Difference." *Feminism and the Critique of Colonial Discourse.* Inscriptions 3–4. Center for Cultural Studies, University of Santa Cruz, 1988.

30. Barad, "Diffracting diffraction," 170.

31. Haraway, *Simians.*

32. Maxine Sheets-Johnstone, *The Primacy of Movement* (Philadelphia: John Benjamins, 1999).

33. Karen Barad, "Posthumanist Performativity: Toward an Understanding of How Matter Comes to Matter," Signs: Journal of Women in Culture and Society 28:3 (2003), 801–31. doi:10.1086/345321.

34. Rick Dolphijn and Iris van der Tuin, "Matter Feels, Converses, Suffers, Desires, Yearns and Remembers: Interview with Karen Barad," in *New Materialism: Interviews & Cartographies* (Ann Arbor, MI: Open Humanities Press, 2012). doi:10.3998/ohp.11515701.0001.001.

35. Ibid.

36. Ibid.

37. Isoke Ndeya Femi used the phrase "affective muscle" when we had breakfast at Professor Elenita Strobel's home in Sonoma County, California, May 13, 2017.

38. Isoke Femi, in her sixties when I met her in May 2017, told me of a day she was at a carnival, feeling free-spirited and generous to the point of calling white people her sisters and brothers. Her day was quickly ruined when she saw an offensive statuesque figure caricaturizing black people with protruding lips and wide open eyes. In her words, she felt an uncontrollable rage and needed a place to hold it. She quickly sought out her one of her "white allies," to whom she screamed the words "I hate white people!" while the friend sat there and received these difficult expressions of intergenerational hurt. "What would you like me to do?" her friend

responded, when she was done belching her tearful rage. "It takes a lot to do that kind of work," Isoke Femi would later tell me. "One needs affective muscles." When Isoke told me her remarkable story, I felt it served as a noteworthy example of how nontarget populations can meet oppressed others halfway ... allowing for a healing that is otherwise truncated when we essentialized negative feelings and ascribe labels as a result.

39. Elizabeth Grosz, "The Future of Feminist Theory: Dreams for New Knowledges," *Revista Eco-Pós* 13:3 (2010), 52.

LETTER 5

1. Augustine Nwoye, "Memory Healing Processes and Community Intervention in Grief Work in Africa," *Australian and New Zealand Journal of Family Therapy* 26:3 (2005), 149–50. doi:10.1002/j.1467-8438.2005.tb00662.x.

2. It would be easy here to create a binary by suggesting that modernity is "wrong" and that we must return to "the immediacy of the world at large"—as if the latter were a pristine order of things awaiting occupation. That is not what I mean by making this distinction between modernity and other possible political imaginaries. Modernity itself is not totalizing or complete or monumental; neither are indigenous pasts or future pure and without shadows. As Karen Barad says, "There is no absolute boundary between here-now and there-then" ("Diffracting Diffraction: Cutting Together-Apart," *Parallax* 20:3 [2014], 168–87, doi:10.1080/13534645.2014.927623).

3. Karen Barad, "Diffracting Diffraction."

4. Ibid.

5. Gloria Anzaldúa, *Borderlands/La Frontera: The New Mestiza* (San Francisco: Aunt Lute Books, 1987).

6. C. G. Jung, *Mysterium Coniunctionis: An Inquiry into the Separation and Synthesis of Psychic Opposites in Alchemy* (Princeton, NJ: Princeton University Press, 1963), 345.

7. Barad, "Diffracting Diffraction."

8. Stanton Marlan and David H. Rosen, *The Black Sun: The Alchemy and Art of Darkness* (College Station, TX: Texas A&M University Press, 2015), 16.

9. Elizabeth Lloyd Mayer, *Extraordinary Knowing: Science, Skepticism and the Inexplicable Powers of the Human Mind* (New York: Bantam, 2007).

10. Alethea, I thought to mention that it is very easy to fall into the trap of seeking to naturalize African and indigenous practices as some kind of default ontology we should all adopt, while denaturalizing the West as "old" and needing transformation. But none is truer than the other. Even modernity is not some backward notion we must leave behind in order to find the new ahead of us. I wouldn't want to create some kind of "successor regime" dynamic here. Each performs the world differently, but are themselves subject to revision. For instance, African cosmologies in their current iteration think of the dead as disembodied spirits in ancestral realms, which shares a humanistic distinction with Judeo-Christian thought. I think more in terms of dust and nonhumans around us. Our souls are locked up in the ordinary things that condition us. While I am enabled to think that way, agential realism becomes a strategy for me to revisit and return to the so-called "old."

11. Nwoye, "Memory Healing Processes," 147.

LETTER 6

1. Rahul Kalvapalié, "Arizona Woman Finds Note from 'Chinese Prisoner' in Walmart Purse," Global News, May 6, 2017, http://tinyurl.com/loaqddk.

2. Ursula K. Le Guin, "The Ones Who Walk Away from Omelas," in Robert Silverberg, ed. *New Dimensions 3* (New York: Nelson Doubleday, 1973).

3. Ibid.

4. Ibid.

5. A few kilometers north of where your grandfather is born, in northern Nigeria, the Kanuris are known for the long tribal marks they make on their faces. It is also a familiar though fading tradition in Yorubaland for people to mark their bodies in rituals of scarification. These changing bodies are instigated by particular ethical imaginaries (sorry if that

sounds like gibberish. Let me try again). What I mean to say is that some imperatives are acted out and materialized in form of the bodies we take on—and these imperatives are the contributions of place, of history, of story, concepts of beauty, animal others, time, imagination, and hope. Particular Yoruba tribal-marked bodies came to be that way as a response to the transatlantic slave trade; it was a way to identify kith and kin.

6. Chinua Achebe, *No Longer at Ease* (Portsmouth, NH: Heinemann, 1987), 151.

7. Remember that "thought" is transcorporeal—which basically means it jumps from bodies to bodies, or melts through. It is not a human attribute. If we were to follow the performative traces of thinking in its ongoing flow, we might notice how thinking decenters the human figure. Some thinking is possible while others are impossible—due to specific intra-active configuration of bodies. This is why I say how to think of some phenomena may not be available yet.

8. In pivoting my explorations around agential realism, the new materialist theory that rethinks truth, boundaries, and bodies (whether conceptual or material or political bodies) as ongoing reiterative intra-actions, I am in fact saying that—in some queer sense—agential realism cannot overly exert itself as some kind of newfound truth, for the moment it does, it undermines its own premises as a way of seeing how entangled performances produce the world.

9. John Shotter, "Agential Realism, Social Constructionism, and Our Living Relations to Our Surroundings: Sensing Similarities Rather than Seeing Patterns," *Theory & Psychology* 2:3 (2014), 306. doi:10.1177/0959-3543-1351-4144.

10. Astrida Neimanis and Rachel Loewen Walker, "Weathering: Climate Change and the 'Thick Time' of Transcorporeality," *Hypatia*, submission to Climate Change Special Issue (2013), doi:10.1111/hypa.12064.

11. Andrea Thompson, "Earth's Clouds Alive with Bacteria," Live Science, February 27, 2008, http://tinyurl.com/mna8kbu.

12. Ibid.

13. A different way means a different crisis, not the same one. If the apparatus changes, then the meaning changes as well.

14. Narrowness here is not a way of saying it is "wrong" or inadequate, except I am speaking from the vantage point of a different framework.

15. Ibid.

16. Grosz, "Future of Feminist Theory," 52.

17. There is a story about a man who faithfully hammered a nail. Every day, without fail. Tap, tap, tap. It was his sacred duty, and he did it without question. One day, the hammer's head fell off from overuse. There were no blacksmiths in his town, and no one knew what to do about his broken hammer. Distraught, he heard that there was a powerful medicine man who could help fix his problem—a man with answers. So he went to him and complained about his hammer and how much time had already been lost in not hitting the nail. The healer's eyes beamed, and he jumped up, declaring "I might have just the thing you're looking for!" He rushed into his hut, and came back with a feather. "That's a feather," the seeker murmured. "Yes, I see that," the healer noted. "But how can I achieve my nail-hitting practice with this feather?" he continued, exasperated. "Who said anything about achieving that? Who said anything about solving your problem?" the healer asked. "Well, isn't that what you are supposed to do—solve problems? Provide answers?" "Oh, no!" the healer cried. "I don't give answers. I help you ask different questions." "Other places of power" is not shorthand for "indigenous augmentation of modern objectives."

18. Barad, *Meeting the Universe Halfway*, 10.

19. Chris Mowles, *Managing in Uncertainty: Complexity and the Paradoxes of Everyday Organizational Life* (Abingdon, UK: Routledge, 2015).

20. Barad, "Quantum Entanglements," 251.

LETTER 7

1. David Whyte, *The Sea in You: Twenty Poems of Rojuited and Unrequited Love* (Langley, WA: Many Rivers Press, 2015), http://tinyurl.com/y9dmnrlc.

2. Julia Zorthian, "Stephen Hawking Says Humans Have 100 Years to Move to Another Planet," *Time,* May 4, 2017, http://tinyurl.com/k4sv5w7.

3. There was a time prior to your arrival that I was so enamored by accounts of extraterrestrial civilizations and stories about little "grays," beings from other dimensions that visited earth and crash-landed in the legendary Area 51—only to be retrieved by the American military. In one story I read—which I cannot verify to be authentic—a scientist that interviewed a surviving EBE (extraterrestrial biological entity) disclosed that the entity told him that he was a future iteration of humans, and that he had indeed traveled back in time—to our time—to help prevent the future event that leads to the "rapture-like" event. Having relocated to a distant planet at a yet-to-be-determined future date, we would go on to become the large-eyed, hugged-headed, three-fingered, flying-saucer-piloting, miniscule beings that have animated popular imagination. I am not one to dismiss stories about other worlds—even though this reads as a fantastical plot for a woo-woo sci-fi novel. Having let go of my need to believe in a geocentric, anthropocentric universe, I find it highly likely that life isn't as "special" or as isolated as mainstream thinking presumes it to be, or—at least—is loath to allow alternative ideas about. What is of note here is that moving from "here" to "there" contains greater logistical implications than the modalities of the journey takes into account. Because we are porous beings, intersectional becomings, moving from here to there is never simple. There is no preset "there" frozen in wait. We collectively make "here" and "there." Earth makes its humans.

Bibliography

Achebe, Chinua. *No Longer at Ease*. Portsmouth, NH: Heinemann, 1987.

———. *Things Fall Apart*. London: William Heinemann, 1968.

Adriaens, Fien. "Post Feminism in Popular Culture: A Potential for Critical Resistance?" *Politics and Culture* 4 (2009). http://tinyurl.com/y947tgr3.

Aiyejina, Funso. "Èsù Elegbara: A Source of an Alter/Native Theory of African Literature and Criticism." Lecture at the Centre for Black Art and African Cultures, Lagos, 2010. http://tinyurl.com/y95ajurr.

Akomolafe, Adebayo C., Molefi Kete Asante, and Augustine Nwoye, eds. *We Will Tell Our Own Story!* New York: Universal Write, 2016.

Alaimo, Stacy, and Susan Hekman, eds. *Material Feminisms*. Bloomington, IN: Indiana University Press, 2007.

Alupuoaku, Igwe. "Osu Caste System in Alaigbo." *Osondu Newsletter* 4. http://tinyurl.com/l3c8vaa.

Anzaldúa, Gloria. *Borderlands/La Frontera: The New Mestiza*. San Francisco: Aunt Lute Books, 1987.

Armah, Ayi Kwei. *The Beautyful Ones Are Not Yet Born*. Boston: Houghton Mifflin, 1968.

Augustine. *The Confessions*. Translated by Henry Chadwick. Oxford, UK: Oxford University Press, 2009.

Barad, Karen. "Diffracting Diffraction: Cutting Together-Apart." *Parallax* 20:3 (2014), 168–87. doi:10.1080/13534645.2014.927623.

———. *Meeting the Universe Halfway: Quantum Physics and the Entanglement of Matter and Meaning*. London: Duke University Press, 2007.

———. "Posthumanist Performativity: Toward an Understanding of How Matter Comes to Matter." *Signs: Journal of Women in Culture and Society* 28:3 (2003), 801–31. doi:10.1086/345321.

————. "Quantum Entanglements and Hauntological Relations of Inheritance: Dis/continuities, SpaceTime Enfoldings, and Justice-to-Come." *Derrida Today* 3:2 (2010). doi:10.3366/E1754850010000813.

————. *What Is the Measure of Nothingness? Infinity, Virtuality, Justice.* Ostfildern, Germany: Hatje Cantz, 2012.

Casalini, Brunella. "The Materialist Bent in Contemporary Feminist Theory." *Periódico do Núcleo de Estudos e Pesquisas sobre Gênero e Direito Centro de Ciências Jurídicas, Universidade Federal da Paraíba* 2 (2015), 134–47. https://goo.gl/5SROkl.

Dolphijn, Rick, and Iris van der Tuin. "Matter Feels, Converses, Suffers, Desires, Yearns and Remembers: Interview with Karen Barad." In *New Materialism: Interviews & Cartographies.* Ann Arbor, MI: Open Humanities Press, 2012. doi:10.3998/ohp.11515701.0001.001.

Feibel, Carrie. "Heart with No Beat Offers Hope of New Lease on Life." NPR, June 13, 2011. http://tinyurl.com/6hyjrox.

Frost, Samantha. "The Implications of the New Materialisms for Feminist Epistemology." In *Feminist Epistemology and Philosophy of Science: Power in Knowledge,* edited by Heidi E. Grasswick. New York: Springer, 2011.

Gabriel, Markus. *Why the World Does Not Exist.* Cambridge, UK: Polity, 2015.

Gordon, Avery. *Ghostly Matters: Haunting and the Sociological Imagination.* Minneapolis: University of Minnesota Press, 2004.

Gray, Madison. "Philip Emeagwali: A Calculating Move." *Time,* January 12, 2007. http://tinyurl.com/y8uerurn.

Grosz, Elizabeth. "The Future of Feminist Theory: Dreams for New Knowledges." *Revista Eco-Pós* 13:3 (2010), 52.

Haraway, Donna. "Tentacular Thinking: Anthropocene, Capitalocene, Chthulucene." *E-flux* 75 (September 2016). http://tinyurl.com/ycrw63wf.

Hekman, Susan. *The Material of Knowledge: Feminist Disclosures.* Bloomington, IN: Indiana University Press, 2010.

Igwe, Leo. "The Osu Caste System." Mukto-mona. http://tinyurl.com /k3kq7a9.

Imhotep, Asar. "Understanding *Ase* and Its Relation with *Esu* among the Yoruba and the *Ase.t* in Ancient Egypt." January 4, 2012. http://tinyurl .com/ybruv33m.

Johri, Ankita Dwivedi. "Africans attacked in Delhi: Tracing the Faultlines of Open Racism and Distrust." *The Indian Express,* June 14, 2016. http:// tinyurl.com/htxlq42.

Jung, C. G. *Mysterium Coniunctionis: An Inquiry into the Separation and Synthesis of Psychic Opposites in Alchemy.* Princeton, NJ: Princeton University Press, 1963.

Kalvapalié, Rahul. "Arizona Woman Finds Note from 'Chinese Prisoner' in Walmart Purse." Global News, May 6, 2017, http://tinyurl.com /loaqddk.

Le Guin, Ursula K. "The Ones Who Walk Away from Omelas." In Robert Silverberg, ed. *New Dimensions 3.* New York: Nelson Doubleday, 1973.

Lovecraft, H. P. "The Call of Cthulhu." *Weird Tales.* February 1928.

Marder, Michael. *Dust.* New York: Bloomsbury Academic, 2016.

Marlan, Stanton, and David H. Rosen. *The Black Sun: The Alchemy and Art of Darkness.* College Station, TX: Texas A&M University Press, 2015.

Mascarenhas, Anuradha. "Sex Determination: An Old Law, a New Debate." *The Indian Express,* February 4, 2016. http://tinyurl.com/y8ph7hg5.

Mathis-Lilley, Ben. "The Short but Intriguing History of White Americans pretending to be Black." The Slatest, June 12, 2015. http://tinyurl.com /pvuhrxs.

May, Mike. "The Reality of Watching." *American Scientist* 86:4 (July–August 1998).

Mayer, Elizabeth Lloyd. *Extraordinary Knowing: Science, Skepticism and the Inexplicable Powers of the Human Mind.* New York: Bantam, 2007.

Minh-ha, Trinh T. "Not You/Like You: Post-Colonial Women and the Interlocking Questions of Identity and Difference." *Feminism and the*

Critique of Colonial Discourse. Inscriptions 3–4. Center for Cultural Studies, University of Santa Cruz, 1988.

Mowles, Chris. *Managing in Uncertainty: Complexity and the Paradoxes of Everyday Organizational Life*. Abingdon, UK: Routledge, 2015.

Neimanis, Astrida, and Rachel Loewen Walker. "Weathering: Climate Change and the 'Thick Time' of Transcorporeality." *Hypatia*. Submission to Climate Change Special Issue (2013). doi:10.1111/hypa.12064.

Nunnally, Wave. "What Did Jesus Mean by 'Many Mansions'?" PE News. March 7, 2016. http://tinyurl.com/yatym9db.

Nwoye, Augustine. "Memory Healing Processes and Community: Intervention in Grief Work in Africa." *Australian and New Zealand Journal of Family Therapy* 26:3 (2005), 147–154. doi:10.1002/j.1467-8438.2005. tb00662.x.

Oluo, Ijeoma. "The Heart of Whiteness: Ijeoma Oluo Interviews Rachel Dolezal, the White Woman Who Identifies as Black." *The Stranger*. April 19, 2017. http://tinyurl.com/kfslals.

Onishi, Brian. "Terror and Terroir: Porous Bodies and Environmental Dangers." *Trespassing Journal* 6 (Winter 2017). http://trespassingjournal .com/?page_id=1022.

Perkinson, James W. *Shamanism, Racism, and Hip Hop Culture: Essays on White Supremacy and Black Subversion*. New York: Palgrave Macmillan, 2005.

Rosiek, Jerry. "Critical Race Theory, Agential Realism, and the Evidence of Experience: A Methodological and Theoretical Preface." In *Resegregation as Curriculum: The Meaning of the New Segregation in U.S. Public Schools*, edited by Jerry Rosiek and Kathy Kinslow. New York: Routledge, 2016.

Rotimi, Ola. *The Gods Are Not to Blame*. Oxford, UK: Oxford University Press, 1971.

Roulin, A. "Melanin-Based Colour Polymorphism Responding to Climate Change." *Global Change Biology* 20:11 (November 2014), 3344–50. doi:10.1111/gcb.12594.

Schaff, Philip, ed. *A Select Library of the Nicene and Post-Nicene Fathers of the Christian Church*. Edinburgh: T. & T. Clark, 1896–1900.

Sheets-Johnstone, Maxine. *The Primacy of Movement*. Philadelphia: John Benjamins, 1999.

Sheldon, Rebekah. "Form/Matter/Chora: Object Oriented Ontology and Feminist New Materialism." In *The Nonhuman Turn*, edited by Richard Grusin. Minneapolis: University of Minnesota Press, 2015.

Shotter, John. "Agential Realism, Social Constructionism, and Our Living Relations to Our Surroundings: Sensing Similarities Rather than Seeing Patterns." *Theory & Psychology* 2:3 (2014), 305–25.

Stryker, Susan. "My Words to Victor Frankenstein above the Village of Chamounix." In *States of Rage: Emotional Eruption, Violence, and Social Change*, edited by Renée R. Curry and Terry L. Allison. New York: New York University Press, 1996.

Thompson, Andrea. "Earth's Clouds Alive with Bacteria." Live Science, February 27, 2008. http://tinyurl.com/mna8kbu.

Van der Tuin, Iris. "New Feminist Materialisms," *Women's Studies International Forum* 34 (2011).

Walker, Andrew. "The White Priestess of 'Black Magic.'" BBC News, September 10, 2008. http://tinyurl.com/58bhg8.

Whyte, David. *The Sea in You: Twenty Poems of Rojuited and Unrequited Love*. Langley, WA: Many Rivers Press, 2015. http://tinyurl.com/y9dmnrlc.

Zorthian, Julia. "Stephen Hawking Says Humans Have 100 Years to Move to Another Planet." *Time*, May 4, 2017. http://tinyurl.com/k4sv5w7.

Zou, X. Y., Lei J. Wang, and Leonard Mandel. "Induced Coherence and Indistinguishability in Optical Interference." *Physical Review Letters* 67:3 (1991), 318–21.

About the Author

BAYO AKOMOLAFE left a teaching position as a professor and clinical psychologist in a Nigerian university to pursue "a small and intense life"— a life outside the highways of the familiar, outside of fences. In a sense, his decolonizing journey in the wilds, in the borderlands of globalizing culture, began when he met Ijeoma, his wife of Indian and African descent, and when a healer suggested to him "that I could find my way if I were willing to become generously lost." His quest is to tell the stories of the occluded, to make room for other spaces of power and invite the proliferation of multiple natures. This, his first book is a foray into the ordinary "which the extraordinary is always trying to become." Akomolafe lectures and gives talks internationally, mostly keynote speeches, and is chief curator for an earth-wide commonwealth of curators working from a different ethos of responsivity called The Emergence Network. He currently lives in India with his "life-force," Ijeoma (or Ej), and their two children: Alethea Aanya and Kyah Jayden.

About North Atlantic Books

North Atlantic Books (NAB) is a 501(c)(3) nonprofit publisher committed to a bold exploration of the relationships between mind, body, spirit, culture, and nature. Founded in 1974, NAB aims to nurture a holistic view of the arts, sciences, humanities, and healing. To make a donation or to learn more about our books, authors, events, and newsletter, please visit www.northatlanticbooks.com.